RETURN TO GRACE

Kurt Stasiak, O.S.B.

RETURN TO GRACE

A Theology for Infant Baptism

A PUEBLO BOOK

The Liturgical Press, Collegeville, Minnesota

A Pueblo Book published by The Liturgical Press

Design by Frank Kacmarcik

New Testament passages cited are from *The New Oxford Bible, New Revised Standard Version (NRSV)*.

Excerpts from Psalm 138 (appearing first in ch. 5) are from *The Psalms, A New Translation* (England: The Grail and Wm. Collins Sons & Co. Ltd., 1963).

Library of Congress Cataloging-in-Publication Data

Stasiak, Kurt, 1952–
    Return to grace : a theology for infant baptism / Kurt Stasiak.
      p.   cm.
    "A Pueblo book."
    Includes bibliographical references and index.
    ISBN 0-8146-6155-6
    1. Infant baptism.   2. Catholic Church—Doctrines.   I. Title.
  BV813.2.S73   1996
  234'.1612—dc20   96-34099
                                                                           CIP

Contents

PART TWO
RETURN TO GRACE:

A Theology for Infant Baptism

Preface

"Then Philip began to speak, and starting with this scripture, he proclaimed to him the good news about Jesus. As they were going along the road, they came to some water; and the eunuch said, *Look, here is water! What is to prevent me from being baptized? Nothing,* said Philip, *except paragraphs 7, 20, 21, 34 and 36 of the Rite of Christian Initiation of Adults.*"[1]

Our two-thousand-year-old Ethiopian eunuch would likely have met this response had he wandered into an American parish sometime after 1972, the year the *Rite of Christian Initiation of Adults (RCIA)* first appeared. Although a revised *Rite of Baptism for Children (RBC)* had been published three years earlier, it was the ordo for the initiation of adults that not only caught the attention of but also in many ways set the agenda for the postconciliar Church. The restoration of the order of catechumens; the understanding of initiation as a process assisted by and taking place within the community of the faithful; the renewed emphasis on the paschal character of baptism: these were among the reasons Aidan Kavanagh considered the new ordo "the most explosive pastoral document to be issued since the council." However slowly or with whatever difficulties the *RCIA* was introduced, the baptism of adults would never be the same.

Nor would the baptism of infants or children. For among the adult ordo's many contributions, perhaps the most lasting and significant—the most strategic, to use Kavanagh's term—was that it took the Church seriously. And because it took the Church seriously, the adult ordo demanded that the Church take baptism seriously. Catholic parents today may approach their pastors requesting the baptism of their newborn as automatically as did their parents and grandparents. But those who have seen neither the pastor nor the church for some time may find that their request elicits probing questions

[1]Adapted from Francis J. Buckley, "The Right to the Sacraments of Initiation," 329.

rather than a reassuring smile. The adult ordo has made its mark: it is time to take the Church seriously. And if we take the Church seriously, *we must take baptism seriously.*

Taking baptism seriously—particularly the baptism of infants and children—is the concern of this work.

The five chapters of part 1 report the American Catholic postconciliar discussion of infant baptism. After introducing this section with an overview of the "problem with infant baptism," I outline in chapter 1 the impact the *RCIA* has had upon the understanding and practice of initiation in the postconciliar Church. Although our primary interest is the baptism of infants and young children, the significance of the adult ordo demands more than a passing mention when discussing the postconciliar theology or practice of the sacramental initiation of Christians of any age. This first chapter reviews the writings of the Mature Adulthood School, a school of baptismal thought vigorously promoting the adult ordo, while chapter 2 considers the literature of the Environmentalists, a school whose immediate concern was the baptism of infants and children.[2]

In the first chapter I also establish the five perspectives that structure my presentation throughout part 1. Having emerged early in the postconciliar discussion, these perspectives, or "position statements," on infant baptism (or on the influence of the adult ordo upon the infant baptism discussion) facilitate the review and evaluation of a considerable body of material. These perspectives also guide my examination in chapter 3 of the Sacred Congregation for the Doctrine of the Faith's 1980 *Instruction on Infant Baptism,* which remains the sole major postconciliar document dealing with infant baptism since the 1969 *Rite* itself. While our consideration of this document briefly interrupts our study of the American literature, it does allow us an interesting glimpse of curial reaction to the infant baptism discussion roughly halfway through the postconciliar years we are examining. I continue my report of the American discussion in chapter 4 by examining the literature from 1980 to the present.

My hope is that these four chapters of part 1 might serve as a reference or "handbook" for the American postconciliar discussion on in-

[2]These two schools of baptismal thought were identified and designated by Nathan Mitchell in "The Once and Future Child: Towards a Theology of Childhood," 422–36. For a review and evaluation of the postconciliar debate through 1980, see Paul Covino's "The Postconciliar Infant Baptism Debate in the American Catholic Church," 240–60.

fant baptism. I have tried to present a readable text that narrates the central points of the discussion around the five perspectives set forth in chapter 1. Numerous, sometimes lengthy, footnotes delve into the complexities of the discussion and also allow some fourscore writers to "speak for themselves." Readers familiar with or uninterested in the details of the discussion may avoid these detours from the main text, or they may proceed directly to chapter 5 and my conclusions and observations on the material reported in chapters 1–4.

Having reported the discussion in part 1, I offer my response in part 2. My response in large part finds its roots in a disagreement and a disappointment I experienced often when reviewing the postconciliar literature. I do not agree with Aidan Kavanagh's oft-cited thesis that the adult ordo sets forth "the definitive statement" of the Roman Catholic Church's "norm of baptism." While that thesis certainly speaks some truth, I do not think it speaks the whole truth. Furthermore, when it implies that infant baptism is, at best, a "benign abnormality," I think it has strayed far from the mark. And, convinced as I am that baptism is the ordinary, proper, and "norm-al" means by which infants are initiated into new life with Christ and his Church, I am disappointed in that it seems we rely too much upon theological models or motifs that do not serve our understanding of infant initiation as effectively as they do the conversion and initiation of adults. My response in part 2, then, proceeds from my disagreement and my disappointment. I discuss the unique significance of infant baptism and, in fact, suggest that infant baptism offers something paradigmatic—something normative—for all who seek entrance into God's kingdom. I also propose a model that I believe speaks directly and credibly to the baptism of infants and young children—and, hopefully, to the baptism of adults as well.

Specifically: in chapter 6 I outline a theology of childhood and suggest that while children can learn a great deal from the adult Church, they may have something to teach her as well. In chapter 7 I question whether it is helpful or even possible to hold for "a norm of baptism" and then suggest the concept of adoption (considered from the perspectives of both human experience and theology) as a particularly appropriate paradigm from which to approach the baptism of infants and young children.

After proposing several assumptions at the conclusion of this chapter as to the human act and experience of adoption, I examine in chapter 8 the use of the word "adoption" in the Pauline corpus (in that literature alone is the word found in the New Testament). While Paul certainly did not have infant baptism in mind as he wrote of the Christian's adoption, or *huiothesia* (literally, the "making" or "placing of a son") by God, I believe understanding infant baptism as the adoption of an infant by God, Church, and family both remains true to Paul's teaching and enhances our discussion and appreciation of that sacrament.

Mark Searle once remarked that the sacramental initiation of infants "ought to be seen less as a problem to be grappled with than as an opportunity to be grasped." I attempt to grasp that opportunity in chapter 9. Drawing upon a theology of childhood and the human experience and theological exposition of adoption, I maintain that infant baptism is neither problem nor abnormality but, rather, opportunity and challenge: the opportunity for the Church to see herself, in Nathan Mitchell's words, as "God's once and future child; the challenge for the Church, the sacrament of God's grace, to rediscover within herself the childlike qualities that clearly mark those to whom God's kingdom belongs." In chapter 10 I review and summarize the preceding pages, present my response to the five perspectives of part 1 from my own perspective, and conclude by offering some final reflections—and hopes.

There are many who have assisted me in my efforts, and I offer them my humble thanks. Among my confreres at Saint Meinrad Archabbey, I am especially grateful to the staff of the Saint Meinrad Archabbey Library for their competent research assistance, and to Br. Brendan Moss, o.s.b., for his patient and careful reading of much of this manuscript. I am indebted to Fr. Vincent Tobin, o.s.b., whose expertise with RAM, ROM, and DOS allowed me to survive crashes, viruses, and worst of all, instruction manuals. For their support and encouragement throughout my work on this book, I thank Fr. Timothy Sweeney, o.s.b., now-resigned archabbot of Saint Meinrad Archabbey; Fr. Eugene Hensell, o.s.b., president-rector of Saint Meinrad Seminary; Fr. Ghislain Lafont, o.s.b., of the Abbey of La Pierre-que-Vire, France; the Rt. Rev. Marcel Rooney, o.s.b., abbot of Conception Abbey, Missouri; and Fr. Richard Bourgeois, o.s.b., of Our Lady of Glastonbury Abbey, Hingham, Massachusetts. And a special word of thanks to Mary Boedeker, and to Bing and Bernitha Werne and the people of Saint Henry Parish, Saint Henry, Indiana, for their hospitality and many kindnesses.

Penultimate thanks are due another confrere, Fr. Aidan Kavanagh, o.s.b., and Nathan Mitchell and the late Mark Searle. Although not involved directly in my work, their influence has been great. That their names are mentioned frequently in these pages is but a small reflection of the professional esteem in which I hold these men.

Ultimate thanks—both meanings of the word are fully intended—are due the Colonel and his wife, Joe and Suzanne. This wonderful couple took an infant baptism some forty years ago quite seriously, as they did also all that preceded it and all that follows. It is indeed to such as these that the kingdom of God belongs.

Abbreviations

CIC	*Codex iuris canonici (Code of Canon Law)*
CDWDS	[Sacred] Congregation for Divine Worship and the Discipline of the Sacraments
DOL	*Documents on the Liturgy, 1963–1979*
ICEL	International Commission on English in the Liturgy
JBC	*Jerome Biblical Commentary*
NAAL	North American Academy of Liturgy
NCCB	National Conference of Catholic Bishops (United States)
NJBC	*New Jerome Biblical Commentary*
PA	*Pastoralis Actio (Instruction on Infant Baptism)*
RBC	*Rite of Baptism for Children*
RC	*Rite of Confirmation*
RCIA	*Rite of Christian Initiation of Adults*
RCIC	*Rite of Initiation for Children of Catechetical Age*
SCDF	Sacred Congregation for the Doctrine of the Faith
SCDW	Sacred Congregation for Divine Worship
SCSDW	Sacred Congregation for Sacraments and Divine Worship
USCC	United States Catholic Conference

Introduction:
A "Problem" with Infant Baptism?

"What the value of baptizing infants might be is an extremely obscure question. But one must believe there is some value in it."[1]

"Is Christ's purpose in instituting this sacrament being frustrated by the practice of infant baptism? Do people have valid motives in requesting baptism for their children? To what extent must infants be baptized as soon as possible?"[2]

American Catholics of but a few generations ago would have been as puzzled by St. Augustine's comment as they would have been suspicious of Richard Redmond's questions. Catholic parents, accustomed to arranging for the baptism of their newborn with little preparation and with few questions asked, would have been among the first to affirm the sacrament's value: infants were baptized to "make them Catholic" and to remove original sin. That these infants could not actually profess their faith, let alone consent to their future Christian responsibilities, seldom troubled either priest or parishioner. *That* issue had been settled by St. Augustine and had since been confirmed by centuries of theological commentary and pastoral practice. In the American parochial view in the early 1960s, those contesting infant baptism in favor of a "believer's baptism" were rare, suspect, or Baptist.

In the years following the Second Vatican Council, however, questioning of the contemporary practice of infant baptism became common, credible, and Catholic.[3] While no American Catholic writer

---

[1]St. Augustine, *De quantitate animae*, 36, 80; trans. Mark Searle, "Infant Baptism Reconsidered," 15.

[2]Richard Redmond, "Infant Baptism: History and Pastoral Problems," 79.

[3]More than one period of Church history, of course, has experienced "problems with infant baptism." For a summary of the immediate preconciliar baptismal debates see Aidan Kavanagh, *The Shape of Baptism: The Rite of Christian*

1

explicitly denied the validity of infant baptism, many did challenge the mechanical or perfunctory way the sacrament often seemed to be requested and administered. Augustine had explained that the faith of the sacrament was realized by the infant's parents and the Church, but Richard Redmond asked just what kind of faith these guardians of the infant were professing:

"While the faith of the Church necessarily finds expression at least in the rite itself, often those who represent the Church, i.e., parents, godparents, and the community, show little or no faith. The theological faith of the child finds no environment in which to take root. . . . While we are convinced of the necessity of baptism, many are not convinced of the instruction and formation necessary to make this sacrament fruitful. Even where there is instruction, often it is no more than a veneer. Without formation in the faith, the child can hardly be expected to mature as an apostolic representative of the Church."[4]

Reporting what had been a topic of serious discussion in Europe for a quarter-century, Redmond was also predicting the fundamental issues of the postconciliar American discussion. His questions, cited at the beginning of this introduction, direct our initial consideration of the "problem with infant baptism."

The Parents:
Do people have valid motives in requesting baptism for their children?
    In 1968 Christiane Brusselmans assessed the reasons parents presented their infants for baptism.[5] She found many parents wanted their children *identified,* either as members of society or as one of their family. While the first identification "is a question of putting the child

---

Initiation, 81–101. Stephen D. Cude, "The Barth-Cullman Debate: Baptism in the New Testament," *Resonance 6* (1968) 9–47, offers a detailed summary of one aspect of the discussion.

    The history of infant baptism was not a major factor in the American postconciliar discussion, and there was little interest in reentering the classic expositions of Karl Barth, Oscar Cullmann, Joachim Jeremias, Kurt Aland, Geoffrey Wainwright, and others. American Catholic theologians and liturgists in the postconciliar period were less interested in discussing the origin and evolution of infant baptism in the early Church, preferring to address whether or not the Church should be baptizing infants *now.*

    [4]Redmond, "Infant Baptism," 83.

    [5]Christiane Brusselmans, "Christian Parents and Infant Baptism," 29–48. Citations here are taken from pages 29–30.

in order not with the Church, but with the sociological group to which he is related," the second resembles more a rite of "natural religion . . . [and] as such it helps to celebrate the child's birth."

Brusselmans thought the quest for spiritual or secular *security* another reason many parents sought baptism for their children. Baptism provided spiritual security by removing original sin, while secular security was attained by choosing godparents, a practice that often seemed to indicate "the human role, sometimes very important, that the parents delegate to [the godparents] even while they are themselves alive and especially in the case of a family disaster." Brusselmans believed "the real meaning of the baptism that the Church gives has only a slight connection with what people are requesting."

The Community:
Is Christ's purpose in instituting this sacrament
being frustrated by the practice of infant baptism?

The apparent spurious motives of some parents occasioned a closer scrutiny of "just what kind of faith these guardians of the child are professing," but not all of the responsibility for the alleged unfruitfulness of infant baptism was attributed to the child's immediate family. While Brusselmans had observed that some parents requested baptism for their children to bring the child into a "determined sociological group," other writers questioned the degree of Christian commitment of these groups. Indeed, several writers suggested that contemporary culture and society had imposed its values on Catholicism, and that Christianity, rather than challenging the status quo, had all but surrendered to it. The too-facile, noncritical assimilation of secular culture had encouraged an attitude that being Catholic was not that important—that it was simply something one was "born into." Ralph Keifer was one of many lamenting what we might call the "blurring of American Catholicism":

"We are really less a community of faith now [1974] than we were a decade ago: an extremely brittle authority structure and narrow symbolic focus has cracked, and with it a sense of distinctiveness and belonging which characterized preconciliar Catholicism. As a result to speak of initiation is extremely difficult because there is so little to initiate people *into*, and little or nothing to celebrate. It should not be surprising that so many liturgical services are lackluster, banal,

3

conventional and boring. Boredom, after all, is the experience of having to attend constantly to the insignificant."[6]

Aidan Kavanagh expressed similar sentiments. His oft-cited commentary strongly criticized the attitude that sacramental initiation offers spiritual reassurance to Christians more than it does challenge and direction for their lives:

". . . baptism-confirmation does not initiate the *faith* of an individual, does not *confect* faith on the spot and out of nothing, to inject it like an unheard of miracle drug or a disembodied heart muscle into the vacant veins or chest cavity of a passive receiver. This surgical-pharmaceutical view of faith, and its correspondingly clinical view of Christian initiation, should be called what it is: it is theological heresy because God calls one to faith as he pleases; it is psychological rubbish; it is pastoral myopia; it is ritual magic. . . .

"To reduce baptism-confirmation for neatness' sake to a quasi-magical confection of faith on the one hand or a quasi-surgical excision of the great wart known as original sin on the other, and to attempt to make even this somehow compelling in fifteen minute ceremonies done privately in corners with teacups of water and a smear or two of grease is unacceptable. It reaches tragic proportions when this perfunctoriness is made to bear the additional weight of attempting to reflect, actualize, and predict what a Christian truly is in a compelling way."[7]

Observing that "the reality of what a Christian is is laid open to a large degree in the process by which he gets that way," Kavanagh expressed little surprise that "baptism-confirmation has sunk into a sort of atrophied conventionalism."[8]

The Celebration:
To what extent must infants be baptized as soon as possible?

Attempting to explain the "atrophied conventionalism" into which infant baptism had apparently sunk, some authors called attention to

---

[6]Ralph A. Keifer, "Christian Initiation: The State of the Question," 395–96; emphasis in original. See also his "Faith Community Necessary for Adult Initiation," 161–63.

[7]Aidan Kavanagh, "Initiation: Baptism and Confirmation," 263–64; emphasis in original.

[8]Ibid., 263, 264.

the sacramental celebration of infant baptism itself, observing that an understanding of baptism as initiating one into a countercultural community received little support from the ritual. Prior to the publication of the *RCB* in 1969,[9] the ritual used was an adaptation of the 1614 ritual of the baptism of adults. Rather than offering the kind of creative modifications that would respect the distinct nature and situation of infant baptism, however, the adaptations primarily eliminated features of the rite that were obviously inconsistent with the baptism of an infant (e.g., the lengthy catechesis—a vestige of the early catechumenate). Ironically, then, until the promulgation of the 1969 *RBC* infants were baptized according to an originally adult-oriented rite, while adults in the preconciliar era were most often initiated through this same, now infant-adapted, rite. The inevitable discrepancies are perhaps seen most clearly in the role assigned to the sponsors or godparents of the infant: essential to the structure and process of initiation in the early Church, sponsorship and its responsibilities were retained in the "1614 infant rite"—but at the expense of minimizing the role of the parents.[10]

History had allowed other ritual poverties, due largely to the insistence on *quamprimum* baptism. A higher rate of infant mortality fed spiritual anxieties about original sin, and so infants ordinarily were baptized as soon as possible after birth. Eventually the practice of infant baptism was removed chronologically from the Easter Vigil, which contributed to the theological erosion of understanding baptism as a sacramental dying and rising with Christ. The baptism of

---

[9]An *editio typica altera* of the 1969 ritual was published in 1973. One readily accessible edition that contains these 1973 emendations (as well as those occasioned by the 1983 *Code of Canon Law*) is *The Rites of the Catholic Church*, vol. 1A, *Initiation* (New York: Pueblo, 1988) 359–466. The International Commission on English in the Liturgy (ICEL) is currently in consultation on the Rites for the Initiation of Children, with the hope of completing a thorough revision of these rites within the next few years.

[10]Brusselmans' article is largely a call for the restoration of this sponsorship to the parents, and she proposes a new rite emphasizing this sponsorship. Other writers in the early postconciliar years commenting upon the new rite and emphasizing the restored role of the parents include Frederick McManus, "Ritual of Infant Baptism," 190–99; Richard Guerrette, "The New Rite of Infant Baptism," 224–30; A. Leystan, "New Rite of Infant Baptism," 52–57; and Christopher Kiesling, "The New Rite of Baptism for Children," 262–79.

In my opinion the best commentary on the postconciliar *RBC* is Mark Searle's *Christening: The Making of Christians*.

infants did guarantee large numbers of Catholics, but the desire for quantity often seemed more influential than the concern for quality. Describing the phenomenon, Kavanagh appealed to the Scriptures— and to his distinctive prose. Acknowledging that the Acts of the Apostles reports that after Philip baptized the Egyptian eunuch they both departed never to see each other again, Kavanagh insisted: "It is quite another [thing] to have local churches populated by Egyptian eunuchs. Such churches are anomalous with a vengeance, and their number is legion.[11]

The desire for fewer ecclesial eunuchs and for more active, visible witnesses to the faith led some to advocate the postponement or delay of an infant's baptism. Several grounds for such a decision were proposed, only one of which was sanctioned by the *RBC:* that if there was sufficient doubt that the child would be truly formed and educated in the faith, the baptism was to be delayed until such time as the parents (or others) could guarantee the child's Christian up-bringing (*RBC* 8.3, 4; 25). But others sought to postpone an infant's baptism on the grounds that the sacrament violated the child's free-dom. Describing this position, Monika Hellwig observed: "People want to know what difference it really makes whether a child has been baptized, and whether he ought not to have the opportunity to grow up and find out what religion is all about before getting himself involved in any church obligations." A similar question was on young people's minds, Hellwig noted, for they "frequently want to know by what right others have made a commitment on their behalf about which they were never consulted."[12]

Curiously, "freedom advocates" seem to have existed primarily in the "verbal" discussions of infant baptism. The argument is reported in the literature on a regular basis,[13] but no individual espousing this view is cited and apparently no writer uses it to speak against even the indiscriminate baptizing of infants. Perhaps its origins in popular thought in the United States may be attributed to that nebulous phrase, "the American spirit"—a spirit that has traditionally empha-

---

[11] Aidan Kavanagh, "Christian Initiation for Those Baptized as Infants," 387.

[12] Monika Hellwig, *The Meaning of the Sacraments,* 5. Hellwig is reporting—not supporting—this argument.

[13] See, for example, Norbert Rigali, "New Theology and Infant Baptism," 13–17; Rockford Peterson, "Let's Baptize Babies of Non-practicing Catholics," 14–15; Eugene Maly, "Why Baptize Babies?" 34–38; and Searle, *Christening,* 48–51.

sized personal freedom and individual rights and that received particularly intense expression in the sociological and political climate of the 1960s and 1970s.[14]

A third justification for delaying the baptism of infants was advocated particularly by those who understood the 1972 *(RCIA)* as the norm or paradigm for the "making of a Christian." Some considered that infant baptism, particularly the indiscriminate baptizing of infants, burdened the Church with large numbers of nominal Catholics whose collective apathy was compromising the effective witness of the Church. Others thought that, even when one could reasonably assume that the infant would receive a sound Christian upbringing, infant baptism deprived the future child or young adult of an important psychological moment and force for growth.[15] These concerns encouraged the suggestion that an infant first be enrolled as a catechumen and initiated through baptism at a later and more appropriate time.

"What the value of baptizing infants might be is an extremely obscure question. But one must believe there is some value in it." As we have begun to indicate, this "extremely obscure question" was addressed by many authors in the postconciliar years. Some, emphasizing the vision of Church suggested by the Second Vatican Council (a vision reinforced with the publication of the adult ordo in 1972), considered the baptism of infants as legitimate but abnormal; others saw infant baptism as legitimate *and* as the normal way a faithful family and community initiated one newly born into their Church. We begin our review of the American postconciliar discussion of infant baptism by considering these two principal schools of thought in an effort to detect what, indeed, the answers to this "extremely obscure question" might be.

[14]Maly, "Why Baptize Babies," 35: "Something about [infant baptism] flies in the face of very basic notions in our culture about individual freedom and the importance of personal choice—in short, our insistence on individualism. We want to believe that we choose God (rather than that God chooses us). We want to believe that we can and should save ourselves (rather than that we are saved)."

[15]Searle refers to this argument in *Christening*, 49–51.

PART ONE

MADE, NOT BORN

A Report on the Postconciliar Catholic Discussion
of Infant Baptism in the United States, 1965–1995

Chapter 1

The Making of Christians:
The adult ordo and the
Mature Adulthood School

"Fieri non nasci solet christiana." (Christians are not born, they are made.)[1]

"Augustine and his peers over a century later would have agreed, perhaps extending Tertullian's aphorism to say that Christians do not just pop in off the streets either: they are honed down by the teaching and discipline of the catechumenate until their edges are not only sharp but glow."[2]

The Constitution on the Sacred Liturgy, the first document issued by the Second Vatican Council, called for appropriate revisions and adaptations in the celebration of the sacraments. The *Rite of Baptism for Children (RBC)* was published in 1969, and the opening years of the following decade saw the publication of the *Rite of Confirmation (RC)* (1971) and the *Rite of Christian Initiation of Adults (RCIA)* (1972). Three years later Nathan Mitchell observed that he and his colleagues were engaged in a complex discussion that might best be summarized by the question "Christian initiation—for children or adults?"

"Christians are not born, they are made." But *how* Christians are made—and *when* this making should take place—were the key questions in the American baptismal discussion of the 1970s. While some thought that only adults had the maturity and level of commitment necessary to embrace Christianity, others spoke of the ecclesial and familial environment that would allow a Christian to be made even of the very young. Those advocating the former position eagerly

---

[1] Tertullian, *De testimonio animae*, 1.

[2] Aidan Kavanagh, "The Norm of Baptism: The New Rite of Christian Initiation of Adults," 150. See also his *Shape of Baptism*, 119.

embraced the *RCIA* as an ally. Among these was Aidan Kavanagh, who appraised the new adult ordo not as the latest installment in a long series of liturgical revisions but as the "most mature piece of liturgical reform, the most profound theological statement on the Church, and surely the most explosive pastoral document to be issued since the council."[3] Undeniably the most prolific American writer on Christian initiation in the postconciliar years, Kavanagh was also the most influential representative of what Mitchell had designated as the "Mature Adulthood School":

"Adherents of the [Mature Adulthood School] argue that baptism will diminish in importance unless it is accompanied by the mature adult acts of coming to an explicit, conscious faith and conversion in Christ. In their view this diminishment will lead to the consequence that churches will be filled with baptized catechumens who have never confronted themselves with the costly challenge of the gospel. As a result Christianity will become progressively more flaccid, unable to withstand the assaults of a world profoundly estranged from the values of the gospel. At root the mature adulthood school discerns an ecclesiological problem: indiscriminate infant baptism that ignores the tough work of adult conversion produces a church where largely uncritical, unreflective, unintelligent adherence to 'the faith' becomes a normal condition of life. The result is a placid Christianity of convention not an aggressive Christianity of conviction."[4]

Although our interest here concerns primarily the baptism of infants, it is necessary to consider the major tenets and writers of the Mature Adulthood School. Their exposition of and commentary on the adult ordo revolutionized the American Church's understanding of the nature and consequences of Christian initiation and thus challenged our way of thinking about and celebrating the sacramental initiation of Christians of any age. A discussion of baptism in the postconciliar era, whether it be the baptism of adults or of infants,

[3]Kavanagh, "Those Baptized as Infants," 391.
[4]Mitchell, "Once and Future Child," 429. Covino, "Postconciliar Debate," 242 n. 6, lists the following as representatives of this school of thought: Richard Guerrette, David Greye Perrey, Aidan Kavanagh, Ralph Keifer, Charles Gusmer, the recommendations of the 1973 meeting of the North American Academy of Liturgy, and the articles in *Resonance 6* and *Made, Not Born: New Perspectives on Christian Initiation and the Catechumenate.*

would be incomplete were it not to take their contributions into account. To maintain the focus of our study, I will limit our review of the Mature Adulthood School to two considerations: an overview of their commentary concerning the adult ordo,[5] and their position as regards the practice of infant baptism.

THE 1972 ADULT ORDO:
A PASTORALLY EXPLOSIVE DOCUMENT

"Christians [are not born] . . . they are honed down by the teaching and discipline of the catechumenate until their edges are not only sharp but glow." It would be difficult to overstate the influence of the adult ordo in the postconciliar discussion of *any* matters liturgical or sacramental. As noted previously, the *RCIA* was considered "pastorally explosive"—a document deemed dangerous to the perceived ecclesial status quo because it called for "the radical renewal of the whole of Christian life."[6] Kavanagh insisted that the adult ordo was not one more collection of "incidental liturgical changes that lie at the edges of Christian life," for changing the way a society initiates its members necessarily involves a change in the community's self-awareness: "When one talks of initiation in Christian terms, one is talking therefore of how all else begins and, ultimately, of how all else is sustained."[7]

[5]As mentioned, the most influential representative of the Mature Adulthood School is Aidan Kavanagh. His influence upon the American discussion of Christian initiation is indicated only partially by the extent to which he is quoted in this work and in the works of others throughout the postconciliar period. His many articles and, especially, his 1978 *Shape of Baptism* detail the tenets of this school of thought and provide an extensive analysis of the adult ordo.

For a more detailed investigation of the Mature Adulthood School than that presented here, see Covino's "Postconciliar Debate," 242–47, and his "Question of Infant Baptism in the American Catholic Church: 1965 to 1980." See pages 53–70 of this latter work (upon which "Postconciliar Debate" is based) for Covino's assessment of the school's strengths and weaknesses.

[6]Aidan Kavanagh, "Adult Initiation: Process and Ritual," 5.

[7]Ibid. In "Christian Initiation of Adults: The Rites," 319, Kavanagh observed, "The importance of the new *Ordo* stems therefore not so much from its ceremonial details as from its strategic vision . . . of what the church can become through that continuing renewal process known as Christian initiation." See also his "New Roman Rites of Adult Initiation," 36–37, "Baptism and Confirmation," 262–76, and *Shape of Baptism*, 126–27 and 144–47.

Ralph Keifer listed four areas of "radical reform and renewal" implied by the *RCIA:* the restoration of the baptismal focus of the paschal season; the radical rearrangement of sacramental symbols and priorities; the alteration of pastoral priorities and perspectives; and an end to the harmful estrangement between various ecclesial spheres such as liturgy and life, private devotion and public function, and active ministers and inert laity.[8] He eloquently assessed the consequences for the Church in taking the *RCIA* seriously:

"The program to reform the order of initiation has issued in the promulgation of rites which are, historically and culturally speaking, a massive rejection of the presuppositions of pastoral practice and of most church-goers as to what membership in the church means. This is a revolution quite without precedent because the Catholic Church has never before in its history done such violence to its liturgical practice as to make its rites so thoroughly incongruous with its concrete reality. A step like this is either a statement that rite is wholly irrelevant or that the church is willing to change and to change radically its concrete reality. Such an approach is either suicide or prophecy of a very high order."[9]

Pivotal to the hopes of many liturgists and theologians that the adult ordo would promote a "radical renewal for the whole of Christian life" was the mutually demanding relationship established between catechumen and community. Because adult initiation into the ecclesial community did not consist of being passively absorbed into a community ill defined and (at best) geographically formed, those seeking entrance could not submit as references vague and innocuous claims of "wanting to live a good life." The Mature Adulthood School took the phrase "sacrament of *faith*" seriously, emphasizing that faith must be present to be sacramentalized and that, moreover, faith was not an assent to specific teaching and doctrine as much as it was a faithful embrace of the Christian way of life. Conversion was

---

[8]Keifer, "Christian Initiation," 392–93. Keifer was one of many sharing Kavanagh's esteem for the new ordo: "It is ironic that we have so often cried out for Rome to turn radical, generally expecting instead obscurantism, timeserving and conservatism, that we have been unable to perceive radical revision and drastic change when Rome presents us with it" (392).

[9]Ibid., 402. Keifer's article presents a fine commentary on the American Church's assimilation into the American culture.

about the changing of one's life, not one's mind; it was less the altering of one's religious affiliation than it was the correcting of one's obedience.

The discernment of such a conversion—indeed, its inducement—was primarily the responsibility of the community who supported the candidate through intensive catechesis, or in Kavanagh's words, "conversion therapy."[10] But this catechesis bears little resemblance to the rectory convert classes of days past: "We must learn all over again that proximate preparation for baptism means catechesis, and that catechesis is not about doctrinal or ecclesiastical data, but about conversion."[11] Besides doctrinal instruction, therefore, the therapy of conversion required also the candidates' assimilation into the community's Christian way of life (fasting, prayer, works of mercy), their introduction to a sacramental way of life through their regular participation in public worship, and their sharing in the apostolic work of the community through evangelistic social action and the spiritual and corporal works of mercy.[12]

"Christians are not born, they are made." And yet the *RCIA* was not only about the making of *new* Christians, for initiation "is as of

[10]Kavanagh, "Those Baptized as Infants," 388: "If conversion cannot be induced, then neither catechesis (conversion therapy) nor catechetics (reflection on conversion and its therapy) can take place. Only religious education can happen, and this most often under some threat of external sanction. The results of this, at least so far as initiation is concerned, are highly dubious. It is certain that the effort expended on it rarely is justified by the results. Catechesis, catechetics, and religious education must not be confused."

In "Initiation: Baptism and Confirmation," 265–68, Kavanagh discusses the relationship between evangelization and catechesis. See also Charles Gusmer, "The Revised Adult Initiation and Its Challenge to Religious Education," 92–98, and Thomas Ivory, "The Restoration of the Catechumenate as a Norm for Catechesis," 225–35.

Richard Reichert's "A Catechist's Response to the Rite of Christian Initiation for Adults," 138–46, offers a less enthusiastic assessment of the adult ordo's potential: "[M]ost catechists are neither startled nor overly excited with the RCIA. It is a good document, late in coming. It will not revolutionize their ministry nor the church, viewed in itself" (143). Reichert observes that "the RCIA underscores [our] problem; it did not discover it, nor does it in itself offer a practical solution" (144).

[11]Kavanagh, "Initiation: Baptism and Confirmation," 269. See also his "New Roman Rites," 37.

[12]Kavanagh, "Christian Initiation of Adults," 321–23. See also his "Those Baptized as Infants," 392–93, and *Shape of Baptism,* 129–33.

great, if not greater, importance to the community as it is to the convert."[13] The community could demand such seriousness and conviction of their catechumens throughout the process of initiation
because the presence of catechumens made an equally serious demand of the community. That catechumens approach the Church
seeking a share in its faith implies that the Church has already been
at work in that most subtle yet powerful method of evangelization:
the community is expressing in its actions what it is professing in its
liturgy. Catechumens are, then, "corporate witnesses" who are not
only the object of the Church's ministry but who remind the community that the community itself is in need of constant conversion:

"As a group catechumens occupy an important place in church life
not only because they are recipients of the church's faith in a passive
way through the catechetical teaching process. They also function as
a corporate presence witnessing constantly to the church her need for
continuing conversion in Christ. Without this sustained corporate
witness the church is found to be more sluggish in its own conversion and more resistant to change in general. The catechumen as an
individual and the catechumenate as an order of persons exercise a
true ministry, both passive and active, in the church—a ministry the
church forgoes at her own peril."[14]

This brief overview cannot do justice to the complexity and richness of the adult ordo. It should suffice, however, to illustrate two
points central to the convictions of the Mature Adulthood School:
first, that conversion and subsequent initiation into the Christian
community is a matter of mature faith and of visible evidence of that
faith; and second, that Christian initiation involves the entire Christian community—a community always called not only to initiate but
also to be initiated.

THE MATURE ADULTHOOD SCHOOL:
FIVE PERSPECTIVES ON INFANT BAPTISM

The primary concern of the Mature Adulthood School was the
evangelization, catechesis, and sacramental initiation of adults. They

[13]Kavanagh, "Initiation: Baptism and Confirmation," 268. Subtitled "The Phe-
nomenology of Christian Initiation," the article explores the impact of initiation
upon those who initiate as well as upon those initiated.
[14]Kavanagh, "Norm of Baptism," 147. See also Keifer, "Christian Initiation,"
393.

acknowledged the validity and value of infant baptism when practiced discriminately but ordinarily had little interest in dealing extensively with infant baptism on its own terms. Nevertheless, several
tenets of the school addressed at least indirectly the practice and
common understanding of infant baptism.

I have selected five of these tenets—I shall use the term "perspectives"—to guide not only our review in this chapter of the Mature
Adulthood School's influence upon the discussion of infant baptism
but also of the literature throughout part 1 of this work. These perspectives can be discerned quite readily in the early literature of the
Mature Adulthood School, and for the most part they continue to influence the discussion of infant baptism today. The five perspectives
are (1) that the indiscriminate baptizing of infants is unacceptable; (2)
that the adult ordo presents the definitive statement of the Church's
norm of baptism; (3) that, as initiation is a process and not a single or
isolated "moment" in a Christian's life, continuing education and formation (catechesis) are an integral part of the celebration of the sacrament; (4) that the intrinsic unity among the initiation sacraments of
baptism and confirmation (and Eucharist) must be respected theologically and sequentially; and (5) that the enrollment of an infant
into a catechumenate presents an appropriate alternative to baptism
until such time as the child reaches the age at which a mature decision for the faith is possible.

The first perspective:
The problem of indiscriminate baptism

   The indiscriminate baptizing of infants is unacceptable. "Indiscriminate"
and "unacceptable" are the key words here, for no member of the
Mature Adulthood School challenged the validity of infant baptism.
What was challenged was the often automatic accession to parents'
requests to have their infant baptized, a request many considered
was granted regularly with little consideration of whether the child's
environment would actually foster the making of a Christian.

   Shortly after the 1969 publication of the *RBC*, Richard Guerrette
recognized both the problem of indiscriminate infant baptism and the
legitimacy of the sacrament when administered in the proper context.
Commenting upon the ecclesiological shift from the Tridentine
"Church as kingdom of God on earth" to the Vatican II perspective of
"Church as pilgrim people making their way toward the kingdom,"
Guerrette observed that "while all men are indeed called to the

kingdom, not all men are called to embrace the church." Observing that the quality and character of Christian life had become somewhat obscure, Guerrette felt it essential to reevaluate the practice of infant baptism, since "initiating more and more children into the church with little or no faith-commitment to diakonia on the part of the parents becomes increasingly more difficult to reconcile with the ecclesiological significance of baptism."[15] When new pastoral forms that allow for and encourage "the varying degrees of Christian commitment" that will establish an exemplary consciousness among parishioners are developed, Guerrette thought, infant baptism will serve as a valid *and* instructive sacrament.[16] As the *RCIA* seemed to offer these new pastoral forms, to demand Christian commitment, and to promote an exemplary consciousness among parishioners, the call for a reevaluation of the practice of infant baptism became insistent—as did a growing abhorrence of indiscriminate baptism.[17] The *indiscriminate* baptizing of infants could only be considered counterproductive to the vision of Church supported by the adult ordo: "The enemy against which we must strike is not baptism of infants, but indiscriminate baptism of anyone done for sentimental reasons to support a crumbling *status quo* that is robbing the church of calcium in its bones and the gospel it proclaims of the lean hardness it must have to remain credible. Being a Christian does not mean living passively on divine welfare."[18]

[15]Richard Guerrette, "Ecclesiology and Infant Baptism," 434.

[16]Ibid., 436: "Positing the development of such a renewal in pastoral forms, one can begin to reconcile the administering of baptism to infants with current ecclesiology. With the existence of a genuine Christian community, the celebration of the sacrament conveys its intended ecclesiological significance; and the participants in the liturgy, namely, the community, the child, and the parents, retain their true ecclesial identity."

[17]An American priest writing under the pseudonym David Greye Perrey was apparently the only author who called for the complete elimination of infant baptism. Outlining his views in "Let's Stop Baptizing Babies," 14–15, and *Baptism at 21*, he maintained that a demanding, all-adult catechumenate was the only solution to the Church's number one problem——the failure "to produce Christians on a scale anywhere near the number of Catholics" ("Let's Stop Baptizing Babies," 14). Perrey's extreme position is perhaps seen most clearly in his "allowing" the baptism of an infant in danger of death only as a "practical compromise": "I am not advocating this compromise for any reason other than to make it easier to move the Church in the direction of baptism at 21" (*Baptism at 21*, 100).

[18]Kavanagh, "Process and Ritual," 9. See also his "Those Baptized as Infants," 395–96, and "Norm of Baptism," 145.

As we shall see, dissatisfaction with the practice of indiscriminate infant baptism was one of two perspectives that enjoyed near-unanimous agreement throughout the postconciliar discussion. We turn now to another conviction held strongly by the Mature Adulthood School, a perspective that is one of the better known and frequently quoted tenets of those writing about the adult ordo—and one that led some authors to consider even the discriminate baptizing of infants a practice better tolerated than encouraged.

The second perspective: The norm of baptism

The adult ordo presents the definitive statement of the Church's norm of baptism. Kavanagh's interpretation that the *RCIA* sets forth "the definitive statement of what the Roman Catholic Church's *norm of baptism* is henceforth to be" was one of his major contributions to the discussion, and by the end of the decade the thesis had become practically *de rigueur* in any article dealing with the *RCIA*.[19] The notion of a definitive statement of a norm of baptism is complex and so was subject to misinterpretation, confusion, and criticism (a point to which we shall return below).

Kavanagh defined "norm" not as the frequency with which something occurs but "as the standard according to which a thing is done."[20] He observed, for example, that the council's Constitution on the Sacred Liturgy (nos. 41–42) asserted that the normal performance of the Eucharist "is to be seen in that of the bishop presiding within an event that concretely expresses the whole local church—people, presbyters, deacons and other assistants." This "norm of the Eucharist" obviously does not require that the bishop preside at every Mass, Kavanagh noted, but that "in both theory and practice the eucharist is never to be regarded as anything less than an act of the whole Church, . . . and that this *norm* must to some extent always be achieved, even when the [bishop] does not himself preside."[21]

---

[19]For example, John Gallen, "The Pastoral Celebration of Initiation," 150: "There is no doubt that the norm espoused by the current reform is the practice of adult initiation." Kavanagh thoroughly discusses the normative value of the adult ordo in *Shape of Baptism*, 102–25. The citation in our text is from his "New Roman Rites," 35; emphasis in original.

[20]Kavanagh, *Shape of Baptism*, 108.

[21]Ibid., 107; emphasis in original. Kavanagh later elaborates: "So long as the norm is in place both in practice and in the awareness of those who are engaged in it, the situation is capable of being judged 'normal' even though the norm must

Admitting the council was less clear about positing the adult ordo as normative for baptism, Kavanagh nevertheless detected a definite statement of that normative value in the conciliar documents: "The norm of baptism was stated by the Council . . . to be solemn sacramental initiation done especially at the paschal vigil and preceded by a catechumenate of serious content and considerable duration. This implies strongly, even if it does not require, that the initiate be an adult or at least a child well advanced in years. The conciliar emphasis is clearly on the adult nature of the norm of Christian initiation, deriving as it does from the New Testament doctrine of conversion."[22]

Adult candidates, a lengthy catechumenate, solemn sacramental initiation at the Easter Vigil: this, according to Kavanagh, is what the Church's "*norm of baptism* is henceforth to be." Or, perhaps better, this is the *pastoral* norm—the "standard," the ordinary ways and means—"according to which [sacramental initiation] is done."

But a second interpretation and application of the term "norm" is necessary, one that refers not to *how* or *when* "something is done" but to *why*. For as Kavanagh frequently remarked, the impact of the adult ordo was due not to its rearrangement of ceremonial details or its offering of new "liturgical recipes" but to its strategic vision of initiation and the Church. The adult ordo did not prepare one simply to celebrate the distinct rites of initiation; the thrust of the adult ordo was that toward which the catechumenate and those distinct sacramental rites prepared one: "a *life of faith* in which asceticism, good works, and sacramental engagement could blend in a robust whole rather than languish as mere options, supine before the idiosyncracies of personal taste and piety."[23]

In the light of these pastoral and strategic norms, Kavanagh criticized understanding infant baptism as the "normal way by which

---

be departed from to some extent, even frequently, due to exigencies of time, place, pastoral considerations, physical inabilities, or whatever. Yet to the extent possible, the norm must always be achieved to some extent lest it slip imperceptibly into the status of a mere 'ideal' all wish for but are under no obligation to realize" (108).

[22]Ibid., 109. In n. 12 on this page, Kavanagh refers to the documents *Sacrosanctum Concilium* 64–68, *Lumen Gentium* 14, *Ad Gentes* 13–14, *Christus Dominus* 14, and *Presbyterorum Ordinis* 6.

[23]Kavanagh, *Shape of Baptism*, 105; emphasis in original.

one becomes a Christian."[24] Acknowledging its validity and its constant practice in the history of the Church, he thought the sacramental initiation of infants an "abnormality": a "benign abnormality" when practiced prudently or when pastorally necessary (in anticipation of an infant's death, for example, or when requested by parents committed to the Christian upbringing of their child); a "malign abnormality" when administered because of

"pastoral malfeasance, theological obsession, or the decline of faith among Christian parents into some degree of merely social conformity. The data of neither scripture nor tradition can be made to support infant baptism as the pastoral norm. But those same data clearly support the practice as a benign abnormality in the life of a community whose ministry regularly focuses upon the evangelization, catechesis, and initiation of adults of faith into its midst. Initiatory normality in this sense provides the richest pastoral and theological milieu within which infant baptism can be ascertained for what it really ought to be in the life of the Church—not an unremembered substitute for conversion in faith, but a modest manifestation of God's love for all ages and of the stunning liberality of his grace, especially in difficult circumstances."[25]

Kavanagh's thesis that the adult ordo presented the Church's norm of baptism was a major contribution to the American discussion in the postconciliar years, for it reflected clearly the convictions of the Mature Adulthood School: that Christians are not born but are and

[24]Kavanagh, "Process and Ritual," 8: "That the church has always baptized infants is, I think, unassailable. I also think that infant baptism in itself is theologically legitimate. But that infant baptism should be taken as the pastoral norm for how one becomes a Christian is not in my opinion historically unassailable, and even less is it theologically legitimate or pastorally prudent in the cultural context we find ourselves in today. . . . What I am criticizing here is not infant baptism as such, but its having become in our minds the normal way by which one becomes a Christian."

[25]Kavanagh, *Shape of Baptism*, 109–10. In "Those Baptized as Infants," 391 n. 7, Kavanagh observes: "That infant baptism is abnormal is made clear in the extraordinary qualifications that accompany its administration—namely, the suspension of the baptized's right to the eucharist until the age of reason and the postponement of confirmation until later years." See also his "New Roman Rites," 36, and "Norm of Baptism," 146; these latter articles are contained in sections of *Shape of Baptism*. It is important to note that Kavanagh is neither addressing nor denying the validity of infant baptism.

must be made; that initiation "defines simultaneously both the Christian and the Church";[26] that baptism is "not only a public event in the church but *the* public event";[27] and that the *RCIA* challenges the local parish communities "to become the communities of faith the Second Vatican Council called them to be."[28]

The use of terms such as "malign," "benign," and "abnormality" to describe the practice of infant baptism, however, inevitably attracted criticism of his thesis—criticism, which in some instances seemed to put proponents of infant baptism on the defensive. We will examine this criticism in the following chapters. We consider now a third perspective of the Mature Adulthood School, one that enjoyed the strong support of those whose charge was preparing Christians of any age for baptism.

The third perspective: The necessity of catechesis

Catechesis and formation in the faith are as integral a part and as essential to the baptizing of infants as they are to the process guided by the adult ordo. While the baptizing of infants confers grace and remits original sin *ex opere operato,* it does not automatically assure the subsequent catechesis and formation necessary to fulfill "the true meaning of the sacrament" (*RBC* 3). This distinction between what the sacrament of infant baptism could and could not give was reflected by many authors who emphasized that Christian education and formation do not happen in a vacuum.

Our consideration here of this perspective will be brief, as there was little disagreement as to the essential role catechesis played in the sacrament of infant baptism. Writing in 1976, Charles Gusmer stated the point succinctly: "The issue is not infant baptism, for if all Christians baptized in infancy grew up to be committed adults there would be no controversy."[29] Acknowledging that infant baptism was justified by the faith of the parents and community who brought the infant to the font, Gusmer insisted that parents and community must never cease bringing the faith sacramentally effected at that font to the child in the years following the baptism.[30]

[26]Kavanagh, "The Rites," 333.
[27]Keifer, "Christian Initiation," 393; emphasis in original.
[28]Gusmer, "Revised Adult Initiation," 93.
[29]Ibid., 95.
[30]Ibid., 94: "The theology and practice of the New Testament make it clear that the grace of faith and conversion must be ultimately accepted by a conscious

Catechesis—"conversion therapy"—was central to the process of the *RCIA*. We will explore at greater length the expectation of catechesis as regards infant baptism in the following chapter. We turn now to the fourth perspective of the Mature Adulthood School, one concerning a sacrament few in the preconciliar years would have immediately thought of when speaking of infant baptism.

The fourth perspective: The unity of the initiation sacraments

The intrinsic unity among the initiation sacraments of baptism and confirmation (and Eucharist) must be respected theologically and sequentially. Baptized as an infant; first confession at age seven; first Communion two weeks later; confirmation somewhere before age nine or ten: such is the sacramental experience (and sequence) of many Catholics born after 1910, the year Pope Pius X's *Quam Singulari* lowered the age at which children might receive the Eucharist to "about the age of seven."[31]

Such was not the practice of the early Church, however, and such practice was strongly criticized by many authors in the postconciliar years. A discussion group of the North American Academy of Liturgy (NAAL) in 1973 unanimously concluded:

"The rite of Christian initiation should normally consist of the unified sacramental event in which the three now separated moments (baptism, confirmation, Eucharist) are integrated. The full rite is to be used *at any age* when a person is initiated. . . .

---

adult response. From the beginning the justification for infant baptism has been a pastoral adaptation of the theological meaning of adult initiation whereby children are baptized into the faith of the church as concretized in believing parents (cf. Introduction to revised Infant Baptism, nos. 1–3). This should be the motivation for programs of pre-baptismal catechesis for parents: one way to responsibly ensure the propriety of infant baptism and another striking indication that the parents who present the child for baptism are its primary religious educators." See also Ivory, "Catechumenate as a Norm for Catechesis." As we shall see, these concerns were also among the principal teachings of the Environmentalist School.

[31]Kavanagh, *Shape of Baptism*, 81–101, and, more briefly, Francis J. Buckley, "What Age for Confirmation?" 655–66 (esp. 655–59), explain the developments preceding *Quam Singulari* and the document's impact on the pastoral practice of confirmation and Eucharist. For the history of the separation of the rites of baptism and confirmation, see Kavanagh, *Shape of Baptism*, 35–78, and Nathan Mitchell, "Christian Initiation: Decline and Dismemberment," 458–79.

"For children of responsible Christian parents, two different patterns of initiation might well coexist: the celebration of the full rite of initiation (baptism, confirmation, Eucharist) shortly after birth, to be followed by catechesis appropriate to succeeding stages of development; or enrollment of the infant as a catechumen, with initiation to be celebrated at a later age after catechesis."[32]

The conclusions of NAAL are not only representative of the Mature Adulthood School, they also reflect a concern registered by Aidan Kavanagh: that discussions on Christian initiation must answer strategic rather than tactical questions.[33] Kavanagh believed that the adult ordo clearly addressed an important strategic question in its expression of the intrinsic connection between baptism and confirmation in the adult rite,[34] a connection that was to be maintained no less when celebrating the sacramental initiation of infants:

---

[32]The conclusions of NAAL (Scottsdale, Ariz., December 1973) are reported in John Gallen, "American Liturgy: A Theological Locus," 307. The two paragraphs cited represent conclusions 1 and 5 respectively. The second pattern of initiation, enrollment of the infant as a catechumen, is considered below.

[33]Aidan Kavanagh, "Christian Initiation: Tactics and Strategy" in *Made, Not Born*, 1–6. Kavanagh observes that asking at what age confirmation should be administered is a tactical question and only partially helpful: "[T]he issue raised concerns far more than the appropriate age at which a rite . . . is to be administered. The issue concerns *why* one should be confirmed at all, and *how* one gets to the point of even wanting confirmation. In other words, the issue embraces the whole of the Church's policy on who a Christian is and how he gets to be that way. Phrasing the question of confirmation tactically in terms of age, and responding to it tactically by giving one, not only turns over no rocks and flushes out none of the snakes that lurk there, but also confirms their territoriality and signals our own intent to avoid the area where solutions to our problems may lie hidden. For when we talk about confirmation our conversation is really about baptism; when we are dealing with baptism we are discoursing about Christian initiation; when we are into initiation we are face to face with conversion in Jesus Christ dead and rising; and when we are into conversion in Jesus Christ dead and rising we are at the storm center of the universe" (2; emphasis in original).

[34]*RCIA* 215: "In accord with the ancient practice followed in the Roman liturgy, adults are not to be baptized without receiving confirmation immediately afterward, unless some serious reason stands in the way. The conjunction of the two celebrations signifies the unity of the paschal mystery, the close link between the mission of the Son and the outpouring of the Holy Spirit, and the connection between the two sacraments through which the Son and the Holy Spirit come with the Father to those who are baptized."

24

"The theological point made here is of such seriousness that one feels compelled to ask why and how it can be construed as applying only to adults and not to infants and children, especially if they are baptized at the Easter vigil. Unless the theological point is dismissed as mere rhetoric, it seems inescapable that all who are deemed fit for baptism, no matter what their physical age, should also be confirmed within the same liturgical event. . . . The continued Western practice of deferring confirmation of infants and children, more recently even until adolescence, will have to take account of the theological principle stated clearly in (34)—a thing that would require construal of physical age as 'a serious obstacle' to sacramental reception. But if this is proved then it is inevitable that the same question be posed about baptism of infants: if age is a serious obstacle to receiving confirmation, why then is age not a serious obstacle to receiving baptism? Theological discussion will have to cope with this anomaly."[35]

That the postconciliar Church was struggling with two understandings of initiation—that of adults baptized, confirmed, and admitted to the Eucharist within the same celebration, and that of children or adolescents baptized in infancy and confirmed and communicated some years later—was clear. Kavanagh described the ethos of the former pattern as "splendidly baptismal, paschal, and trinitarian," while considering the latter more the "marking [of] an educational or life-crisis point in the development of the recipients by episcopal presidency at the event."[36] Ralph Keifer was one of many

[35]Kavanagh, "The Rites," 328 (also *Shape of Baptism,* 138–39). Keifer, "Christian Initiation," 394, offers a similar comment: "[M]any who support the maturity-commitment view of confirmation are seriously concerned with a number of values reflected in the rest of the initiatory continuum: a priority is given not only to the experience of transformation which is initiation, but at the same time to responsible acceptance of the gospel and to making the experience of conversion and transformation visible and public before the whole church. But if these priorities are to outweigh the desirability of incorporating the children of Christian homes into the full sacramental life of the church, and even to supersede the witness to God's sovereign grace which infant baptism is, then we must abandon infant baptism, not exalt confirmation. And if we are to retain infant baptism, it seems only logical that it should be followed by infant confirmation and communion."

[36]Aidan Kavanagh, "Christian Initiation in Post-Conciliar Roman Catholicism: A Brief Report," 108. See also his "The Rites," 327–29.

Summarizing the *status quaestionis confirmationis,* John Roberto, "Confirmation in the American Catholic Church," 262–63, described the adherents of these two

25

concurring with Kavanagh in opposing the latter pattern, contending that treating confirmation as a sacrament of commitment and maturity "tends to do violence to the biblical and patristic tradition of baptism, for it makes of baptism a kind of catechumenal preparation for life in the church."[37] Keifer also thought the divorce of confirmation from baptism a theological and pastoral anomaly, for "it separates entry into the body of the risen Lord from the gift of the Spirit, violates sacramental continuum and leads to the catechetical assumption that there are degrees of membership in the church among the baptized."[38]

Theological and pastoral anomaly though it be in the view of many, the theological-maturity model of confirmation does reflect the prevailing practice of today's Church. We will examine in the following chapter the writings of those authors in the immediate postconciliar years who supported this model.

We consider now the final perspective of the Mature Adulthood School concerning infant baptism, a perspective that thought the RCIA's restoration of an ancient Church ordo might effectively address both indiscriminate baptism and the necessity of catechesis.

The fifth perspective:
The catechumenate as a temporary alternative
The enrollment of an infant (child) into the catechumenate presents an appropriate, temporary alternative to baptism. The adult ordo considered catechumens "joined to the Church" and "part of the household of Christ," and so entitled them to Christian marriage and, should they die prior to being baptized, to Christian burial (*RCIA* 47). While the text obviously refers to *adult* catechumens, Kavanagh speculated in 1974 that the recovery of the concept that the catechumen is a *Chris-*

---

patterns of baptismal ethos as belonging, respectively, to the "liturgical initiation school" and the "theological maturity school."

[37]Keifer, "Christian Initiation," 394. As noted, many authors advocated the unified celebration of baptism-confirmation-Eucharist for the sacramental initiation of infants; among others not mentioned at this point in our text are Richard Ling, "A Catechist's Vote for Infant Confirmation," 42–56; Mitchell, "Once and Future Child," 428–30; and Edward Braxton, "Adult Initiation and Infant Baptism," *Becoming a Catholic Christian*, 305–15. Braxton's article, presented at a 1978 symposium on Christian initiation, offers an excellent summary of the major points of the infant baptism discussion from the council to his time of writing.

[38]Keifer, "Christian Initiation," 395.

tianus in fieri would most likely not leave the institution of infant baptism "unaffected indefinitely."[39] Writing three years later of a perceived theological shift in recent years concerning the fate of unbaptized infants—a shift from "a real theological doubt about the salvation of one who dies before baptism" to the confident commendation "of the unbaptized infant to God's mercy"—Kavanagh was more insistent in his assessment as to how the ordo of the catechumenate might influence the practice of infant baptism:

"This theological shift, taken together with the reiteration . . . that a catechumen is not a pagan but already a Christian in incipient communion with Christ in his church, is beginning to enhance the theological legitimacy of enrolling an infant in the catechumenate until such later time when, after serious catechesis is possible, the full rites of initiation might be more effectively and intelligibly celebrated. At the very least, I submit, prudent work on the *pastoral* legitimacy of such a practice can proceed with a certain respectability that would not have been possible twenty years ago."[40]

Prudent work did proceed, and near the end of the decade Julia Upton summarized current theological reflection by stating that an infant-child catechumenate is "at least worthy of serious consideration," as it would allow pastoral flexibility ("indiscriminate baptism exists because there is no other pastoral opportunity"), provide psychological reassurance to parents and pastors ("[removing] the overwhelming concern over infant damnation"), and foster a stronger sense of communal identity ("for it is the community that is responsible for the growth of catechumenal faith").[41] That same year John

---

[39]Kavanagh, "New Roman Rites," 38; see also his "Christian Initiation of Adults," 321ff. The same year Keifer, "Christian Initiation," 395, also suggested the possibility of enrolling children in a catechumenate.

[40]Kavanagh, "Process and Ritual," 9; emphasis in original. The context is the indiscriminate baptizing of infants.

Lorna Brockett, *The Theology of Baptism*, 80–86, offers a fine review of early postconciliar theological reflection concerning the fate of the unbaptized.

[41]Julia Upton, "A Solution to the Infant Baptism Problem," 494–95. Speaking against the claim that infant baptism violates the freedom of an infant, and noting that some (unnamed) advocate the postponement of baptism until an age at which it would be more psychologically effective, Searle, *Christening*, 51, observed that "the grace of [infant] baptism is seriously limited as far as its immediate effectiveness. . . . For this reason, it might be sufficient and, in the face of

Gallen called for the development of a "welcoming ritual" for infants who are catechumenized rather than sacramentally initiated, a ritual that would introduce the infant into the life of the community and ease parents' spiritual concerns about the possible prebaptismal death of their child.[42] Such a rite appeared the following year as David Walsh, echoing the complaint that there was no alternative for bringing a child into the Church other than baptism, offered his "Rite of Welcoming a Christian Child": a rite that was *not* baptism, but that "related to the child's eventual baptism as an adult."[43]

Our last two perspectives have considered two traditional concepts: the unity of baptism-confirmation-Eucharist as sacramentally effecting initiation into the Church, and the salvific admission into the Church effected by enrollment into the catechumenate. As we conclude our examination of the perspectives on infant baptism of the Mature Adulthood School we again cite Aidan Kavanagh who, uniting these two perspectives, insisted that the long-range, strategic vision of Church promoted by the adult ordo must take precedence over tactical responses to short-term pastoral needs:

"Whenever it is deemed advisable to initiate a Christian, regardless of age, that Christian should be initiated fully and completely by water baptism, the 'sealing' of confirmation, and first eucharistic communion. This should hold for everyone, although it may be found pastorally more advantageous to begin the sequence of baptism in its fullness so far as infants and very young children are concerned with solemn enrollment in the catechumenate followed by the sacraments of initiation in full sequence later at some appropriate time. To do this is *not* to 'delay baptism.' *It is to begin baptism in its fullness as soon after birth as practicable, and to celebrate its stages over a*

---

widespread lapsing by those baptized in infancy, more effective, simply to receive the newborn child into the Church as a catechumen, signed with the sign of Christ's cross, as was the custom in the fourth and fifth centuries."

[42]Gallen, "Pastoral Celebration," 151.

[43]David Walsh, "Rite of Welcoming a Christian Child," 8+. Walsh notes: "The service outlined here is seen as the first step in the child's introduction to Christ. As a liturgical rite, it would replace the 'Rite of Becoming Catechumens' in the adult situation. At a suitable time in later life, the person who would have been welcomed by the church as an infant in a celebration of this kind would proceed to the second stage of Christian initiation of adults, viz., the 'Rite of Election and Enrollment of Names.'"

period of years according to the child's growth in faith, rather than to tele-scope the sacraments of initiation into a few minutes or dismember the sacramental sequence altogether.

"As radical as this change in conventional procedure may seem to many Roman Catholics, the notions of the catechumen's being al-ready a Christian in a true degree of communion with Christ in his Church, of the intrinsic place of confirmation *within* the normal se-quence of sacramental initiation, and of the inalienable rights that ac-crue to one baptized by water and the Holy Spirit, together make the change theologically respectable. One also suspects that the demands of Christian existence in a post-Christendom world will make the change pastorally inexorable."[44]

Being a Christian has never been easy—nor was it ever meant to be. To conform one's life to the demands of the gospel and daily heed the call to conversion has, for some generations of Christians, led to persecution and death. For other generations—certainly our own—the challenge is to stand apart from the values of society while yet re-maining a contributing member of that society. "Christians are not born, they are made," as Tertullian said—and *RCIA* advocates in-sisted that today, even if born as cradle Catholics, they are not born into a world sympathetic to gospel ideals. The adult ordo of Chris-tian initiation was considered indispensable to the survival of the Christian Church because it was regarded as essential for the making of Christian individuals and communities.

The Mature Adulthood School thought infant baptism a "benign abnormality" when practiced prudently and appropriately. Apart from the danger of death, prudence and appropriateness meant that the child was in such an ecclesial and familial environment that the pledge sacramentally offered through water baptism would continue to take visible form throughout childhood, adolescence, and adult-hood.

But for many writers, whether they agreed or not with the designa-tion of infant baptism as a "benign abnormality," Tertullian's insist-ence that "Christians are made" was no less true of those brought sacramentally into the Church as infants than it was of those initiated through the lengthy process of the *RCIA*. If the indiscriminate baptiz-ing of infants was thought to be "robbing the Church of calcium in

[44]Kavanagh, *Shape of Baptism,* 175; emphasis in original.

[her] bones," they believed a thoughtful, responsible theology and practice of infant baptism would counter that depletion as effectively as did, presumably, the adult ordo.

Having considered those writers who in the postconciliar period from 1965 to 1980 attended primarily to the potential and promotion of the adult ordo, we turn now to authors of that same period who addressed more directly and extensively the practice and theology of infant baptism.

Chapter 2

Families of Faith:
The Rite of Baptism for Children
and the Environmentalist School

"To fulfill the true meaning of the sacrament, children must later be formed in the faith in which they have been baptized" (*RBC* 3).

"You have asked to have your children baptized. In doing so you are accepting the responsibility of training them in the practice of the faith. It will be your duty to bring them up to keep God's commandments as Christ taught us, by loving God and our neighbor. Do you clearly understand what you are undertaking?" (*RBC* 39).

Nathan Mitchell's description of the Mature Adulthood School introduced our review of the American discussion on infant baptism. A second major school of baptismal thought had developed by the mid-1970s, which Mitchell designated as the "Environmentalist School." We rely upon his description of this school's characteristics and return to our five perspectives to guide our review of its literature:

"In contrast to [the Mature Adulthood School] the environmentalist school emphasizes the importance of initiating children at an early age into the life, faith and worship of the Christian community. Adherents of this position stress the principle that people learn how to think, judge and behave most effectively as Christians through regular participation in the life of the community during all the stages of development between infancy and mature adulthood. To withhold access to the church's worship from children is to deny them the most effective and most widely available means for becoming convinced adult believers. The church, this school contends, is more than a community of transformed adults. It is also a nurturing environment that encourages gradual growth in faith for individuals and groups of all conditions, including children. Thus baptism is not only for adults who have grappled with the painful demands of conversion; it is for any human being who can be nurtured in a community

31

where trust, love and acceptance lead progressively to an adult affirmation of faith."[1]

The first perspective:
The problem of indiscriminate baptism

With few exceptions Environmentalists concurred with the Mature Adulthood School's criticism of the indiscriminate baptizing of infants. The solution was not that of unequivocally refusing to baptize the child of marginal Catholic parents but, following the guidelines offered by the *RBC* (8, 25), delaying the baptism until the parents could be catechized. This delay honored both the more prominent place accorded parents in the postconciliar rite and the renewed appreciation of the sign value of a communal celebration. Acknowledging the confusion and anger of some parents (and pastors) concerning the "new" harshness of these parental requirements, James Challancin observed that seeking a guarantee of parental faith was

[1]Mitchell, "Once and Future Child," 429–30. In "Postconciliar Debate," 248 n. 22, Covino lists the following as representatives of this school: "Christopher Kiesling, William Allen, Norbert Rigali, Charles Keating, James Challancin, Eugene Maly, and Francis Buckley." For Covino's summary and assessment of the Environmentalist School, see his pages 247–53 as well as his "Question of Infant Baptism," 70–82.

In "Postconciliar Debate," 256–59, and "Question of Infant Baptism," 89–95, Covino identifies the emergence of another school in the late 1970s, which he terms the Corresponding Practice School. In "Postconciliar Debate" he writes: "[This school] essentially holds that individuals come to Christian faith in different ways, depending on various circumstances, and that correspondingly different practices of initiation should be employed. In other words, such authors argued that the three new rites of Christian initiation *together* represent Catholic initiatory policy, and that the rite which corresponds to the initiand's circumstances is the one that is 'normal' for him or her. This would take into consideration not only family circumstances (such as practicing or nonpracticing parents), but also the sociological situation: that is, if Christians were such a minority in a certain culture that the Christian upbringing of children might be very difficult, adult initiation might be more appropriate in that context" (257; emphasis in original).

Because many writers from both the Mature Adulthood and the Environmentalist Schools supported the thesis of corresponding practice, Covino lists no specific representatives of the school. Writers of both the Environmentalist and Corresponding Practice Schools were concerned with improving the theological understanding and pastoral practice of infant baptism, and so, for the sake of convenience and economy, I will use the term "Environmentalist" to refer to writers of either school who directly promote infant baptism.

not a recent innovation but an attempt to restore to pastoral practice what had been legislated since the 1917 *Code of Canon Law.*[2]

Although the recovered emphasis on the quality of the parent's faith was not without its critics,[3] a striking and consistent concern

[2]James Challancin, "Infant Baptism: More Difficult Requirements?" 64: "The preponderance of evidence shows that the code's policy toward the baptism of infants has always had two facets: A certain urgency [*CIC* 770], yes, but never without good assurance of Catholic education and upbringing [*CIC* 750, 751]. Pastoral practice may have tended to emphasize only the urgency. One could argue that the changing attitude toward and increasing demands made on those who present their children for baptism is nothing more than an attempt to bring into balance what has always been the policy under the code."

Challancin also demonstrates that canons 750 and 751—we are dealing here with the 1917 code—"actually represent a reversal of legislation. In the 18th century the Sacred Congregation for the Propagation of the Faith ruled that even if parents were indifferent Catholics or otherwise of such a character as to offer little assurance of Catholic upbringing, nevertheless, baptize! The code chose to reverse this decision, making the assurance of Catholic education a requirement for licit baptism" (64). See also Paul Vanbergen, "Baptism of the Infants of *non satis credentes* Parents," 195–200.

[3]We observed in chapter 1 that an extreme position of the Mature Adulthood School was held by David Greye Perrey (pseudonym), who called for the complete elimination of infant baptism. I report here that at least two writers during this period supported even the *indiscriminate* baptizing of infants.

Rockford Peterson, "Let's Baptize Babies," 15, contended that if indiscriminate infant baptism was filling the Church with nominal Catholics, "the answer lies not in refusing infants their share in the life of God but in establishing new priorities in the church." Acknowledging that "sacred Scripture does not specifically tell us what happens to the souls of unbaptized infants when they die," Peterson refers to "a document as liberal as the *Dutch Catechism* [which] advises the Baptism of infants as 'a safer option'" (14). He feared that refusing to baptize infants was penalizing children for the apathy of their parents as well as ignoring those parents "who are most probably apathetic because the church has in the first place ignored them in their deepest spiritual needs" (15). Peterson defended infant baptism "not as the full and final achievement of Christian perfection, but as a valid and complete sign of the *beginnings,* the initiation of a Christian life which *ultimately begins to be* fulfilled in the sacraments of Confirmation, Matrimony, and Holy Orders" (15; emphasis in original).

Paul Donlan, "Second Thoughts on Delaying the Baptism of Infants," 31–33+, also thought that delaying baptism for theoretical reasons (the alternative of the catechumenate) or for practical ones (the lack of spiritual maturity on the part of the parents) placed human activity on a level above the divine: "Usually when baptism is delayed it is for the sake of everyone but the infant—who has to wait to become a child of God until everyone else is accommodated: priests, parents,

when discussing the possibility of delaying baptism was that "the bruised reed not be crushed nor the smoldering wick extinguished." Acknowledging that parents sought baptism for their children for a variety of religious, sociological, and psychological reasons, many authors urged that respect for theological and liturgical ideals be tempered with respect for the psychological and spiritual capabilities of the parents. Even prior to the publication of the 1969 rite, Brusselmans had insisted that even simple "human" motivations should not be condemned, for "they can well serve as stepping stones to a further education of the faith of the parents who ask the Church for the baptism of their children."[4] Yet perhaps no writer expressed this concern as eloquently—and, with the assistance of Cyril of Jerusalem, as traditionally—as did Mark Searle, who counseled both pastoral support *and* challenge for those parents whose motives for requesting baptism for their infants might be less than ideal:

"Today, as in the past, there are all sorts of reasons why people might seek baptism for themselves or their children. Family and social pressures continue to operate as well as superstition and an unchristian fear of divine punishment. Yet it would be unrealistic to ask always for the purest motivation and a fully articulated sense of purpose. The Church has always recognized this and, while turning away those whose motives were clearly wrong and seemingly incorrigible—'those who cannot hear,' as Hippolytus called them—she has been prepared to work with the Spirit to lead them on to a fuller appreciation of what they were asking. Such a generous policy was clearly that of Cyril of Jerusalem, the fourth century bishop who hoped that contact with the Christian community and its liturgical celebration would help such people:

'We, the ministers of Christ, have admitted everyone: acting as doorkeepers, we have left the door open. This means you have been free to enter in a sinful condition and with dubious motivation. You have entered. You have passed in and been enrolled. Do you see how imposing this assembly is? Look at her order and discipline, the reading of the Scriptures, the religious who are present, the course of instruction. Let the place affect you; let yourself be changed by what you

---

godparents and the 'faith community'" (38 n. 5). We will consider Donlan's comments concerning a child catechumenate below.

[4]Brusselmans, "Christian Parents and Infant Baptism," 30.

see. Go promptly away now and come back tomorrow in a better mind.'"[5]

Most Environmentalists agreed with the Mature Adulthood School that the indiscriminate baptizing of infants was unacceptable. But consensus was not reached on the next perspective we will examine: for the "adult ordo as norm" thesis implied to some a devaluing of the practice of infant baptism that was clearly inadmissible.

The second perspective: The norm of baptism

While the value offered the Church by the *RCIA* was evident, Aidan Kavanagh's portrayal of the adult ordo as "the definitive statement" of the Church's "norm of baptism" was at times more captivating than clear. Richard Reichert expressed his support of the new adult rites but criticized Kavanagh's insistence that the *RCIA* was "normative"—and especially that infant baptism was "abnormal."[6]

Reichert thought Kavanagh's understanding of the concept "normative" both too literal and theoretical. A more accurate interpretation of the normative value of the adult ordo, he believed, was that of considering its *ultimate* goal: the realization of a mature, adult faith within the community.[7] Acknowledging that this "normative goal" is ideally accomplished when dealing with the people and through the process envisioned by the adult ordo, Reichert argued that deviating

---

[5]Searle, *Christening*, 34. The citation from Cyril of Jerusalem is from the *Procat.*, 4. Concerning the necessary balance between pastoral sensitivity and liturgical integrity, see also Redmond, "Infant Baptism," 88; Buckley, "Right to the Sacraments," 331–32; and Anthony Sherman, "Baptismal Preparation: Where Parents Are At," 8–9.

[6]Reichert, "A Catechist's Response," 141: "If its normative value were taken seriously, 'abnormal' practices like infant baptism and the inverted order of receiving first communion and confirmation *would have to be abolished!* Catechesis would be directed exclusively to adult catechumens. A church of mature, adult believers would be assured. Thus reasons a liturgist" (emphasis in original).

[7]Ibid.: "The normative value of the RCIA as stated above seems to be derived primarily from its goal of achieving adult faith within a faith community. All pastoral efforts at initiation *must* respect that goal as normative" (emphasis in original).

Earlier in his article Reichert had observed: "In summary, the RCIA is rightly seen as normative in two ways: the theology and psychology of initiation upon which the document is founded is truly paradigmatic for catechetical ministry especially in its emphasis on coming to faith in a faith community; the goal of conversion of life in an adult church is likewise paradigmatic" (140).

from the process is neither abnormal nor counterproductive to attaining that goal:

"This does not mean all pastoral decisions to deviate from that order—decisions made precisely to achieve the goal in very concrete and less than ideal circumstances—automatically result in abnormal practices. The historical development of the practice of infant baptism within our Western tradition can be judged pastorally normal even though deviating from the more ancient order outlined in the RCIA. We have an equally official document which sets down the rite for infant baptism."[8]

Reichert seems to have been the first to disagree with Kavanagh's choice of vocabulary, although, as we shall see in chapter 4, several authors in the early 1980s challenged the norm-of-baptism thesis (or at least Kavanagh's characterization of it). In the closing years of this first full postconciliar decade, however, several authors offered more nuanced statements concerning the normative value of the adult ordo, statements that seemed to emphasize more the goal, or vision of the Church, toward which that ordo was oriented. Francis Buckley, for example, spoke of the sacraments as "part of a lifelong process of initiation into the mystery of God." Noting that "God is ever at work, summoning and enabling us," he observed that the *RCIA* was "a model for this lifelong process, which proceeds by stages: attraction, reflection, conversion, commitment, action—all carried on with the active support of a community of fellow believers and searchers."[9] Similarly, Mark Searle introduced his book *Christening* by explaining that while his work dealt primarily with the *RBC*, frequent reference would be made to the adult ordo, "since in many respects these [rites] reveal more clearly the full implications of becoming a Christian."[10]

---

[8]Ibid., 142.

[9]Buckley, "Right to the Sacraments," 330.

[10]Searle, *Christening*, vii. Searle subsequently expressed the normative value of the adult ordo in a way that challenged, rather than unintentionally belittled, the practice of infant baptism: "What it means to lose faith in the wisdom of the world and find faith in Christ is therefore best seen in the experience of adult conversion, but the same conviction has to be engendered even in those who are born of Christian parents. For them, the sacraments of initiation may commence in infancy and be spread out over several years as they grow up, but the program of the sacraments can never divorce itself from the process of formation. *The end*

The next perspective we will consider is one in which consensus between the two major schools of baptismal thought was reached. This perspective also allows us to explore at some length the views of those directly advocating the discriminate baptizing of infants.

The third perspective: The necessity of catechesis

The Christian initiation of adults was prepared for and, in part, effected, by the *RCIA*-guided journey through faith toward the sacrament. But Environmentalists also considered baptism a "sacrament of *faith*," and maintained that the postbaptismal journey of a child was no less important and no less required than the journey expected of the adult catechumen. Writing prior to the publication of the 1969 *RBC*, Christopher Kiesling clearly dismissed the "instant confection" mentality some associated with infant baptism:

"Christian initiation is the whole situation and process wherein the Christian family and community devote themselves to the Christian rearing of the child and the child humanized and socialized in a Christian way. This initiation is as long a process as initiation into, let us say, the American community. It takes years and leads gradually through many phases to adult faith and love. For a child to be given and to assimilate such an initiation into a community of faith and love, reversing the sinful human condition, cannot be called anything other than a gift of God's grace."[11]

And yet what exactly *was* the grace of infant baptism? Many Catholics saw it as that which removed the stain of original sin and thus opened the gates of heaven to their children. That immediate (and, as understood by some, *only*) effect of baptism, with its manifest emphasis on the individual infant, made it difficult for many to understand infant baptism as anything but a private matter between God and child. Infant baptism was considered a remedy to "the

---

of both is the same: the obedience of faith, whereby a person commits his whole self freely to God in Christ and the Church. In that sense, the rites of the Christian initiation of adults are *normative for our understanding of what initiation is all about*" (18–19; emphasis mine).

Robert Hovda, "Hope for the Future: A Summary," 157, observed: "This *process [RCIA]* is proposed again as normative, even though the *sacraments* of initiation continue to be celebrated for infants and children. This *norm* effectively shifts the focus of initiation from the individual to the community" (emphasis in original).

[11]Christopher Kiesling, "Infant Baptism," 624.

childhood infection of original sin, rather than a life-long challenge to a continual conversion of dying and rising in Christ."[12]

As noted above, apparently only two American writers appealed to the "childhood infection of original sin" to justify even the *indiscriminate* baptizing of infants. But consideration of original sin was by no means absent from the literature.[13] Indeed, many felt that the "continual conversion of dying and rising in Christ" was a never ending battle precisely because of the influence of original sin. Writing with keen pastoral sensitivity, Mark Searle suggested that anyone taking the word of God to heart could not help but realize how unintentionally divided the human heart could be: "Small wonder, then, that the New Testament speaks of the Christian life in the images of warfare, struggle and the endurance of the long-distance runner. We know enough of what this is about from our own experience, recognizing perhaps wryly enough that the doctrine of original sin is one of the most obvious truths of the Christian faith."[14]

---

[12]Gusmer, "Revised Adult Initiation," 95. Braxton, "Adult Initiation and Infant Baptism," 304, writing as late in the decade as 1979, observed, "There is very little doubt that most ordinary Catholic lay people are of the persuasion that all infants should be baptized and that the central reason for this is to free the infant from the constraints of original sin."

[13]Specific and detailed considerations of original sin include William Hamilton, "New Thinking on Original Sin," 135–41; James L. Connor, "Original Sin: Contemporary Approaches," 215–40; and Brian O. McDermot, "The Theology of Original Sin: Recent Developments," 478–512.

In 1973, four years after the initial promulgation of the *RBC*, the SCDW issued an *editio typica altera*. Interestingly, three of the four modifications dealt with original sin. The only change in the text of the rite involved the alternate prayer for the exorcism and anointing before baptism (*RBC* 49-B [also 221]): the phrase "bring these children *out of the power of darkness*" was amended to read "cleanse these children *from the stain of original sin*," thereby making specific the mention of original sin in both of the two possible prayers of exorcism. Similarly, two phrases in "Christian Initiation: General Introduction" were altered to allow a clearer allusion to, or specific mention of, original sin: no. 2, originally reading "raised *from their natural human condition*," was amended to read "rescues us *from the power of darkness*"; and, to a description of the effects of baptism in no. 5 was added the phrase "washes away every stain of sin, original and personal." For a brief commentary on these modifications, see Paul Turner, "Baptism and Original Sin," 81–83. We will consider additional changes mandated by the 1983 *Code of Canon Law* in chapter 4.

[14]Searle, *Christening*, 53. Searle's excellent treatment of original sin—an entire chapter in *Christening* (53–66)—is particularly helpful in that it situates an understanding of original sin within the context of the *RBC* itself.

Among the first of the American writers to enter the postconciliar discussion on infant baptism, Kiesling sought to shift the focus of the relationship between infant baptism and original sin away from its preconciliar, predominantly negative understanding (baptism *removes original sin, the obstacle to heaven, from an individual*) to a more positive one (baptism *inserts one into a community* committed to living in reverse of this sinful orientation). Indeed, the reorientation of one's life—in the case of infant baptism, the acceptance of the infant by and into a community where that reorientation was a primary commitment—could be considered the grace of infant baptism:

"[The] baptism of an infant concerns the parents and the Christian community as much as it does the infant. Baptism of an infant is not simply a matter of the parent's presenting a child to the church which offers baptism to the infant as a kind of thing which becomes his property to be acknowledged when he is older. Baptism of an infant is a pledge on the part of parents and the Christian community to reverse, in the rearing of the infant, that orientation to sin which affects all mankind, which is inherited with birth into the human race, and which is actualized in the process of personality development."[15]

That infant baptism concerned the parents and Christian community as much as it did the infant was central to the baptism discussion throughout this period.[16] Born into a Christian family, an infant is baptized through and because of that family's faith. That baptized infant Christian must still be *made* an adult Christian, however, for the grace of initiation is neither exhausted nor brought to fruition at

[15]Kiesling, "Infant Baptism," 622–23.

[16]Ibid., 618–19: "But we still think of baptism as offered by the church for the individual to express his subjective faith. The baptism of infants is still embarrassing, for although baptism of an infant expresses the subjective faith of the Christian community, this is no help to the infant for his salvation through his faith, as long as the subjective faith of the baptized person is of primary importance in baptism. The idea of baptism as incorporation into the church is not taken seriously as a grace from God for salvation quite apart from a concomitant act of faith and love. Yet this social dimension of baptism is, I believe, a key to appreciating the value of infant baptism." See also Guerrette, "Ecclesiology and Infant Baptism," and Fred Krause, "Infant Baptism and the Domestic Church," 25–30.

As we have seen, that baptism affected/effected the already initiated as well as the neophytes was also emphasized by the Mature Adulthood School.

the baptismal ceremony: the infant's faith is not "confected on the spot," nor is it guaranteed in and for the years to come. Environmentalists agreed that committed Christians are not born but made and that they are made primarily through their living with other committed Christians. It is the family of the infant and the ecclesial community to which they belong who bring their faith to and immediately bear the burden of the baptism of their infants.[17] Far from offering the Church the soft and subtle security of steadily increasing numbers, infant baptism challenges the community to consider well and hard their willingness to live the gospel they profess. Infant baptism bound the community to faith, not the infant: it called the community to live its faith so that it would, indeed, be the Christian faith of the community that determined the environment in which the child would be reared and formed.[18]

This emphasis on the communal nature of infant baptism is reflected in Mitchell's naming of the "Environmentalist School."[19] Kiesling reminded his readers that contemporary theology emphasizes that God's grace is given visible form in the world around us and that, as

[17]That it is the faith of the Church and parents into which the infant is baptized is clear from the *RBC*, for example, "Christian Initiation: General Introduction," 9: "[Godparents and parents are present] to profess the Church's faith, in which children are being baptized." See also the excerpts from *RBC* 3 and 39 that introduce this chapter.

[18]Brian Haggerty, "Adult Initiation and Infant Baptism," 159: "[Infant baptism] means that a community of Christians commits itself, not to ensure that the infant being baptized will adopt its faith and the forms through which it is expressed, but rather to share its values and its insight into faith with that child. What infant baptism conceived in a communitarian context presupposes is not faith on the part of the infant recipient but faith on the part of the Christian community. The solemn commitment made when an infant is baptized does not bind the infant to faith; it binds the community to demonstrate a faith so alive and dynamic that the child baptized may eventually find fulfillment in it."

[19]Covino, "Postconciliar Debate," 250: "The tenets of this school were fundamentally theological, stressing the work of the Spirit in the actions of the Christian community, the corporate nature of sin and grace, and a 'high' sense of ecclesiology in which the Church or Christian community was seen as the environment in and through which an individual is formed in the Christian faith. Participation and membership in this community were the means to eventually making a mature commitment to the faith." Covino quotes Krause, "Infant Baptism and the Domestic Church," 26–27, who remarked: "The community assumes the responsibility to provide both the instruction and the environment which will make [a later act of personal faith] a real possibility for this child."

grace is given us in the Church, "to belong to the Christian community is to be in some degree 'in grace.'" For a child to belong to a committed Christian community is *not* natural, Kiesling observed: "It is grace, a gift from God."[20] The environment, the Christian community within which the child was expected to be raised, is a visible sign of God's grace, just as the educational and formative contributions of the community are considered as the effecting of that grace.[21]

Because infant baptism concerns the community as much as it does the infant, the community "effects itself" when baptizing an infant no less than when discerning and guiding the conversion of an adult. Charles Keating wrote that "baptism sets our boundaries" and observed that the baptism of an infant is both the celebration of, and a challenge to, the faith of a mature adult: "[By baptizing] this child we commit ourselves to be what we proclaim: a community whose unity visibly communicates that Christ is of the Father."[22]

While Keating wrote that when we baptize an infant "we commit ourselves to be what we proclaim," Nathan Mitchell argued that infant baptism challenged us to see in the child *who we must become*. "It is not childhood we are destined to lose," Mitchell asserted, "but rather adulthood, that frightening arrogance of life that seeks to dominate, control and blame God for having cheated us of so much."[23] Mitchell appears to be the first American Catholic writer to elaborate

---

[20]Kiesling, "Infant Baptism," 621.

[21]Ibid., 623. "We can say that the visible form in which the grace of God is given to the infant in baptism is the Christian community and Christian parents or guardians who commit themselves by baptism to rear the child in the way of faith and love. Incorporation into the church is not a by-product of individual salvation given in baptism but an integral element of salvation. In fact, for the child it is prior to any personal acts of faith and love; it is the grace which makes possible the acts of faith and love when maturity is reached."

Later in the same article, Kiesling concluded: "Thus baptism is a *sign* or *symbol* of grace because it expresses God's graciousness-to-this-child incarnate in the rearing which Christian parents give and to which they pledge themselves along with the community. It is an efficacious symbol because in the very activity of expressing this incarnate graciousness, it is effected: Christian parents and community undertake the Christian development of their child, thus cooperating with God's grace extended to the child, though the undertaking may have begun before, and continues after, the moments of the rite which declare it" (624–25; emphasis in original).

[22]Charles Keating, "Baptism Sets Our Boundaries," 102.

[23]Mitchell, "Once and Future Child," 433.

a theology of childhood,[24] and the title of his article—"The Once and Future Child"—suggests his thesis that childhood is not to be seen solely as a "provisional prelude to mature and adult faith." Children represent the future of the Church not simply because they will become the adult community of the next generation but because it is in their childhood that the Christian community sees its ultimate destiny and goal. Mitchell maintained that "one could almost define Christianity itself as the state of childhood, the surrendering openness to God as the absolute future of man, the future that comes forward to meet men in unconditional love and acceptance."[25] His thesis addressed what others had perceived as a theological hazard of focusing too exclusively on the initiation of adults.[26]

Finally, while parental involvement was always assumed when considering the community's responsibility for and after the baptism of an infant, several authors stressed the more prominent role given the parents by the *RBC*.[27] Many considered the parents and family as the infant's primary community of faith. As mentioned above, Brusselmans' article was largely a plea for the restoration of parental sponsorship, and she was among the first to encourage a reevaluation and strengthening of the role of parents through a renewed appreciation of their sacramental marriage.[28] And Kiesling specified that it was "precisely the rearing of the child by the parents" that was

[24]Covino, "Question of Infant Baptism," 28, observed, "In 1975, Nathan Mitchell offered a unique defense of infant baptism that was based on a 'theology of childhood.' While this particular argument was not discernably echoed by other authors, it is important in this discussion of the diachronic progression of the debate because it can be seen as 'setting the stage' for a future line of argument that would stress the important place which infant baptism plays in the total Catholic initiation polity."

[25]Mitchell, "Once and Future Child," 428.

[26]See, for example, Hovda, "Hope for the Future," 159: "Historical efforts to return to the practice of adult baptism only have not been terribly successful, both because such efforts fail to 'interpret and support the place of the child in the church' and because 'there is something normative about a child in the life of the kingdom.'" (Hovda is quoting from Daniel Stevick's "Christian Initiation: Post-Reformation to the Present Era.") We will return to Mitchell's argument in chapter 6.

[27]*RBC* 5.3 details the special roles enjoyed by parents in the actual celebration of their child's baptism. Among those sections of the *RBC* dealing with parental roles and responsibilities *after* baptism are nos. 5.5, 39, 56, 64, and 70-A.

[28]Brusselmans, "Christian Parents and Infant Baptism," 38, had remarked, "If we want parents to rediscover and resume with full knowledge the role which

"the grace of God counteracting original sin. . . . The grace of God overcoming human nature's sinful orientation is embodied in the interaction between parents (first the mother) and the child. . . . If the parents treat the child in a truly Christian way, they will develop in him a Christian personality; or more precisely, God through their instrumentality will develop a Christian personality in the child.

"Baptism calls explicitly into consciousness of the parents and the Christian community what God would do for this child if they cooperate with him. . . . The benefit for the child in being baptized is his gaining Christian parents *explicitly conscious of their responsibility and pledged to fulfilling it,* and thus an open channel, so to speak, for the grace of God extended to him."[29]

Just as catechesis, or "conversion therapy," was indispensable to the goals of the adult ordo, there was virtually unanimous agreement among the Environmentalist and Mature Adulthood Schools that continuing catechesis and formation in the faith was essential in bringing about the true meaning of the sacrament of infant baptism. The next perspective we will examine also spoke to the continuing unfolding of the grace of baptism—although the precise theological meaning of that grace and its appropriate liturgical expression were widely contested.

The fourth perspective:
The unity of the initiation sacraments
The *RBC* considered the celebration of an infant's baptism and confirmation within one liturgical event an exceptional circumstance. As we observed in chapter 1, however, many writers of the Mature Adulthood School insisted that Christian initiation (celebrated at any age) should include the conferral of confirmation and the reception of

---

the Church confides to them, an indispensable need is a pastoral theology of the family and of infant baptism which will present to parents the dignity of marriage and the responsibilities which flow from their state of christian parenthood for the building up of the body of Christ." Others dealing specifically and extensively with the role and responsibility of the parents include Kiesling, Rigali, Keating, Krause, Sherman, and Friedman.

[29]Kiesling, "Infant Baptism," 622; emphasis in original. See also Searle, *Christening,* 49. Perhaps nowhere in the *RBC* is parental responsibility stressed more clearly than in the citations that open this chapter and in the words addressed to the parents and godparents that introduce the "Renunciation of Sin and Profession of Faith" (no. 56).

the Eucharist within one unified rite. In his study of the American postconciliar discussion on infant baptism, Paul Covino offered the succinct conclusion that, just as authors of the Environmentalist and Mature Adulthood Schools agreed that the indiscriminate baptizing of infants was a problem, "so they also came to agree on reintegrating the rites of initiation. In fact, no direct opposition to this point appeared during this period."[30]

But brevity is often the enemy of clarity, and so perhaps a more nuanced assessment is required. In addition to the Mature Adulthood School's consistent call for a unified celebration of the initiation sacraments, several other positions concerning initiation unity were evident. For example, some writers simply accepted Church legislation and practice, which ordinarily separated confirmation and infant baptism. As the explanation (or defense) of infant baptism was their primary concern, these authors dealt with confirmation from the perspective of what the celebration of that sacrament could reveal about the baptism that had preceded it by several years.[31] And at least two authors not only accepted the prevailing practice but *encouraged* the separation of confirmation from infant baptism. Noting that confirmation is usually conferred at the age of reason, Norbert Rigali suggested that an even later reception of the sacrament might be more appropriate.[32]

---

[30]Covino, "Postconciliar Debate," 256. The context is Covino's designation of the fourth and last of the major baptismal schools of thought, the Initiation Unity School. He had earlier explained that "[this school] was not primarily an argument for or against the practice [of infant baptism]. It was, rather, a position which advocated the celebration of the three now separated rites of initiation (baptism, confirmation, Eucharist) in one unified rite. Many authors from both the Mature Adulthood and Environmentalist Schools also espoused the positions of this school" (254).

[31]See the review of Rockford Peterson's position in note 3 of this chapter. Monika Hellwig's *Meaning of the Sacraments* is another example of an approach that accepts the current practice of the Church and that explores the pastoral and theological meanings of that practice. Her focus is readily discerned in the titles of her chapters "Baptism and the Community Commitment" and "Confirmation and the Personal Dimension."

[32]Rigali, "New Theology and Infant Baptism," 17: "But today, when responsibility is understood, not so much in terms of 'the rational animal' and 'the age of reason,' as in terms of 'the person-in-relation-to-others' and the person's 'self-disponibility,' there are good reasons for thinking that a later age would be more fitting for confirmation." Rigali's argument occurs in the context of a metaphor

Francis Buckley concurred. Agreeing that the (1917) *Code of Canon Law* maintained the rights of the baptized to be confirmed, he insisted that the question as to when confirmation should be conferred should not be answered solely by appeals to liturgical preferences or the earliest historical precedents. Rebuking liturgical historians who blamed the rapid growth of the early Church and the resultant pastoral unavailability of the bishop for the disintegration of the original unity of the sacraments of initiation,[33] Buckley recognized historical, pastoral, and theological reasons for maintaining the current separation between baptism and confirmation.[34] The concern should not be whether delaying confirmation to a more mature age might deprive a particular individual of sacramental grace, thought Buckley, "but whether the church would be deprived of a truly effective and responsible witness by conferring it too early."[35] Buckley is a forceful

---

comparing children in Christian families with novices in a religious order—a metaphor he admits has "great limitations."

[33]Buckley, "Right to the Sacraments," 333: "This is too simplistic a position. The liturgy of initiation from the third to fifth centuries is beautiful—but it did not work. It did not successfully initiate newcomers into the community. In fact the community broke down under the influx of too many inadequately prepared and motivated converts."

[34]Ibid. Buckley emphasizes the ancient tradition concerning the symbolic and central role of the bishop in the Church community as well as the "classic theology of confirmation, rooted in the New Testament, [which explained] the sacrament as conferring a *special* (not exclusive) gift of the Spirit, for the task of *bearing witness* and continuing the messianic mission of Jesus" (emphasis in original). In "What Age for Confirmation?" 662, he argues against the position that children be confirmed as early as possible (the second or third year of life) and maintains the distinct purpose of each of the initiation sacraments: "Baptism is the beginning of the spiritual life, the Eucharist is its nourishment. Confirmation has another purpose, the social good of the whole Church."

Buckley's emphasis upon the role of the bishop and upon confirmation as a sacrament of Christian maturity allowed him in "What Age for Confirmation?" (written prior to the publication of the 1972 adult ordo) to advocate the separation of confirmation from baptism also in the case of adults: "Adult converts should come together for confirmation from all the parishes of the diocese to the cathedral. They will have been baptized at the Easter vigil in their own parishes, where they were welcomed into the larger family of the parish. On the vigil of Pentecost they will gather in the center of the diocese to be fully incorporated into the church" (665).

[35]Buckley, "Right to the Sacraments," 334; also "What Age for Confirmation?" 662.

proponent in this period for delaying confirmation until an age when the valid pastoral and theological sign of the sacrament can be credibly given.[36]

Finally, some writers, clearly preferring the reunification of the initiation sacraments, proposed various rites that would fill the perceived pastoral gap were infants to be baptized, confirmed, and communicated within the same liturgical celebration. As early as 1974 Ralph Keifer had suggested studying the practice of the American Episcopal Church, a practice "which unifies initiation but provides for a repeatable rite which is a reaffirmation of the baptismal commitment."[37] Writing at the end of the decade, John Gallen echoed Kavanagh's preference for posing *strategic* questions—perhaps revealing as well a certain weariness with the *tactical* question of the proper age for confirmation:

"I do not think that it is pastorally helpful for us to devote our attention much longer to asking questions about the appropriate age for a confirmation liturgy that is separate from baptism and Eucharist. The better, the real, question is: when do we wish to celebrate the liturgy of initiation in its fullness? The model offered by the reform of Vati-

---

[36]In "What Age for Confirmation" Buckley criticizes six major arguments for the early conferral of confirmation—from birth to "as early as possible"—and concludes: "[A]t what age should confirmation be given to those who are baptized in infancy? It should be given when they have sufficient psychological and spiritual maturity. For most Catholics this will occur around the time they leave school and enter the world of business and labor. Some few may mature earlier. . . . Let the reception of confirmation not come at some fixed age but when the recipient feels ready and freely asks for it. It will then be a moment on which he can look back in later life and say: 'That was the time when I freely chose of my own accord to be an adult Christian with all that this implies. That was when I first reached Christian maturity'" (666).
Buckley's criticism of what he might consider "indiscriminate confirmation" would undoubtedly find agreement among the Mature Adulthood School, although they would of course refer the argument back to the advisability of infant baptism. Our treatment here cannot do justice to the intricacies of Buckley's argument.

[37]Keifer, "Christian Initiation," 395. Keifer continued by suggesting the alternative of an infant or child catechumenate until full initiation could be celebrated at a later age. See also Tad Guzie, "Should We Cancel Confirmation?" 17–23. Guzie also refers to the Episcopal rites and suggests, "We may very well need a rite of passage into adulthood or a ceremony of Christian commitment, perhaps during the high-school years" (23).

can II is adult initiation. It is not a model or norm that excludes the option for infants."[38]

Acknowledging that infant baptism-confirmation-Eucharist was a valid and proper pastoral option, Gallen also recognized the need for a future liturgical celebration that would "focus and crystallize [the already sacramentally initiated person's] mature commitment of faith," and suggested that a more creative and comprehensive use of the Paschal Vigil might serve this purpose better than the development of a new rite of Christian maturity.[39] There was, then, considerable disagreement as to the unified celebration of the sacraments of initiation. While most agreed that confirmation was intrinsically related to baptism, strikingly divergent views emerged as to the exact relationship between these two sacraments—as well as to when that relationship would be best expressed liturgically. Discussion concerning the effective expression of the initiation of an infant or child into the Church is also the point of our fifth and final perspective. Our examination here will be brief, as there was minimal comment from the Environmentalist School in this first full postconciliar decade concerning the concept of the infant or child catechumenate.

The fifth perspective:
The catechumenate as a temporary alternative to baptism
As we observed in the previous chapter, Aidan Kavanagh's prediction that the restoration of the catechumenate would influence the practice of infant baptism proved prophetic, as several authors

[38]Gallen, "Pastoral Celebration of Initiation," 152. Braxton, "Adult Initiation and Infant Baptism," 310–11, offers a brief but intriguing rumination concerning when to initiate.

[39]Gallen, "Pastoral Celebration of Initiation," 152: "Each year at the vigil, I suggest, a special place, a special time, a special importance should be accorded to those members of the community who now make that protest of love in the renewal of baptismal vows for the first time since their initiation in infancy or young childhood. This first public profession of faith is not a matter of incidental and 'matter of course' ceremonial, but ought to be a milestone in the Christian journey and be recognized as such. It should be prepared for with enormous care and undertaken with all the seriousness that arriving at the moment of maturity demands. From this moment on, all the responsibilities of young adulthood in the life of the Christian community belong to the newly dedicated Christian."

suggested that the enrollment of an infant in a catechumenate could serve as a theologically legitimate and temporary alternative to baptism. There was, apparently, only one writer in the 1970s who opposed this suggestion.

Appealing to magisterial and papal teaching, canon law, and revelation, Paul Donlan insisted that baptism (of water, blood, or desire) was the sole means for the remission of original sin and warned that denying baptism to infants was jeopardizing their eternal salvation. Although he readily admitted that the divine mercy and action were not limited to the sacraments, Donlan considered relying upon extra-sacramental means, illegitimate appeals to theological opinions, and dangerous liturgical experiments. Experiments and opinions were clearly what he considered a children's catechumenate[40] and, as he thought it clear that children who have not reached the age of reason "cannot be true catechumens for they do not have the 'explicit intention'" required by the Church, their (nonsacramental) initiation rite into a catechumenate could only and necessarily be sacramentally ineffective.[41]

Donlan's criticism of the infant/child catechumenate suggestion stands alone in the 1970s, but the 1980 *Instruction on Infant Baptism* and several authors thereafter also opposed the concept for various theological and liturgical reasons. We consider the instruction in the following chapter, and we will return to the American literature in chapter 4. I conclude this chapter by summarizing our review of the first fifteen years of American Catholic postconciliar writing on the subject of infant baptism.

[40]Donlan, "Second Thoughts," 37: "To begin with, there can be no experimentation which would jeopardize the salvation of souls. Baptism is necessary for salvation. There can be no experimentation with necessary means. In medicine, when there is a serious illness involving danger of death, the doctors do not experiment on the patient, nor would the family allow such a thing. They all realize that the patient is not a guinea pig. The same common-sense approach should prevail in the supernatural life which is at stake depending on whether baptism is administered or not."

[41]Ibid., 38: "[I]t is important to point out that catechumens are united to the Church by virtue of an explicit desire to join her [*Lumen Gentium* 14]. . . . Consequently, children who have not use of reason cannot be true catechumens for they do not have the 'explicit intention.' These unbaptized children remain in the same position with respect to grace and salvation as non-baptized children of non-Catholic parents."

CONCLUSIONS AND OBSERVATIONS

Our study of the American postconciliar discussion on infant baptism has thus far followed Nathan Mitchell's 1975 delineation of the two major American baptismal schools of thought. Our utilization of five perspectives, discerned in the early postconciliar literature, has structured our review of the teachings of each school concerning the theology and practice of infant baptism. Prior to summarizing our findings from chapters 1 and 2, a caveat is in order.

Mitchell's categorization and our subsequent treatment of the two schools should not encourage the conclusion that the Mature Adulthood School opposed the baptism of infants. Such an assertion would be as erroneous as the claim that the Environmentalists dismissed the publications of the Mature Adulthood School or the importance of the adult ordo. The primary difference between the two schools was their immediate focus (the initiation of adults or of infants), but their long-range or strategic interests (the quality of life in the Church) coincided. Many Environmentalists would have agreed with Aidan Kavanagh, for instance, that the enemy of a mature adult Church was not infant baptism but the sentimental and indiscriminate baptizing of infants, which was "robbing the church of calcium in its bones." And, although Tertullian's adage is associated more frequently with the Mature Adulthood School and the adult ordo, the Environmentalists also held that "Christians are not born, they are made."

Our first set of observations, then, reflects fundamental principles shared by writers of both schools. That these observations appear "seasoned" to us a generation later should but remind us of their continuing influence on ecclesiology and sacramental-liturgical theology. The observations are two:

1. Baptism (or any sacrament) is not a matter involving simply the individual who receives the sacrament and the God whose grace is conferred. The celebration of baptism (sacraments) has significance for the entire Church because the liturgical celebration is an act of the entire Church.

2. Because of this, the entire community is involved and "re-made" as it initiates an individual. This involvement of the community, and the challenge given the community through its practice of sacramental initiation, is expressed more clearly in the lengthy and obviously public nature of the adult ordo. But this involvement and challenge is no less essential to, and no less efficacious of, the continuing outpouring of the grace of the sacrament in the baptizing of an infant.

There is no confecting of faith on the spot in either celebration, for the personal and communal significance of one's baptism—of which the sacramental ceremony is but one part—continues to unfold throughout the life of the individual.

A second set of observations concerns the distinctive contributions of the respective schools. Regarding the adult ordo as normative for Christian initiation, the Mature Adulthood School emphasized the recovered paschal focus of Christian initiation and, furthermore, insisted that infants and children (as well as adults) receive full sacramental initiation into Christ's death and resurrection through the unified celebration of baptism, confirmation, and Eucharist. It considered the restored catechumenate a vital order in the public life of the ecclesial community—an order that visibly compelled the community to live and be forever challenged by the faith it professes.

Consonant with the above principles and challenged by the Mature Adulthood School's consistent appeal that Christians are *made*, Environmentalists sought to remove infant baptism from the predominantly individualist approach of preconciliar times and to understand the sacrament as an act and pledge of faith on the part of parents and community. No longer considered a sacramental remedy to be sought as quickly as possible to ward off the spiritual dangers ensuing from an untimely death, infant baptism was understood as the symbolic and efficacious initiation into a spiritual environment that would form, sustain, and challenge the individual (and community) throughout life.

We review now the five perspectives, which have guided the discussion in chapters 1 and 2.

The problem of the indiscriminate baptizing of infants

There was virtually unanimous agreement between the two schools that the indiscriminate baptizing of infants was unacceptable. Because their primary concern was the "environment" of infant baptism, writers of the Environmentalist School were quick to urge that, while theological and liturgical ideals were important, insufficiently prepared or motivated parents be treated with charity and dignity—and with a hope toward the parents' own future and further growth in the faith. A theologically pessimistic view of the fate of unbaptized infants did not seem to play a significant part in the discussion.

The norm of baptism

The Mature Adulthood School saw in the adult ordo the Church's norm of baptism. Stated in its extreme position, anything other than the initiation process of a mature, conscious adult was seen as falling short of the norm and was considered, therefore, an anomaly. Environmentalists, however, considered infant baptism as both legitimate and as normal: the normal and acceptable way for practicing Catholic families to bring their children into the Church and to begin the life-long education and formation in the Christian faith implicit in such a baptism and assumed by such a family. While the concept of the adult ordo as norm appeared in the literature throughout the decade, the closing years saw a growing acknowledgment that there was no *one* way of making Christians, and a number of authors spoke of the goal or vision of the Church, as reflected in the *RCIA*, as the adult ordo's normative value. Mention is due Nathan Mitchell's distinctive attempt to elaborate a "theology of childhood," and thereby consider the significance children and childhood might have for the Church. Ironically (in the light of the "norm controversy"), one writer in the closing years of the decade suggested there might be something normative in the life of the kingdom about a child.

The necessity of catechesis

Consensus was reached on this issue, although the particular expressions varied. Whereas the Mature Adulthood School naturally emphasized the communal "conversion therapy" realized through the adult ordo, Environmentalists stressed the primary role of the parents in the Christian education and formation of their children (an emphasis with which the former school would certainly agree).

The unity of the initiation sacraments

The Mature Adulthood School consistently counseled that the unity among the initiation sacraments of baptism, confirmation, and Eucharist must be respected theologically and liturgically. As we have seen, however, several Environmentalists not only accepted Church legislation (which separated the sacramental celebrations) but also maintained there were valid pastoral, theological, and historical reasons for maintaining such a separation.

The catechumenate as a temporary alternative to baptism

This suggestion was based on the restoration of the order of the catechumenate as called for by the *RCIA*, which clearly considered a catechumen as already joined to the Church and thus entitled to Christian burial. The possibility of enrolling an infant or a child into the catechumenate seemed, on the one hand, to avoid the worst evils of indiscriminate baptism and, on the other hand, to alleviate the concern of parents and pastors (at least in the minds of the writers) regarding the fate of the unbaptized. Apparently only one American writer in the 1970s contested this suggestion on theological grounds.

This, then, was the terrain of the American discussion on infant baptism at the conclusion of the first full decade following the publications of the postconciliar rites of adult and infant initiation. As is evident, writings were many and views were diverse. Moreover, terms and concepts not associated with the preconciliar practice or understanding of infant baptism had taken firm root in the discussion: deferral, anomaly, community, initiation unity, catechumenate.

In the light of such writings and speculations an official intervention could be presumed and, in late 1980, the Sacred Congregation for the Doctrine of the Faith issued the first major curial document dealing with infant baptism since the 1969 promulgation of the *RBC*. It is to this congregation's instruction that we now turn.

Chapter 3

A Curial Response to the Discussion:
The 1980 *Instruction on Infant Baptism*

"Contemporary theological investigation is considering the sacramental initiation of infants by water-baptism as problematical. . . . One of the possible obstacles to revising church practice in this area of initiation and making it more credible in the contemporary situation is the absence of any means of introducing infants to the life of the church other than by full water-baptism."[1]

"In view of this [questioning of traditional sacramental practice] and in response to the many petitions received, the Sacred Congregation for the Doctrine of the Faith . . . has prepared the present Instruction . . . to recall the principal points of doctrine in this field which justify the Church's constant practice down the centuries and demonstrate its permanent value in spite of the difficulties raised today. The document will then indicate some general guidelines for pastoral action" [3].[2]

Canonists of the previous decade had observed that the closer scrutiny given parents requesting baptism for their children was due not to changes in Church legislation but to greater attention given to canonical legislation already in force. Not surprisingly, the revised *Code of Canon Law (CIC)*, on which work had begun in the mid-1960s, clearly reflected this emphasis.

Some two years prior to the promulgation of the 1983 code, however, the Sacred Congregation for the Doctrine of the Faith (SCDF) published its *Instruction on Infant Baptism*. Although addressed to the universal Church, *Pastoralis Actio (PA)* responded to many aspects of

[1]Walsh, "Rite of Welcoming a Christian Child," 8, as an example of those calling for a reexamination of, or alternatives to, traditional sacramental baptism.

[2]The *Instruction on Infant Baptism (Pastoralis Actio)* was published by the SCDF on October 20, 1980. An English translation may be found in *Vatican Council II: More Postconciliar Documents*, gen. ed. Austin Flannery (Collegeville: The Liturgical Press, 1982) 103–17. Bracketed numbers in our text refer to the paragraph numbers of the document.

the infant-baptism discussion in which American authors had engaged, and thus it allows us some insight into curial reaction to that discussion.

The goals of *PA* are set forth clearly in the document's introduction. Acknowledging the difficulties of educating and raising the young in the faith, the instruction notes that parental and pastoral concerns have prompted suggestions that endanger "so essential a doctrine as that of the necessity of baptism."[3] *PA* sought to reaffirm the traditional Catholic teaching concerning the baptism of infants, evaluate contemporary discussion on the subject, and propose guidelines for pastoral practice. We will review the document according to these three goals.

PASTORALIS ACTIO 4–15:
TRADITIONAL DOCTRINE ON INFANT BAPTISM

The instruction justifies the practice of infant baptism with numerous appeals to tradition and magisterial teaching. Our concern is with what I have designated this section's "two conclusions," for their import is reflected throughout the document. Noting that Jesus' command to transmit the faith and to baptize the nations (Matt 28:19) has always been seen as an essential part of the mission of the Church, the instruction maintains that the Church likewise has always understood Jesus' conversation with Nicodemus (John 3:5) "to mean that children should not be deprived of baptism" [12]. The document then sets forth its "first conclusion":

"The Church has thus shown by her teaching and practice that she knows no other way apart from baptism for ensuring children's entry into eternal happiness. Accordingly, she takes care not to neglect the mission that the Lord has given her of providing rebirth "of water and the Spirit" for all those who can be baptized. As for children who die without baptism, the Church can only entrust them to God's mercy, as she does in the funeral rite provided for them" [13].[4]

---

[3]*PA* 2: "Some think it better to delay the baptism of children until the completion of a catechumenate of greater or less duration, while others are asking for a reexamination of the teaching on the necessity of baptism, at least for infants, and wish the celebration of the sacrament to be put off until such an age when an individual can make a personal commitment, perhaps even until the beginning of adult life."

[4]Although *PA* had reaffirmed the doctrine of original sin in nos. 6 and 7, this is the only time the instruction addresses directly the fate of infants dying prior to baptism. An accompanying footnote refers to the 1969 *Rite of Funerals* (82, 231–37),

After a paragraph reaffirming the Augustinian and Thomistic teachings that infants are baptized in the faith of the Church, *PA* offers its "second conclusion":

"Although the Church is truly aware of the efficacy of her faith operating in the baptism of children, and aware of the validity of the sacrament that she confers on them, she recognizes limits to her practice, since, apart from cases of danger of death, she does not admit a child to baptism without its parents' consent and a serious assurance that after baptism it will be given a Catholic upbringing. This is because she is concerned both for the natural rights of the parents and for the requirements of the development of faith in the child" [15].

These two conclusions—the reaffirmation of the necessity of baptism for salvation and the acknowledgment of limits to sacramental practice—orient the document's response to those challenging infant baptism and structure *PA*'s pastoral recommendations and prohibitions.

PASTORALIS ACTIO 16–26:
ANSWERS TO DIFFICULTIES BEING RAISED TODAY

The document answers (literally, "judges": *iudicare*) five contemporary challenges to the legitimacy or desirability of infant baptism. The instruction reports, first, that the New Testament sequence of "preaching-faith-sacrament" is interpreted by some as the "rule" or sequence for baptism and that, "apart from cases of danger of death, they would apply this rule to children, and would institute an obligatory catechumenate for them" [17].[5] *PA* 18 responds by appealing to

---

which warns that allowance of the funeral rite must not be construed as compromising the necessity of baptism. No. 82 stipulates that, with the permission of the local ordinary, funeral rites may be celebrated for an infant if the parents intended to have the infant baptized; this rubric accompanies the relevant prayers in the Sacramentary and appears in modified form in the 1983 *CIC* (1183, §2). See also the revised 1989 *Order of Christian Funerals*, 237 n. 1. We observe the absence throughout the document of any reference to limbo, the theological opinion of which would have provided a traditional (if not, for many, unsatisfactory) answer as to the eternal fate of the unbaptized infant. We will comment further on this in subsequent chapters.

[5]This and the following challenge addressed by the document are among the views of the Mature Adulthood School. More comprehensive responses to these first two challenges than the brief instruction allows are found in the writings of the Environmentalists cited in our chapter 2; see especially the articles by Kiesling and Haggerty.

the apostolic origins of the practice of infant baptism, noting once again that the Church provides the faith in the baptism of infants. Citing the Council of Trent, the document then asserts that baptism is a *cause* (and not merely a sign) of faith.

A second challenge addressed by *PA* questions infant baptism on the grounds that an infant cannot consciously accept or appropriate the grace of the sacrament [19]. The instruction maintains that while children may be incapable of freely accepting God's grace, they are capable of becoming children of God and co-heirs with Christ—powers that will be at their disposal as they grow in consciousness and freedom [20].

In what is arguably the document's finest response to a contemporary challenge, *Pastoralis Actio* offers three points countering the view that baptism violates an infant's freedom [21].[6] It asserts, first, that there is no such thing as a human freedom pure and untouched by outside influences and that one of the responsibilities of parents is to orient the life of their child toward the values they themselves consider true. The document then remarks that every person, whether baptized or not, is bound by indefeasible duties (*officium*) to God, and that the New Testament portrays entry into Christian life "not as a form of slavery or constraint but as admittance to true freedom" [22]. Finally, the document admits that individuals may in later years reject their baptismal rights and responsibilities but consoles parents that their educational and formative efforts may yet bear fruit as "the seeds of faith sown in the child's soul may one day come to life again" [22].

The Church must consider the realities and influences of social structures, which pose the fourth challenge cited by the instruction [23].[7] But *PA* insists that sociological principles such as homogeneity and pluralism are not normative principles but merely pointers and are, therefore, inadequate for the resolution of religious questions that are by nature "a matter for the Church and the Christian family"

[6]For arguments supporting (and predating) the document's response on this issue, see especially Searle, *Christening,* 48–51, and Rigali, "New Theology and Infant Baptism."

[7]Keifer's "Christian Initiation" is one example of a commentary on the weakening of Catholic identity and the consequent difficulties of faith maturation in contemporary society; see also, passim, the writings of Kavanagh. These articles, and those by Kiesling and Keating, represent predocument responses from different viewpoints.

[24]. The document notes that such sociological criteria would have paralyzed the missionary expansion of the early Church and insists that in today's world, precisely because the gospel is no longer normative for society, "it is therefore of great importance that in questions connected with infant baptism, the Church's own nature and mission should be taken into consideration before all else" [24].

Finally, the instruction considers the criticism that the practice of infant baptism, with its concomitant preoccupation with numbers and social establishment, reflects more the Church's desire to administer a sacrament than it does her mission of awakening faith and promoting the spread of the gospel [25].[8] Affirming that the Church's apostolate "should aim at stirring up lively faith and fostering a truly Christian life," the instruction insists that the pastoral and sacramental requirements expected of adults "cannot be applied unchanged to children who, as mentioned above, are baptized 'in the faith of the Church'" [26]. The document again emphasizes the necessity of the sacrament, "a necessity that has lost none of its importance and urgency, especially when what is at stake is ensuring that the child receives the infinite blessing of eternal life," and maintains that a preoccupation with numerical membership is not an evil if properly understood: for the mission of the Church is "to wish to give to everyone, children no less than adults, the first and basic sacrament of baptism." Infant baptism is "truly evangelical," the paragraph continues, "since it has the force of witness, manifesting God's initiative and the gratuitous character of the love with which he surrounds our lives." The paragraph concludes by observing that, even in the case of adult baptism, salvation comes "in virtue of [God's] own mercy" and "not because of deeds done by us in righteousness."

PASTORALIS ACTIO 27–33:
SOME PASTORAL DIRECTIVES

Pastoralis Actio did not simply reaffirm the teaching of the necessity of infant baptism for salvation but recognized limits to the Church's sacramental and pastoral practice. While insisting that certain suggestions proposed could not be accepted (for example, "the definitive abandonment of infant baptism and freedom to choose, whatever the reasons, between immediate baptism and deferred baptism"), *PA*

---

[8]This criticism is frequently expressed by the Mature Adulthood School. The article by Donlan parallels (and predates) *PA*'s response.

clearly acknowledged "the need for a pastoral effort pursued in greater depth and renewed in certain aspects" [27]. Four of the five perspectives established in chapter 1 guide our review of the document's pastoral prohibitions and recommendations.[9]

The first perspective:
The problem of indiscriminate baptism

The instruction offers two "great principles" to govern the pastoral practice of infant baptism, both of which are based upon the two conclusions found in section 1. The first principle again reaffirms the necessity of baptism for salvation:

"Baptism, which is necessary for salvation, is the sign and the means of God's prevenient love, which frees us from original sin and communicates to us a share in divine life. Considered in itself, the gift of these blessings to infants must not be delayed" [28.1].

The second principle, which *PA* clearly subordinates to the first, speaks of the limits of the Church's practice and against the indiscriminate baptizing of infants:

"Assurances [*cautio*] must be given that the gift thus granted can grow by an authentic education in the faith and Christian life, in order to fulfil the true meaning of the sacrament.* As a rule, these assurances are to be given by the parents or close relatives, although various substitutions are possible within the Christian community. But if these assurances are not really serious there can be grounds for delaying the sacrament; and if they are certainly non-existent the sacrament should even be refused" [28.2].[10]

The following paragraph, a subsection entitled "Dialogue Between Pastors and Believing Families," emphasizes parental presence, participation, and preparation as regards their child's baptism. As the 1983 *CIC* (867, §1, §2) will subsequently mandate, *PA* calls for the prompt *(sine mora)* baptism of an infant in danger of death, adding that "otherwise, as a rule, 'an infant should be baptized within the first weeks after birth'" [29].

---

[9]The instruction does not address the unity of the initiation sacraments.

[10]An accompanying footnote (*) refers to *RBC* 3. *Cautio* is translated throughout the document as "assurance(s)."

Paragraphs 30–31 address the "dialogue between pastors and families with little faith or non-Christian families." A clear stand is again taken against the indiscriminate baptizing of infants,[11] and when it is clear the Christian upbringing of the child cannot be guaranteed the baptism is to be delayed. This "educational delay" *(paedagogica dilatione)* is to be construed as neither pressure nor discrimination but rather as an opportunity to "[help] the family to grow in faith or to become more aware of its responsibilities" [31]. This paragraph also addresses the issue of the infant catechumenate, to which we shall return below. It concludes by upholding the rights of responsible parents to have their children baptized even when regional pastoral plans legitimately and ordinarily postpone baptism in areas dominated by large numbers of "families of little faith or non-Christian families."

A final comment concerning the "assurances" and the "well-founded hope" is appropriate. Paragraph 29 specifies that the two "great principles" form the basis upon which "concrete cases will be examined in a pastoral dialogue between the priest and the family," and refers to the *RBC* for the "rules for dialogue with parents who are practicing Christians" (5.1,5 and 8.2). In the paragraph that deals with "families with little faith or who are non-Christian" [30-31], assurances considered sufficient for baptism without delay are "the choice of godparents who will take sincere care of the child, or the support of the community of the faithful," and "any pledge giving a well-founded hope for the Christian upbringing of the children"— conditions seemingly suffering in force when compared with the "serious assurances" required by *PA* 28.2 but which seem an appropriate pastoral accommodation and strategy for situations the instruction considers akin to mission territory. This accommodation is best understood in reference to the document's second section, in which contemporary challenges to the legitimacy of infant baptism are addressed.[12]

---

[11]*PA* 30: "In fact the Church can only accede to the desire of these parents if they give an assurance that, once the child is baptized, it will be given the benefit of the Christian upbringing required by the sacrament. The Church must have a well-founded hope [*spes fundata*] that the baptism will bear fruit." The document again refers to *RBC* 3.

[12]For example, *PA* 24 states: "In a society whose mentality, customs and laws are no longer inspired by the Gospel it is therefore of great importance that in

The second perspective: The norm of baptism

As we discussed in chapters 1 and 2, the normative value of the adult ordo was interpreted in various ways. Without reentering the intricacies of that discussion here, we note that *PA* clearly rejects one implication derived from the "adult ordo as norm" thesis: "that the initiate be an adult or at least a child well advanced in years."[13] Acknowledging that the *Rite of Initiation for Children of Catechetical Age* is intended for nonbaptized children "capable of receiving and nurturing a personal faith and of recognizing an obligation in conscience (*RCIA* 252)," the instruction specifies what the existence of that rite does *not* imply: "[I]t must be stated clearly that the existence . . . of a Rite of Initiation for Children of Catechetical Age [RCIC] in no way means that the Church considers it preferable [*malle*] or normal [*ordinarius*] to delay baptism until that age" [31].[14]

The above citation immediately follows the document's directives concerning the enrollment of a child for a "future catechumenate"—a logical progression, since the *RCIC* is the desired outcome of such an enrollment. But by placing its commentary on the catechumenate and the *RCIC* in the subsection of the document entitled "Families with Little Faith or Non-Christian Families" (and not in the preceding subsection, "Believing Families"), the instruction, in addition to reinforcing its previous statement denying the "freedom to choose . . . between immediate baptism and deferred baptism" [27], infers that baptism during infancy is the ordinary ("norm-al"?) time and means for the sacramental initiation of children.

---

questions connected with infant baptism the Church's own nature and mission should be taken into consideration before all else"; and again, *PA* 26, which contends that if properly understood a preoccupation with numbers "is not a temptation or an evil for the Church but a duty and a blessing."

[13]So, for example, Kavanagh, *Shape of Baptism*, 109.

[14]This clarification from *PA* is undoubtedly at least part of what Covino refers to in "Postconciliar Debate," 242. Observing that many members of the Mature Adulthood School raised the "apparent incongruity of baptizing infants who were incapable of faith," he remarks: "In the very last months of 1980, tenets of [the Mature Adulthood School] drew official criticism from the [SCDF], an action which indirectly served to acknowledge that this had become a serious position in Catholic baptismal thought." As we shall see, the child catechumenate as an alternative to sacramental baptism—another tenet of the school—also merited specific comment from the instruction.

The third perspective: The necessity of catechesis

Catechesis supports the well-founded hope that infants be formed and educated in the faith in which they are baptized. *PA* emphasizes "the presence and active participation of the parents in the celebration," noting their "priority over the godparents" and their responsibilities to "inform their pastors of the coming birth and prepare themselves spiritually" [29]. In addition, *PA* clearly does not consider the infant's baptism as the end or accomplishment of the Church's mission, nor does it consider the infant as the only "target" of that mission. The document urges that the pastoral effort leading up to the baptism of infants "should be part of a broader activity extending to the families and to the whole of the Christian community" [32]. Calling for individuals and groups within the ecclesial community to be involved in the pastoral care afforded engaged and young married couples, the instruction implies that preparation for marriage is directed partly toward preparation for the baptism of one's children, and it exhorts priests to "give this apostolate an important place in their ministry" [32].

Acknowledging the active participation of the community "which has already come into use in the [initiation] of adults," *PA* insists that such participation is no less essential in the initiation of infants. The instruction would agree that even those baptized as infants must be "made" Christian:

"This active participation by the Christian people, which has already come into use in the case of adults, is also required for the baptism of infants, in which 'the people of God, that is the Church, made present in the local community, has an important part to play' [*RBC* 4]. Finally, the community's work will continue, after the liturgical celebration, through the contribution of the adults to the education of the young in faith, both by the witness of their own Christian lives and by their participation in various catechetical activities" [33].

The last perspective:
The catechumenate as a temporary alternative

In its introduction *Pastoralis Actio* acknowledged that a proposed solution to the "problem" of infant baptism was "to delay the baptism of children until the completion of a catechumenate of greater or less duration" [2]. As the document sets forth its pastoral directives, this suggestion of enrolling a child in a catechumenate is evaluated.

Addressing the situation in which "families with little faith or non-Christian families" request baptism for their children, the instruction advises priests who prudently decide to delay baptism to maintain contact with the parents in an effort to obtain "the conditions required on their part for the celebration of the sacrament." *PA* then suggests "as a last recourse, that the child be enrolled in a catechumenate to be given when the child reaches school age" [30].

PA remarks that these guidelines "have already been made and are already in force, but they require some clarification" [31].[15] Writing three years prior to the instruction, Paul Vanbergen had summarized the context of the 1970 SCDF response that occasioned those guidelines and had made a pertinent observation:

"[On July 13, 1970, the SCDF] takes up the question of the baptism of the children of non-Christians or of irregular Christians . . . and suggests that the registration of the child with a view to eventual baptism be proposed to the parents if the conditions for proceeding with baptism are not sufficient. *But nothing is said about the status of a child thus registered (catechumen? pre-catechumen?) nor about the significance of the registration (administrative transaction? first part of baptism?)."*[16]

PA clarifies questions of status and significance by specifying the *nature* and *limitations* of a child's "enrollment":

"Enrollment for a future catechumenate should not be accompanied by a specially created rite which would easily be taken as an equivalent of the sacrament itself. *It should also be clear that this enrollment is not admittance to the catechumenate and that the infants enrolled cannot be considered catechumens with all the prerogatives attached to being such.* They must be presented later on for a catechumenate suited to their age" [31; emphasis mine].

By distinguishing clearly between *enrollment for* and *admittance to* the catechumenate and by specifically disavowing that an infant en-

---

[15]An accompanying footnote reads: "These rules were first given in a Letter of the [SCDF] replying to a request by the Most Reverend Barthélemy Hanrion, Bishop of Dapango, Togo, and they were published, together with the Bishop's request, in *Notitiae* No. 61 (volume 7, year 1971), pp. 64–70." For the text of the SCDF's letter, see *DOL* 732–33.

[16]Vanbergen, "Baptism of Infants of *non satis credentes* Parents," 200 n. 1; emphasis mine.

rolled for a future catechumenate enjoys "all the prerogatives attached to being [a catechumen]," *PA* seemingly weakens the argument of various authors who, deeming an infant catechumen as one already joined to the Church and therefore entitled to Christian burial, had proposed the child catechumenate as a legitimate response to the pastoral quandary surrounding the "fate of the unbaptized." Finally, it should be noted that *PA* considers an enrollment for a future catechumenate clearly within the context of "families with little faith or non-Christian families," and not as an option for "believing families." This again reinforces the document's contention that "certain suggestions being put forward today cannot be accepted."

CONCLUSIONS

As regards *Pastoralis Actio* and our *perspectives* on infant baptism, we offer the following conclusions:

The problem of indiscriminate baptism. Maintaining the necessity of baptism for salvation, *Pastoralis Actio* recognized limits to the sacramental ministry of the Church and required parental "assurances" that a child presented for baptism would be formed and baptized in the Catholic faith. In cases where a sufficient "well-founded hope" could not be discerned, the instruction permitted an "educational delay" oriented toward the future spiritual growth of the infant's family and encouraged pastors to maintain contact with the family.

The norm of baptism. PA did not address the thesis of the adult ordo as norm in any detail. In its second section ("Answers to Difficulties Being Raised Today") it did address several positions associated with the Mature Adulthood School (for example, the relationship between baptism and act of faith-personal reception of grace [17–20] and baptism in contemporary society [23–24]).

In offering its pastoral directives in section 3, *PA* stated clearly that the Church "in no way . . . considers it preferable or normal to delay baptism" until an age when children are able to consciously receive and profess a personal faith. In the case of infants born into "believing families," baptism during infancy is considered the "norm."

The necessity of catechesis. PA frequently referred to the necessity of preparing and catechizing parents and families prior to and after the baptism of their infants. The instruction encouraged a broad pastoral effort oriented toward the newly married and those preparing for marriage and urged that appropriate groups within the parish community be involved in that preparation. The importance of baptismal preparation and catechesis was seen to justify an "educational delay" in some instances, and PA clearly attributed to parents (assisted by pastoral efforts) the responsibility "of awakening their children's faith and educating it." Finally, the instruction held that the community is itself affected through the baptism of its infants and that communal responsibility for and involvement in the lives of those baptized should not be confined to the sacramental celebration alone.

The catechumenate as a temporary alternative to baptism. In cases in which a well-founded hope on the part of the parents could not be discerned—and in the context of "families with little faith or non-Christian families"—PA allowed as a last resort that the child might be enrolled in a catechumenate to be given when the child reaches catechetical age. In its clarification of a 1970 decision of the SCDF, the instruction stated that such an enrollment "should not be accompanied by a specially created rite" that might be understood as baptism itself, and that infants enrolled for this future catechumenate were *not* catechumens and did not, therefore, enjoy the prerogatives associated with the catechumenate.

A BRIEF ASSESSMENT

PA sought "to recall the principal points of doctrine" concerning infant baptism [2], "to judge certain views . . . which question its legitimacy as a general rule" [16], and "to indicate the principles and fundamental guidelines" concerning its practice [27]. These objectives were met. Maintaining the necessity of infant baptism "for ensuring children's entry into eternal happiness" [13], the document upheld infant baptism as the normal practice for believing families [31], required a well-founded hope for the future Catholic education and formation of an infant coming from families with little faith or non-Christian families [30], emphasized the essential role of parents and community in the baptizing of infants [32–33], and clarified that an infant enrolled for a future catechumenate was not considered a catechumen [31].

But the precise influence of *Pastoralis Actio* upon the subsequent American discussion of infant baptism is difficult to determine. Although such an analysis lies outside the scope of our work, I offer several observations to conclude our discussion of the document.

As the instruction clearly supported two of the perspectives we have identified in the American discussion on which consensus had been reached (that the indiscriminate baptizing of infants was unacceptable and that pre- and post-baptismal catechesis was an intrinsic element of the meaning and celebration of the sacrament), it is no surprise that a number of authors in the following decade refer to *PA* to explain the necessity of catechesis, or the "educational delay."

In contrast to this, there also are indications in the literature that the document was not well known or that, once read, it slowly found its way into the less-accessible areas of files and bookshelves. The absence of references to *PA* in many articles in the following decade may indicate unfamiliarity with the document—or represent a tacit appraisal of *PA*'s actual contribution to the discussion in the United States. While *PA* did lend a certain "hierarchical authority" to writers and pastors calling for catechesis and prebaptismal discernment,[17] with one exception (the clarification concerning the child catechumenate) it did not really add anything new to the 1969 *RBC:* calls for catechesis, prebaptismal discernment, and the educational delay are found in the ritual's introduction (nos. 3–8). And it is interesting that most authors who subsequently criticized the "child catechumenate as alternative" suggestion refer to *PA* only in passing if at all. And one author, encouraging that the child catechumenate be considered an alternative to the problem of indiscriminate baptism, refers to the "door opened" in the 1970 "Togo Letter"—unaware, apparently, that the question she poses in 1990 was clearly answered by *PA* 31 in 1980.

While *Pastoralis Actio* did clarify certain aspects of the Church's teaching on the "extremely obscure question" of the value of baptizing

[17]Francis G. Morrisey, "Papal and Curial Pronouncements: Their Canonical Significance in Light of the 1983 Code of Canon Law," *Jurist* 50 (1990). Pages 102–25 address the comparative authoritative weight of the numerous "Roman documents." Morrisey describes "instructions" as a "rather common form of pronouncement by the Roman curia . . . which clarifies the prescriptions of laws and elaborates on and determines an approach to be followed in implementing them" (115) and concludes: "It is this form of document, along with the declaration, that has given rise to the greatest difficulty in interpretation in the post-conciliar era. Since the texts are not strictly speaking legislative—at least according to their nature—their application certainly allows for more leeway than would a decree" (116).

infants, it by no means put an end to the discussion. In the following chapter we resume our review of the American postconciliar discussion.

Chapter 4

Infant Baptism Reclaimed:
The literature from *Pastoralis Actio*
to the present

"The baptismal waters have calmed since Aidan Kavanagh and others claimed that adult initiation is the 'norm.' It seems clear that this does not necessarily exclude the baptism of infants, but it does question indiscriminate infant baptism and raises other possibilities. The conversion and growth of the adult envisioned in the RCIA is the norm, and anything done earlier should contribute to that growth."[1]

"If there is any reason for not admitting an infant to faith and baptismal life in the communion of the Church, it may only be that the child's own God-given household is not faithful."[2]

As the 1980s began, the *Rite of Baptism for Children* was itself approaching the adolescent age of twelve—an age that typically sees human beings beginning their hesitant, sometimes frantic, search for identity and meaning. As the title of this chapter suggests, however, the literature of this decade reveals a more stable and less defensive approach to the initiation of infants and young children. The preceding years of challenge and reflection seem to have resolved some of the early postconciliar growing pains of the sacrament, and authors continued to explore the possibilities and opportunities posed by the baptizing of infants.

We examined the Mature Adulthood and Environmentalist Schools at some length in chapters 1 and 2, and so the fundamental tenets and interests of the schools are familiar. In this chapter we will not segregate authors according to schools of thought, therefore, but will allow the five perspectives established in chapter 1 to guide our review of the literature from 1980 to the present.

---

[1] James Dunning, *New Wine, New Wineskins: Exploring the RCIA*, 101.
[2] Mark Searle, "Infant Baptism Reconsidered," 44.

The first perspective:
The problem of indiscriminate baptism

The indiscriminate baptizing of infants continued to be fought in the literature—and sought in the parishes—throughout the 1980s.[3] To initiate sacramentally without establishing pastorally the requisite well-founded hope presumably furthered the depletion of calcium from ecclesial bones and, moreover, was considered by some to be a liturgical lie, a "betrayal" of the ritual that robbed the liturgical symbols of their integrity.[4]

Lawrence Mick contended that even a well-founded hope, if understood merely as a kind of generic belief in Christ or a conventional desire to "live right," might not be sufficient. Because baptism was "fundamentally initiation into the Church," Mick considered active Church membership a "prerequisite," and held that parents "who never or only rarely worship with the community and who have no concrete sense of belonging or commitment to the local Church cannot honestly promise to raise their children in the Church." Celebrating baptism under these circumstances, Mick believed, would be "a travesty of the sacrament, saying in ritual something that is not true in fact."[5]

Mick is admirably resolved to keep calcium in Church bones and integrity in its rituals, but perhaps he widens the gap between what the Church can legitimately demand of parents and what some parents might be capable of giving. This gap had been sensitively described some years previously by John Garvey, who, while agreeing wholeheartedly that the sacraments were not mere social occasions, remained uncomfortable with the stricter requirements. Garvey felt the relationship between ritual honesty for the strong and pastoral

[3]For example, Joseph M. Champlin, "Why It's Not as Easy to Get Kids Baptized," 25–26, and Daniel Lowery, "Should Every Baby Be Baptized?" 14–19. Addressing Catholic parents, both authors refer to *Pastoralis Actio* in justifying the prebaptismal inquiry. Others referring to *PA* include Tad Guzie, *The Book of Sacramental Basics* 98–103, and William Engel, "Pastoring Marginal Catholics: Another Look at Infant Baptism," 18–22.

[4]Joseph Martos, "Let's Deny Baptism to Babies of Fallen-Aways," 14–15. See also Julia Upton, *A Church for the Next Generation: Sacraments in Transition*, 71: "[B]aptizing the child of anyone who requests the sacrament, facilely accepting even a questionable degree of faith as sufficient, can rob the sacrament of its ritual dynamism. . . . [I]t does not give full expression to the sacramental reality and ought to be discouraged."

[5]Lawrence Mick, *Understanding the Sacraments Today*, 26.

concern for the weak was not mutually exclusive, and he touched that delicate nerve linking the urgency of gospel commitment with the need for pastoral understanding—and for pastoral humility:

"I am not entirely comfortable with the point I want to make. It seems reasonable to ask for a commitment to Catholic practice before admitting people to Catholic sacraments. But the church is not always free of responsibility for the distance some people feel from Catholic practice. In any case, the church ought to feel some responsibility and some sense of mission towards the people who, for whatever reason, live at the edges of the church."[6]

Noticeably absent among Garvey's concerns is the fate of an infant dying without the sacrament. He feared, rather, that the potential value of the "educational delay," the understanding of which had been evolving at least since the publication of the 1969 *RBC*, might be mutating into a too-rigid pastoral approach that would result in a readily discarded pile of crushed reeds and quenched wicks. As such, his concern is primarily for the parents' tenuous, though somehow felt, relationship with the Christian tradition and community.[7]

[6]John Garvey, "Turning People Away: More Fastidious Than Jesus?" 679. Peggy Ellsberg, "'Let the Little Children . . . ,'" 16, offers a personal and poignant reflection along these same lines.

[7]Garvey, "Turning People Away," 8, makes this point: "Demands that the marginal first prove themselves and conform before they can share in the sacraments and services of the church can be experienced as excessive and crushing. The very fact that they turn to the church can, for the reasons we noted above, be a sign that God's grace is already at work in them. And that divine working is better nourished by the sacraments than by human heavy-handedness. We who minister in the name of the church are also modeling the church. And welcoming the fallen and marginal should be a part of that model as much as the challenge to reform."

Having explained in his 1982 article, "Why It's Not as Easy to Get Kids Baptized," Joseph Champlin addressed the downside of the discernment of the prebaptismal inquiry in "Welcoming Marginal Catholics: Pastoral Challenges of Baptism and Matrimony," 3–8. He addresses the Church's concern for marginal Catholics at greater length in *The Marginal Catholic: Challenge, Don't Crush.*

Joan Torres, "Uncommitted Catholic Parents and Children's Baptism," 49–50, and Greg J. Humbert, "Welcoming Unmarried Parents: Mysterious Grace of Baptism," 15–17, offer interesting reflections concerning actual experiences with the "educational delay."

Robert Kinast, *Sacramental Pastoral Care: Integrating Resources for Ministry*, 108–30, offers pastoral examples and recommendations concerning "whether to

In the parish, however, many parents were concerned more about the destiny of their unbaptized child after death than about their own relationship with a faith community on earth. Acknowledging the traditional doctrine of the necessity of baptism for salvation, authors sought to reassure parents by appealing to the equally traditional teaching that God's power is not limited to the sacraments and by emphasizing the Church's trust in God's loving mercy—as expressed, for example, through the Christian burial allowed infants dying prior to baptism.[8]

As in the previous decade, most authors considered the indiscriminate baptizing of infants unacceptable. Those insisting that infants be

---

baptize" and "delayed baptism." He believes "it is rare that the parents' level of faith development is such that baptism should be postponed" (129).

[8]See, for example, Upton, *Next Generation*, 69–70, and Mick, *Understanding the Sacraments Today*, 27–28. As regards the fate of unbaptized infants, Gerard Austin, *The Rite of Confirmation: Anointing with the Spirit*, 142, speaks for many theologians: "While theologians today generally reject any notion of limbo as in no way demonstrable from the New Testament and as contradictory to the general divine will of redemption, nevertheless, this thinking has yet to trickle down to the popular level. Catechesis and preaching must face up to this problem."

We noted in the previous chapter that *Pastoralis Actio* is silent as regards the notion of limbo, stating only that the Church "knows no other way apart from baptism for ensuring children's entry into eternal happiness" and that, concerning children who die without baptism, "the Church can only entrust them to God's mercy, as she does in the funeral rite provided for them" (13). Similarly, no reference to limbo is found in the 1979 letter of the SCDF, "On Certain Questions Concerning Eschatology" *(Recentiores Episcoporum Synodi)*, although this letter reaffirms the teaching on hell and purgatory. (For the text, see *More Postconciliar Documents*, 500–504).

In light of this, Basil Cole's "Is Limbo Still in Limbo?" 56–64, is puzzling in that he tries to show that "the theory of limbo is so consistent with accepted Catholic teaching on the state of infants dying without benefit of baptism, that it is certain, not a mere theological opinion or a mere product of scholastic reasoning, extraneous to sacred scripture and sacred tradition but a theological term intrinsic to revelation itself" (58). The pastoral recommendations with which Cole concludes his article are, in my opinion, unfortunate.

The recently published *Catechism of the Catholic Church* (English trans. for the U.S., 1994, USCC) no. 1261, reiterates the statement found in *PA* 13 and adds the following statement: "Indeed, the great mercy of God who desires that all men should be saved, and Jesus' tenderness toward children which caused him to say: 'Let the children come to me, do not hinder them,' allow us to hope that there is a way of salvation for children who have died without Baptism." Consistent with the ecclesial documents cited above, no teaching on—or reference to—limbo is found in the *Catechism*.

formed in the faith in which they had been baptized received clear support from the revised *Code of Canon Law*, promulgated in 1983: in addition to requiring the consent of at least one parent or guardian, canon 868 specified a "founded hope" as a requirement for the licit baptism of an infant.[9]

But while the 1983 *CIC* and consequent emendations to the *praenotanda* of the 1969 *RBC* may have filled a certain lacuna inherited from the previous code regarding weak or nominal Catholics, canonists did not necessarily find consistency when canon 868 was considered *in toto*. John Robertson noted the apparent contradiction between §1.1° and §2 of the canon. While *CIC* 868, §1.1°, required consent from at least one parent or guardian for the licit baptism of an infant, *CIC* 868, §2, waived this requirement in danger of death.[10] Explaining how "in the process of formulating the present law, the circumstances in which an infant in danger of death could be baptized were reversed,"[11] Robertson acknowledged that canons 867 and 868 reaffirm

---

[9]*CIC* 868, §1,2° reads: "[It is necessary that] there be a founded hope that the infant will be brought up in the Catholic religion; if such a hope is altogether lacking, the baptism is to be put off according to the prescriptions of particular law and the parents are to be informed of the reason."

Paul Counce, "The Deferral of Infant Baptism According to Canon 868, §1,2°," 338–39, notes the influence of the revised code on *RBC* 8 and observes that "[the change] in the ritual clarifies the ecclesiastical law by the removal of any ambiguity. It is evident that the deferral of infant baptism, in both Code and ritual, is not only lawful but actually compulsory in certain circumstances, said circumstances to be determined by particular law." He concludes: "It is clear that the practice of the Church as regards delaying the baptism of infants has undergone a gradual but ultimately radical change during the past century, from an unwillingness to put off baptism except in the face of unequivocal absence of a hope for future Christian faith to now a clear directive to defer the sacrament in circumstances determined in particular law" (339). Counce details the evolution of the canonical requirements concerning the deferral of baptism from the 1917 code to the present.

New Zealand canonist Brendan Daly provides additional detail in "Canonical Requirements of Parents in Cases of Infant Baptism According to the 1983 Code," 409–38.

[10]*CIC* 868, §1,1° reads: "[For the licit baptism of an infant it is necessary that] the parents or at least one of them or the person who lawfully takes their place gives consent"; *CIC* 868, §2 reads: "The infant of Catholic parents, in fact of non-Catholic parents also, who is in danger of death is licitly baptized even against the will of the parents."

[11]John Robertson, "Canons 867 and 868 and Baptizing Infants Against the Will of Parents," 637: "Initially the study group [1971] proposed that infants were not

the necessity of baptism for salvation—a necessity without burden for Christian parents who would certainly want their child baptized were death imminent. He thought the situation different, however, when dealing with parents who do *not* want their child baptized. Asking to what Church or community an infant baptized in such circumstances would belong, Robertson inched the lid of this Pandora's box up an inch or two by warning that "[t]he question could become especially significant if the infant survives."[12]

The second perspective: The norm of baptism

The "adult ordo as norm" thesis, which enjoyed considerable momentum and acceptance in the first full postconciliar decade, was challenged by at least two writers in 1981. Considering Kavanagh's "concept of the normativity of adult initiation [as] highly questionable," Paul Covino noted that the *RCIA* clearly was "intended for adults," and that to extend the principles of an adult ordo to the Church's entire practice of Christian initiation was "an unfounded assertion." The fact that neither the *RCIA* nor the *RBC* referred to the

---

to be baptized against the will of parents (or those who take the place of parents) since the parents, in virtue of the natural law, are the ones who freely seek baptism for their children. After the first general consultation [1981] the provision was changed to indicate that in danger of death any infant is licitly baptized unless there was a danger of aversion to religion. Finally, [1983 *CIC*] all qualifications were dropped so that in danger of death any infant may be baptized licitly even against the will of the parents." As does Robertson, Daly, "Canonical Requirements of Parents," 413–23, provides extensive commentary and documentation concerning the evolution of these canons.

[12]Robertson, "Canons 867 and 868," 638: "[T]here is a difference when parents, especially non-Catholic parents, are opposed to the baptism of their child even when the child is in danger of death. In view of the teaching of the Declaration on Religious Freedom that no one may be forced to embrace the Christian faith against his or her own will, it is more difficult to justify baptizing an infant, even in danger of death, when the parents (or those who take their place) are opposed."

See also in this regard Daly, "Canonical Requirements of Parents," 425–28, who also considers the issue of an infant in danger of death. As regards *CIC* 868, §2, he observes: "The canon does not say the child must or should *(debet)* be baptized, merely that it can be, but even the fact that provision is made for the lawfulness of such an action seems somewhat contrary to the Church's teaching on religious freedom and freedom of conscience" (426). On page 427 Daly cites letters written in 1986 by the Congregation for the Sacraments and the SCDF criticizing, from different perspectives, those who would diminish the force of the canon.

practices of the other, he contended, "would seem to imply the actual exclusiveness of each rite's independent principles."[13]

Observing that the conciliar documents with which Kavanagh supported his thesis "do not indeed state anything about the normativity of adult initiation,"[14] Covino thought Kavanagh's comparison of the Church's norm of Eucharist to that of baptism "especially problematic," since, as used in the conciliar documents, "norm" does not refer to adult baptism. Furthermore, he criticized the "unfair analogy" by which Kavanagh likened infant baptism to a private low mass: when celebrated as presented in the rites (that is, within the Christian community), Covino maintained that infant baptism "does not deviate from any stated norm."

Kevin Irwin believed the "two clearest flaws in Kavanagh's argumentation concern the church's teaching and practice on which he grounds his statements about the adult norm and the inherent logic of his thesis."[15] Also faulting Kavanagh's use of the conciliar documents, Irwin maintained that "to argue from these texts in order to establish the norms of baptism is indeed to stretch the stated meaning of these texts."

As did Covino, Irwin took issue with Kavanagh's utilization of the Eucharist as an example of a sacramental norm—not because of what Kavanagh said about the Eucharist but because of "what is adduced in regard to baptism." Noting that both the *RCIA* and *RBC* assume "some form of Christian assembly" even in cases of emergency, Irwin thought this a clear indication that both rites "are meant to be public celebrations with a variety of ministers involved in rites of maximum symbolic significance" and concluded that "the parallel between private Mass and infant baptism on grounds of liturgical abnormality is more than a bit strained."

Referring to the recent emphasis given the principle *legem credendi lex statuat supplicandi*, Irwin submitted that the long and continuing

---

[13]Covino, "Question of Infant Baptism," 66–67.

[14]For the documents referred to, see our chapter 1, note 21. As we observed, Kavanagh acknowledged the council was less clear about positing the adult ordo as normative than it was in describing the norm of the Eucharistic celebration.

[15]Kevin Irwin, "Christian Initiation: Some Important Questions," 4–24; the citations in our text here are from pages 7–11. Irwin also addresses "the church's understanding of infant baptism as drawn from the revised rituals," and "the sustaining values which should be present in a catechumenal structure designed for adults to be initiated or for parents presenting children for initiation."

liturgical tradition of infant baptism argued against considering any *one* form of baptism as the norm:

"One wonders, therefore, why the RCIA alone should now become the norm since it co-exists with the infant rite which is experienced by more in the church than is the adult rite. Instead of determining *a priori* that a form of initiation that has not been the church's lived expression of baptism for centuries should now become the church's norm for theology and practice, what would be more helpful is to allow both forms of initiation to co-exist and to utilize both in developing the theology of initiation. Elements which are characteristic or emphasized in one form may well be needed to balance aspects missing or deemphasized in the other. The juxtaposition cannot but be healthy for theology and church practice alike for both form the contemporary expression of the church's *lex orandi.*"[16]

Irwin's final criticism of the thesis is perhaps the most telling—the term "norm" itself. Acknowledging the usual clarity and precision of Kavanagh's writing, Irwin thought the technical use of "norm" "so conflicts with common usage that it produces little real clarity" and is also laden with overtones of "affirmation and obligation"—and in the case of infant baptism, of abnormality.[17]

Responding directly to Irwin's article, Lawrence Mick agreed that Kavanagh's use of the term "norm" is confusing and also preferred terms such as "model" or "pattern" to explain the "normative value" of the adult ordo. Mick agreed with Kavanagh, however, that the *RCIA* "with its vision of a catechumenate which fosters conversion and celebrates it with a variety of rites is the model which best portrays Christian initiation" and thus "presents the premier example of the Christian initiation process." Acknowledging that specific circumstances and pastoral needs necessitate a variety of approaches to conversion and initiation, Mick observed that these other approaches "are derivative from the premier model, and their adequacy can be evaluated on how well they achieve the same goals as the model

---

[16]Ibid., 9–10.

[17]Acknowledging that "vocabulary is not the overriding concern in this critique of the adult norm," Irwin characterized the use of the word "norm" as "unhelpful" and suggested other words "that appear to do at face value what 'norm' does in this case, after explanation": "paradigm," "model," "guide," "type," "pattern." (See our discussion of the second perspective in ch. 2.)

even though they address different circumstances." Mick also argued against Irwin's interpretation and application of the *lex orandi* principle, believing "issues of initiation are more complex than Irwin's comments might suggest." Reporting his experience that "the paradigmatic character of adult initiation asserts itself very quickly when both adult and infant rites are adequately implemented," Mick considered this a "very healthy state of affairs," as "it supports the continued practice of baptizing children of believing parents and at the same time calls the entire assembly to a deeper commitment to the conversion process that should mark not only the catechumenate but also the life of every member of the church."[18]

The next year marked the tenth anniversary of the initial publication of the *RCIA*. At the 1982 NAAL meeting, Raymond Kemp assessed the pastoral needs and academic challenges of the next ten years and observed that the still-developing understanding of the *RCIA* continued to pose a challenge to the practice of infant baptism:

"From ecclesiology to baptism to catechesis for conversion. The rite of Christian initiation for adults clearly indicates over and over that conversion has to be evident before sacramental celebrations are held. . . . [One question this raises] is how are you to explain what happens when we baptize infants even if we would immediately confirm and invite them to Eucharist. And I do not want to hear about *ex opere operato*."[19]

Mark Searle said not a word about *ex opere operato*, but in responding to Kemp's remarks he did take issue with the practice of "speaking of the RCIA as 'normative' for Christian initiation in general." Searle specified four "stumbling blocks" and three "misgivings" pertaining to the interpretation and implementation of the *RCIA* and maintained (as had Irwin) that both the *RCIA* and the *RBC* would be better served if considered as complements to one another rather than as competitors.[20] Neither baptismal ritual by itself, Searle

---

[18]Lawrence Mick, "Christian Initiation: Separate-But-Equal Doesn't Work," 14–18.

[19]Kemp's address at the January 1982 NAAL meeting was published as "The Rite of Christian Initiation of Adults at Ten Years," 309–26; citation is from page 320.

[20]Searle's response appeared as "Response: The RCIA and Infant Baptism," 327–32.

insisted, can exhaust "all that baptism means, all that is involved in the mystery of sharing the life of God in Christ." We approach the mystery of baptism more fully not only by considering the diverse liturgical traditions of East and West, Searle asserted, but also by accepting and evaluating "the diversity of baptismal candidates." Acknowledging that all baptisms were not equal, Searle suggested the inequality points not to the greater value of one form over another but to the unique richness waiting to be discovered in each particular celebration:

"Baptism at the age of seventeen is not the same as baptism at the age of seventy or at the age of seven years or seven weeks. The situation of the candidate contributes to the significance of a given celebration and this is as true of an infant being baptized as it is of an adult. In our enthusiasm for the 'meaningfulness' of an adult baptism celebrated as the climax of a lengthy catechumenate, we should be careful not to overlook the significance of the baptism of an infant. Indeed, it is an urgent pastoral-theological task to explore with parents and godparents the significance of each and every infant baptism. The RCIA should help us to learn how to do this, rather than being promoted as an alternative to infant baptism."[21]

A firm believer that the RCIA journey of faith is truth-bound, Searle believed further truth awaited a deeper exploration of a "theology of childhood and of the child's place in the Church." Taking childhood seriously, Searle believed, "would not mean neglecting the importance of conversion but would broaden our concern to include the ethos of conversion."[22] In a major study on infant baptism that

[21]Ibid., 329–30. Searle continues: "It is doubtful how useful it is to speak of two initiatory theories and politics, rather than of two poles with a whole spectrum of ritual practice and theological interpretation, but it would seem in any case more helpful to maintain the tension rather than collapse the meaning of Christian initiation into a single standardized economy."

[22]Ibid., 331. Searle concludes by again addressing the "ethos of conversion," and offers a challenge to the practice of both adult and infant baptism: "The moral would seem to be that the postponement of baptism does not, on its own, guarantee a confessing Church at the service of the kingdom, truly separated from the State and innocent of civil religion. Ultimately, the question we are confronted with is not how individuals may best be initiated, but how we can create an ethos of conversion" (332). Searle's call for a theology of childhood supports Nathan Mitchell's 1975 article, "Once and Future Child," which we will address at some length in part 2.

Searle subsequently wrote for and edited, he addressed more fully the place of the child in the Church and family, suggesting that infant baptism "ought to be seen less as a problem to be grappled with than as an opportunity to be grasped."[23]

Authors continued to reflect upon the value and influence of the adult ordo, and opinions as to the meaning of "norm" continued to emerge. As in the closing years of the previous decade, some writers understood the term as referring to the goal or vision of the Church, toward which the *RCIA* was oriented. For example, James Dunning stated that "the conversion and growth of the adult envisioned in the RCIA is the norm, and anything done earlier should contribute to that growth."[24] Ten years later Kieran Sawyer echoed this statement: contending that the *RCIA* and *RBC* are "equally authoritative, since both are based on official ecclesial documents," she held the *RCIA* as "the 'paradigm' because the goal of initiation is adult faith, [and] not because the RCIA model is the only or best path to arrive at adult faith."[25]

That the process of the *RCIA* was seen as an effective model upon which to structure programs for religious education and preparation for confirmation was evident, and for many this proposed catechetical structure and its hoped-for results was the norm of the adult ordo.[26] Aidan Kavanagh, however, insisted that whatever the benefits to such programs the *RCIA* model might contribute, such benefits were secondary to the significance of the "adult ordo as norm" he understood from the conciliar reforms. He observed that the *RCIA* was meant to serve "as the paradigmatic norm for the reform of [infant baptism and confirmation]," and is thus "the normative document that translated into liturgical practice the Council's fundamental outlook on basic initiatory procedure."[27] The main purpose of this

[23]Searle, "Infant Baptism Reconsidered," 50.

[24]Dunning, *New Wine, New Wineskins*, 101.

[25]Kieran Sawyer, "A Case for Adolescent Confirmation," 40.

[26]This is a major premise underlying two publications appearing in 1991: Kubick's *Confirming the Faith of Adolescents*, and Robert D. Duggan and Maureen A. Kelly's *The Christian Initiation of Children: Hope for the Future*.

[27]Aidan Kavanagh, "Theological Principles for Sacramental Catechesis," 318–19. Michael Balhoff, "Age for Confirmation: Canonical Evidence," 549–87, examines the documents of the 1964 study commission charged with revising the baptismal rites in the Roman Ritual. He concludes, in part, that "the history of the

outlook, Kavanagh remarked, "was to restore and integrate those sacraments that crown the whole grace-laden way of coming to faith in a faithful church."[28]

Kavanagh's understanding of "norm" has particular import for the fourth perspective, which we will consider below. The continuing influence of his thesis as well as the seemingly inevitable confusion it invites is reflected by one writer's observation that "[t]he RCIA has termed adult Baptism the norm," but many "have been hard pressed to give definite meaning to this statement."[29]

The third perspective: The necessity of catechesis

Although the cloud of "sacramental magic" that had long enveloped infant baptism had not entirely dissipated at the parochial level, the literature provided scant indication that baptism was considered an instant confection of faith existing apart from what had preceded and would follow it. Baptism is the sacrament of faith, and the continuing conversion effected by the infant's family and faith community continued to be seen as the most visible expression of that faith. This echoed the fundamental conviction of the previous

---

drafting process rather clearly reveals that *the rite for adults was developed first so that the principles might be clear for the later rites—baptism of infants* and confirmation when celebrated separately" (560; emphasis mine). Balhoff provides full references and extensive commentary throughout his article. As regards the reasons given why the reform of the Roman Ritual was to begin with the order of adult baptism and not that of infants, see, especially, page 558 and notes. Documenting the series of inclusions, rearrangements, and revisions of the various drafts that led to the final promulgation of the 1983 code, he observes that "the *exemplary* character of the rite of adult initiation stands out more clearly than at any time in the postconciliar reform" (573; emphasis mine).

[28]Kavanagh, "Sacramental Catechesis," 318–19. In context, Kavanagh's main concern is the sequence of the initiation sacraments (Eucharist following confirmation as the culmination of baptism) and the celebration of confirmation with baptism within the same liturgical event. The theological reasons behind such a sequence and celebration are, Kavanagh maintains, the "internal logic and grammar" of the sacraments of initiation, to which the *RCIA* "gives voice" and places "as the central norm of the entire sacramental system" (319).

[29]Edward Jeremy Miller, "Confirmation as Ecclesial Commissioning," 120. Miller adds his own definition of, and reason for, holding the *RCIA* as the norm: "The present practice of separating Baptism from imposition of hands for children retains some merit even when adult Baptism is affirmed as the norm. It is the norm because the immediate implication of being baptized is to work for the Kingdom."

decade: that baptism is not something done "to the baby" but is the grace of God sacramentally celebrated and effected—and, necessarily, continually effected by parents and community as they themselves are reinitiated continually through the baptism of their young.[30]

Writers continued to address the relationship between baptism and original sin, and the idea that baptism suddenly snatched an infant from Satan's power continued to yield to that of understanding baptism as initiation into a community constantly struggling to fight against the orientation and influence of original sin. That baptism washed away original sin signaled that Christian life and responsibility had begun, not that the meaning of the sacrament had been fulfilled. The joy surrounding an infant's baptism is due not so much from the understanding that the infant has been freed from limbo as that the child is freed by the grace of Christ to live and grow in that grace:

"Removing original sin in baptism means that one is graced to engage in a struggle with sin in the world. It means that a beginning is made, grounded in the grace of Christ, continued by his grace throughout life, and ritualized in moments of need and growth in other sacramental and liturgical celebrations. Life's journey in faith implies a constant struggle and encounter with aspects of that sin we call original. Neither infant nor adult initiates are exempt from the struggles of the Christian life after exorcism, washing and anointing.

[30]Searle, "Infant Baptism Reconsidered," 43, observed: "Thus it is not so much that baptism infuses faith into a child as that baptism is the deliberate and conscious insertion of the child into the environment of faith, which faith is the faith of the Church, which in turn is the faith of Christ himself. If the Church did not continue to live by the pattern of Christ's own faith in its dying and being raised to life, it would cease to be Church. Such existential faith constitutes the identity of the Church and the identity of the family as domestic church. It is into this faith that the child is baptized when it is baptized in the faith of the Church."

In her 1968 article "Christian Parents and Infant Baptism" Christiane Brusselmans had stressed the need for a "pastoral theology of the family and of infant baptism which will present to parents the dignity of marriage and the responsibilities which flow from their state of christian parenthood for the building up of the body of Christ" (38). And see again Searle, "Infant Baptism Reconsidered," 36–38, who considers "the vision of the family as a domestic church, *ecclesiola in ecclesia,* in virtue both of baptism and of the sacrament of marriage," as the "key to a new understanding of baptism."

They are, however, thus graced by God in initiation and given in baptism an horizon of hope and a grounding in God's love."[31]

Yet while original sin was very much alive in the literature and undoubtedly quite vibrant everywhere else, some writers suggested that the removal of original sin was only a secondary effect of baptism,[32] that original sin could not be considered a constitutive factor for a theology of baptism,[33] and that "the practice of baptizing infants does not depend for its legitimacy upon the belief that without baptism infants are excluded forever from the vision of God."[34] Searle provides an apt description of current thinking on the infant baptism-original sin linkage, a description in which the idea of relationship is primary:

[31]Irwin, "Important Questions," 15–16. Stephen J. Duffy's article, "Our Hearts of Darkness: Original Sin Revisited," 597–622, and Roger Haight's, "Sin and Grace," *Systematic Theology: Roman Catholic Perspectives*, vol. 2, ed. Francis Schüssler Fiorenza and John P. Galvin (Minneapolis: Fortress, 1991) 77–141 (esp. 85–107), are representative of more recent reexaminations of the doctrine, reality, and effects of original sin.

[32]Mick, *Understanding the Sacraments Today*, 27: "Moreover, baptism does not remove original sin in some magical way. We are freed from sin in baptism because we die to sin with Christ and rise to new life. While many people still see baptism as fundamentally the removal of original sin, that is only a secondary effect of baptism. Baptism is most basically an incorporation into the death and resurrection of Christ, brought about by initiation into the community that lives out that death and resurrection every day. It is in that daily dying to sin and rising to new life that the freedom from sin which is celebrated in baptism takes root and bears fruit."

[33]Kenan B. Osborne, *The Christian Sacraments of Initiation: Baptism, Confirmation, Eucharist* 59: "[O]riginal sin is not mentioned at all in the New Testament insights into baptism. Therefore, original sin cannot be seen as a constitutive factor for a theology of baptism." Speaking of the new rites later in his work, Osborne observes: "Adults do not have the option of limbo, and thus original sin is no longer operative in an adult. For children, however, baptismal theology prior to the new rite [1969] was somewhat dominated by the original sin concept. The fact that it is mentioned only once is indicative of the Church's official stance: namely, a distancing from the emphasis on the original sin approach [concerning baptism]" (103). (But see our ch. 2 n. 13 and ch. 3 n. 4.)

[34]Searle, "Infant Baptism Reconsidered," 47. Searle continues: "But [infant baptism] does suppose the possibility that infants *as infants* might be called to share the divine life in the Body of Christ, a possibility which, as we have argued, derives substantial support both from the fact that the Church has always baptized infants and from the insights into the nature of childhood gained from the research of the human sciences" (emphasis in original).

"A newly baptized infant is not merely one who is delivered from sin and from the threat of damnation, but one claimed by the irrescindable Word of God to be an adopted child of God, a living member of Christ, a temple of the Holy Spirit. The child in baptism enters into a new set of relationships with God, with the Church, and—we have argued—with its own family. In this instance, at least, water is thicker than blood!"[35]

The fourth perspective:
The unity of the initiation sacraments
One contribution of the postconciliar liturgical reform to sacramental-liturgical theology and ecclesiology was the recovery and restoration of the intrinsic relationship among the three sacraments of initiation. Observing that "no single sacrament is as calculated to demonstrate the importance of process in the Christian life as is the sacrament of baptism," Searle suggested that the term "sacraments" of baptism might be more correct, for "baptism, confirmation, and Eucharist belong together and together they belong to a larger initiatory process."[36]

That the sacraments of initiation belong together, and that the larger initiatory process to which they belong should not be interrupted by non-initiation sacraments, was expressed somewhat more forcefully by Raymond Kemp. Kemp likened an initiatory cycle begun by baptism but not immediately completed by confirmation and Eucharist to an "excommunication" and considered "then requiring reconciliation ['first confession'] to the table of the Lord before initiation to that very table [to be] nonsense."[37] Convinced that "what we are doing with our young . . . smacks of sacraments looking for a theology from coast to coast," he asserted: "Penance before Eucharist shows no understanding of baptism. Confirmation at the end of

[35]Ibid., 45.
[36]Ibid., 11. Aidan Kavanagh, *Confirmation: Origins and Reform,* 96, notes that the postconciliar reform of confirmation had two principle goals: "First, it was meant to bring confirmation into a closer relationship to baptism. . . . Second, confirmation reform was meant to reiterate this sacrament's relationship to the eucharist, which consummates both baptism and confirmation." The respective studies on confirmation by Kavanagh and Austin provide ample historical-liturgical evidence and commentary on the intrinsic relationship among the initiation sacraments.
[37]Kemp, "Rite of Initiation at Ten Years," 319. For the requirement see *CIC* 914.

baptism, alleged reconciliation and Eucharist shows no understanding of baptism. Adolescent confirmation ratifying infant baptism in the eighth, tenth, twelfth or fourteenth grade is the pure destruction of baptism."[38]

Recognizing that current Church legislation did not allow infant baptism-confirmation, some writers recommended celebrating confirmation prior to first Communion so as to "[respect] the order and sequence, if not the inherent unity, of sacramental initiation which is found in [no. 215 of] the RCIA."[39] Commenting upon the adult ordo's unifying portrayal of the sacraments of initiation, Osborne held that a "non-baptismal theology of confirmation is basically erroneous" and

[38]Kemp, "Rite of Initiation at Ten Years," 319. Dunning, *New Wine, New Wineskins*, 104, is equally forthright in his assessment of initiation unity: "[I]t is time to confront head-on those who claim that the restoration of Baptism-Confirmation-Eucharist as one rite of initiation is archaic and not good pastoral practice. They have co-opted the word 'pastoral'; but it should be clear by now that to tie Confirmation as a separate 'maturity rite' to any time in early or late adolescence is pastoral nonsense. Perhaps we need to celebrate a 'puberty rite of passage,' but let us not load that baggage onto Confirmation."

Kavanagh, *Confirmation*, 88, calls such tampering with the initiation sequence a "*ritus interruptus* which cannot but cause serious warps in theology and pastoral practice." See also Austin, *Rite of Confirmation*, 129–33.

M. Francis Mannion, "Penance and Reconciliation: A Systematic Analysis," 98–118, agrees it is difficult to make sense of penance-understood-as-reconciliation for children prior to their first Communion: "It is, in our opinion, however, possible to make *penitential* sense out of confession before first communion. While it cannot be assumed that children, even at the age of reason, could be serious sinners needing reconciliation with the church, the rite of confession can be seen as an appropriate way for children to recall, renew, and grow in their baptismal faith as they prepare for the completion of initiation into the church's life through the eucharist. In this penitential conception of first penance before first communion, there is less of a disruption of the baptism-eucharist initiation process. This will be the case especially if first confession has the context of an ongoing exposure to penitential practices and celebrations going back to the very beginning of religious formation, both in the home and in church or school education programs. Again, however, there is underlined here the necessity of devising a rite of penance for children which would include a declaration of blessing rather than of absolution" (115–16; emphasis in original).

[39]Michael Downey, *Clothed in Christ: The Sacraments and Christian Living*, 73.

The "initiation sequence" for infants is a frequently cited example of the *RCIA's* "normative" or "modeling" value for the understanding and practice of Christian initiation. In addition to Downey see also Balhoff, "Age for Confirmation," passim; Austin, *Rite of Confirmation*, 145 and passim; Catherine Dooley, "Catechu-

insisted that "[t]o theologize on one without the other is to separate the unity of the paschal mystery."[40]

There was considerable agreement among many liturgists and theologians, then, as to a unified celebration of initiation of infants: a unity that should be respected sequentially if not simultaneously. But this agreement did not always reflect the realities of parish life:

"At one end of the line we find an adult making the fully aware, deliberate commitment envisioned by the RCIA. . . . At the other extreme we find a disinterested teenager who has attended CCD classes sporadically over the years and can barely name the seven sacraments, a group of reluctant junior highs who have been dragged through a series of confirmation classes, and a class of seven-year-olds enthusiastically renewing their baptismal promises by chanting, in response to the ancient questions, 'We *do* believe! We *do* renounce him!'"[41]

Kieran Sawyer distinguished two models of faith formation: the *RCIA* model (generally consistent with the stages of the adult rite from initial inquiry to and after mystagogy) and the *RBC* model ("the spiritual journey of the cradle Catholic, which is based on the Rite of Baptism for Children and all that it entails")[42] and believed that the unique characteristics and requirements of these two formations should be honored. Acknowledging that "rituals are essential to the process" of initiation, Sawyer considered them as "secondary to the process" and warned that "restoring the sequence of the rituals

---

menate for Children: Sharing the Gift of Faith," 307–17; Kavanagh, *Confirmation,* 110–11 and passim; and Upton, *Next Generation,* 85–87.

Acknowledging that baptism-confirmation is currently permitted only in children of catechetical age and admitting the "anomaly of having full communicants whose baptism has not been 'confirmed,'" Guzie, *Book of Sacramental Basics,* 111, is one of several suggesting that "another way to restore the traditional order would be to put confirmation together with first eucharist, and celebrate the two in a single ceremony."

[40]Osborne, *Christian Sacraments of Initiation,* 101. See also Kavanagh, *Confirmation,* 86. Austin, *Rite of Confirmation,* 128, remarks: "Our present separation of the three sacraments of initiation is more than just a departure from the early liturgical tradition. It is a theological impoverishment. Eucharist must not be viewed merely as the transubstantiation of the elements; it is the fulfillment of baptism, and leads to the actualization of the church."

[41]Kieran Sawyer, "Readiness for Confirmation," 335; emphasis in original.

[42]Ibid.

without restoring the sequence of the process disrupts the intrinsic unity of process and ritual."[43] Sawyer felt that the RBC model (baptism, confession, Communion, and confirmation) respected the actual process by which those baptized in infancy developed and matured in the faith[44] and that when dealing with those baptized as infants, the Church would be better served were the sequence of the rituals to be determined by the actual process of conversion. That Eucharist preceded confirmation in this model does not deny the unity of the initiation sacraments, Sawyer contended, since that unity "is found in their connection to the total initiation process rather than in their temporal proximity."[45]

Thomas Marsh also believed that the concept of unity should not be oversimplified and urged particularly that "it should not be confused with the unity we associate with a moment of time." Acknowledging that the unified celebration of baptism, confirmation, and Eucharist "is entitled to be regarded as the standard and norm," Marsh noted that this entitlement "presupposes a particular set of circumstances: the adult convert, the catechumenate, the full rite of initiation." Marsh held, as did Sawyer, that the distinctive context and circumstances surrounding infant baptism, "with all its implications for the unity of the initiation sacraments, has to be respected."[46]

---

[43]Sawyer, "A Case for Adolescent Confirmation," 27, 43.

[44]Ibid., 40: "When we pay less attention to restoring the traditional sequence of the rituals, and take as our primary principle the unity of process and ritual, then the value of the RBC approach to the initiation of children becomes apparent. This approach looks first at the actual process by which a child baptized in infancy comes to mature faith, and adapts the sequence of the initiation rituals to suit that process." Commenting upon the RCIA model, Sawyer had observed that "Baptism-confirmation-eucharist is the 'correct' sequence [for adults] because it suits the process by which an adult comes to mature faith in the church" (37). Sawyer presents eight "principles of initiation" derived from her study of recent ecclesial documents referring to initiation, which "shed light on some of the key issues in the confirmation dialogue, particularly the sequence question" (25).

[45]Ibid., 41. Upton, Next Generation, 86, is one of many insisting that the Church is *not* well served by such a determination: "It is not only inconsistent, but also pedagogically unsound to have two different theological understandings of the same sacrament—one for infants and another for adults. . . . [W]hat is involved in the resolution of these issues is not revision of confirmation practice, but renewal of the initiation process. Such a renewal, we know, is afforded the Church in the RCIA."

[46]Thomas Marsh, *Gift of Community: Baptism and Confirmation;* citations in our text at this point are from page 188. Implying the reception of confirmation *after*

What that respect for the set of circumstances particular to infant baptism means is that the child, baptized as an infant, is growing up and into the community "and therefore growing in the Spirit which fills the community."[47] Marsh believed that a later age for confirmation—he suggests "some period in mid-teenage"—would "enable the ecclesial character of the sacrament to stand out more clearly," as confirmation would then appear "as the completion of the rite and process of christian initiation giving full entry into and membership of the Church." Just as baptism constituted the Christian community while "effecting" an individual Christian, Marsh held that confirmation so celebrated would be "both a significant reminder to the community of its own identity and promise it is offering the candidates and an invitation to the candidates to appreciate this concept of the Church."[48] Marsh insisted that this understanding of confirmation and unity did not contradict the norm for the celebration of the initiation sacraments for adults.[49]

Eucharist, Marsh had previously noted: "Confirmation is a sacrament of initiation; it is not a later sacramental event in the life of the fully initiated Christian." What the determining factor must be, he observes, is "the recognition that the fully initiated member of the Church is the mature member. This is the *terminus ad quem* in the light of which the whole process of initiation has to be assessed" (187).

[47]Ibid., 191: "There is a developing and dynamic giving of the Spirit throughout this process until it is completed. In the context of infant baptism, baptism expresses the beginning of this gift and growth in the Spirit and confirmation its completion. The pneumatological reference thus pervades, implicitly or explicitly, the whole rite of initiation. But the theme of the Spirit is particularly appropriate to the conclusion of the process which heralds entry into mature and responsible membership in the Church."

[48]Ibid., 192. Perhaps anticipating the complaint that preconfirmation catechetical programs often lead many young people "to regard confirmation as the special event which marks their 'graduation' from ecclesiastical constraint into the apparent freedoms of secular life" (so Kavanagh, *Confirmation*, 110, and the text cited by n. 54 below), Marsh adds: "It is important, of course, that the candidates' subsequent experience of the Church should not contradict this meaning and promise" (192). In Marsh's view, confirmation completes the sacramental sequence (though not the lifelong process) of Christian initiation, for he recommends that children begin receiving the Eucharist at (presumably) the age of seven.

[49]Marsh, *Gift of Community*, 196–97: "While there are differences between the two contexts [infant and adult baptism], these are not as substantial as they appear at first sight. It is the same *concept* of christian initiation which is in question

In an effort to lend credibility to the unified celebration of the initiation sacraments for adults *and* to their (chronologically) non-unified celebration in the case of baptized infants, Edward Jeremy Miller suggested understanding confirmation as a type of lay ordination and ecclesial commissioning "in which the one ordained [confirmed] represents the corporate group and extends its self-understanding by taking up the commission."[50] Miller thought that if confirmation were thus seen as "the ecclesial mandate (commission) to accomplish the mission of being the Church," then the "delayed" conferral of the sacrament for those baptized as infants would be as credible a practice as the simultaneous conferral of baptism-confirmation (and Eucharist) upon adults completing the *RCIA*. Although Miller does not specify an age for confirming those baptized as infants, he does say that confirmation as ecclesial commissioning "is best celebrated at an age when responsibility can be assumed."[51]

William O'Malley agreed. Puzzled that a Church that "would not allow a 12-year-old, much less a child of seven, to vow a life of celibacy . . . not only allows but encourages a child before puberty to assume the responsibilities of confirmation," he believed the sacrament should be delayed "until individuals want to be confirmed because they have in fact had an adult conversion."[52] Acknowledging that those advocating the unified or early celebration of confirmation enjoyed an argument that was "theologically unchallengeable," O'Malley insisted their stance "both denies the receptivities of candidates so young and misses a golden opportunity to evoke adult conversion at a later age—which seems more desirable than the theological nicety."[53]

---

in both situations. It is the actual working out and application of this concept to the different circumstances which give rise to the differences. The differences themselves are not fundamental" (emphasis in original). See also his "Christian Initiation: Practice and Theology," 13–24. Frank C. Quinn, "Confirmation Reconsidered: Rite and Meaning," 354–70, offers a comparative assessment of the views of Kavanagh and Marsh.

[50]Miller, "Confirmation as Ecclesial Commissioning," 118.

[51]Ibid., 120.

[52]William J. O'Malley, "Confirmed and Confirming," 16, 19.

[53]Ibid., 19. Joseph J. Martos, "A Modest Proposal," 30–31, also sees confirmation as the sacrament "for those who are willing to go forward into active participation in the life of the local Christian community. Such active participation would usually take the form of some kind of regular service in the church." He con-

We return to Aidan Kavanagh and his insistence that the legitimate need for effective pastoral responses to the Church's youth does not legitimize using confirmation preparation and celebration as a catch-all for religious or secular rites of passage:

"After being brought to full sacramental initiation in the Church no later than the age of reason, subsequent catechesis of those baptized in infancy would then be free to focus not on confirmation but on their assuming an increasingly knowledgeable public capacity in the Church sometime between the age of reason and young adulthood. Such a procedure could culminate in a liturgy of reconciliation to the Church (if needed) and a solemnization of holy communion. The cate-chetical focus would then be where it ought to be: on the eucharist as

---

cludes: "Those who are baptized as infants, [then], would see Confirmation as the time when they are willing to take the last step in the initiation process to active adult membership in the church." In line with this see Dan Grippo, "Confirma-tion: No One Under 18 Need Apply," 31–32.

Gérard Fourez, "Celebrating the Spirit with Adolescents: More on Confirma-tion," 199–206, explores confirmation as a "mutual recognition" between the com-munity and those confirmed of the presence of the Spirit in each. Speaking of the often tense and distrustful relationship between the adult and younger members of the community, Fourez suggests that the time for confirmation would be "around the age of twelve [when] the relationship between the young and the adults begins to change. . . . At the very moment when the youth and the adult tend to antagonize each other, would it not be meaningful to be called to a cele-bration that will help avoid adultism and lead to the recognition that we can, young and adult, mutually receive the Spirit of God from one another?" (206).

Christopher Kiesling, "Confirmation: The Rite Not the Age," 25–28, asserting that the "entire parish community needs to be reminded from time to time of the marvel of grace bestowed on it through baptism, namely, the very Spirit of the Father and Son, and the Spirit's infinite power" (27), believes the norm for decid-ing when to celebrate confirmation in a parish is "whether the whole parish com-munity has reached a need to celebrate again the sacrament of the Holy Spirit in its midst, renew its appreciation of the indwelling Spirit, and pass that gift and its appreciation on to another generation of baptized people" (28).

Mark Searle's "Confirmation: The State of the Question," 15–22, addresses the American discussion and outlines the views of Anglican and European scholars. Marsh, Sawyer, Fourez, and Reichert develop their views in Kubick, ed., *Confirm-ing the Faith of Adolescents*. Sawyer, "The Confirmation Dialogue Continues," (1986) 215–21, offers a catechist's assessment of Marsh's *Gift of Community*, Austin's *Rite of Confirmation*, and the articles by Miller and Balhoff. See also *Con-firmed as Children, Affirmed as Teens*, and *When Should We Confirm?* both edited by James A. Wilde.

the sacrament of Christian maturity par excellence. Sacramental sequence is thus kept intact and the educational and therapeutic needs of the young are free of having to be seen always in terms of confirmation. If it is decided that the Church's ministry to its youth needs formal celebrations of puberty, of the reception of one's driver's license, of graduation from programs of religious education, of spiritual awakening, and of civil majority, then paraliturgical rites to fill such needs can be developed without having to make confirmation cover them all, to the confusion of many. Votive masses, Bible services, *Te Deums*, marriage, penance, and solemnized communion are all strictly liturgical options for such needs as well. Why confirmation must substitute for all these is a question which finally has no compelling answer."[54]

In light of the above, Michael Balhoff defines understatement anew by introducing his study of the canonical evidence for the age for confirmation with the remark, "Discussion about the age for confirmation has proved confusing in recent years." Balhoff provides an invaluable study of the "age of confirmation" issue, tracing the question from its origins in the postconciliar confirmation study commissions to the subsequent 1972 and 1984 decisions of the United States National Conference of Catholic Bishops (NCCB). Disavowing that his article is "a critique of the NCCB's decisions about age for confirmation," Balhoff does admit there are several things "worthy of note" in the NCCB's 1984 decision to allow the age for confirmation in each diocese to be determined by the local ordinary. We cite here four of Balhoff's six "precise conclusions":

"1. The central issue is not age for confirmation, but rather the unity and sequence of the initiatory sacraments. To view age as a primary question or to consider the possibility of faith-affirmation (maturity

---

[54]Kavanagh, *Confirmation,* 111–12; see also pages 97–101. Austin, *Rite of Confirmation,* 135–36, cites the work of social historian Joseph Kett, who noted that the concept of adolescence was given shape at the turn of the century by "psychologists, urban reforms, educations, youth workers, and parent counselors." Kett implies that the concept of adolescence was "invented" rather than "discovered." Commenting upon those theologians who "identify the initiation sacraments with distinct moments in the life cycle," Austin warns: "It would seem imperative to guard against building a theology of confirmation on such a relative and elusive concept as adolescence." Upton, *Next Generation,* 82–85, also comments briefly on the "mis-uses" of confirmation.

rite) alone is not true to the conciliar and postconciliar reform, which consistently reinforced a system in which there was connection and succession among the sacraments of initiation.

"2. The statement of the specific and narrow law is found in the Rite of Confirmation, n. 11, and in the [CIC], canon 891, which require, after infant baptism, conferral of confirmation at the age of discretion and at a Eucharistic service, presumably at First Eucharist.

"3. The exceptional situation is permitted where there is a postponement of confirmation *at the discretion of the episcopal conference,* and apparently no such determination has yet been made by the NCCB. It does not appear that the exception was intended to be at the discretion of the individual bishop. The evidence indicates that such a decision by the episcopal conference is not necessarily as desirable as is popularly thought.

"4. A bishop who is the local ordinary may presently allow for postponement of confirmation possibly by virtue of customary practice or at least by virtue of his power to dispense from certain universal laws of the Church according to the norms of canon 87, §1. But dispensations are not really intended to be used as an habitual avoidance of the universal law, and such a use of the canon could not be recommended."[55]

Assessing Balhoff's documentation and conclusions, Kavanagh observed that allowing individual bishops to establish the age of confirmation "appears to violate the spirit and letter of canon 891."[56] Given canonical intricacies, principles of initiation, and episcopal prerogatives, one can debate whether the spirit of *CIC* 891 is being violated; *that* the Spirit is conferred at ever-later ages is clear. A 1984 NCCB survey revealed that dioceses in the United States were confirming individuals from grades three through twelve and that the majority of candidates were confirmed during or after their eighth grade of

---

[55]Balhoff, "Age for Confirmation," 586–87; emphasis in original. Balhoff documents every stage of the "age for confirmation" issue and includes excerpts from minutes of NCCB meetings.

[56]Kavanagh, *Confirmation,* 121–22 n. 29. He continues: "And where an individual decision has the effect of putting reception of confirmation *after* first reception of holy communion there appears to be an ignoring of the doctrine expressed in canon 842:2" (Kavanagh here refers the reader to Balhoff, "Age for Confirmation," 580–82). See Kavanagh's pages 81–122 for an extended commentary and discussion on Balhoff's findings.

school. This trend toward delaying the sacrament until the age of thirteen or beyond seems to reflect both the experience and preference of many involved in the area of preparation for confirmation. For example, Sawyer is convinced that "many of the readiness problems surrounding confirmation could be resolved by establishing late adolescence as the minimum age for the sacrament."[57]

Aidan Kavanagh advises keeping the focus of catechesis "on the eucharist as the sacrament of Christian maturity par excellence," and so warns that confirmation must not be made to bear the weight of "formal celebrations of puberty, of the reception of one's driver's license, of graduation from programs of religious education, of spiritual awakening, and of civil majority."[58] William O'Malley laments "the reluctance to delay [confirmation] as another example of sound theology defying sound psychology," and complains that "[a]cademic rightness tyrannizes over the jaw-to-jaw experience of those of us who have not only to explain the faith but lead truculent students to interiorize a need for it."[59] And Paul Turner demonstrates both insight and dry wit, offering his recent study and assessment of seven models of the sacrament under the title *Confirmation: The Baby in Solomon's Court*.[60] Solomon's sword remains poised, and a steady and certain stroke does not seem soon. The controversy and conflict surrounding confirmation continue, as consensus on both strategic (nature) and tactical (age) questions remains elusive.[61]

[57]Sawyer, "Readiness for Confirmation," 339. Sawyer's "The Confirmation Dialogue Continues," 219, provides a grade-by-grade breakdown of the results of the survey, to which 106 dioceses responded. In line with this, see again her "Readiness for Confirmation," 337–38.

[58]Kavanagh, *Confirmation*, 111, as cited above.

[59]O'Malley, "Confirmed and Confirming," 18.

[60]Paul Turner, *Confirmation: The Baby in Solomon's Court*.

[61]On April 29, 1994, the NCCB was notified that the Congregation for Bishops had confirmed the NCCB's June 1993 approval of the norm for the age of confirmation. The norm reads: "The [NCCB] hereby decrees that the sacrament of confirmation in the Latin rite shall be conferred between the age of discretion, which is about the age of 7, and 18 years of age, within the limits determined by the diocesan bishop and with regard for the legitimate exceptions given in canon 891, namely, when there is danger of death or, where in the judgment of the minister grave cause urges otherwise." The decree from the Congregation for Bishops stated that "in consideration of the vote of the bishops, the above-mentioned norm is approved for five years [July 1, 1994–July 1, 1999] in order that the bishops, with the lapse of time and the addition of new perspectives, may again

The fifth perspective:
The catechumenate as a temporary alternative

Authors throughout the 1980s continued to suggest an infant-child catechumenate as a temporary alternative to infant baptism,[62] and Julia Upton again provides an end-of-the-decade *status quaestionis*. Asking whether an infant-child catechumenate could coexist with infant baptism, Upton observed that they do exist in today's Church "experientially if not theologically," and reiterated her conviction of the previous decade: that such a peaceful coexistence could only strengthen the Church pastorally, sociologically, and psychologically.[63]

But while the suggestion continued to be discussed, it also began to meet its first sustained criticism. The 1980 SCDF instruction *Pastoralis Actio* had deemed "unacceptable" the "freedom to choose, whatever the reasons, between immediate baptism and deferred baptism" [*PA* 27] and had clearly stated that an infant could not be considered a catechumen or enjoy the prerogatives of the catechumenate [31]. In addition to this criticism (and, as we discussed in the previous chapter, the instruction's influence is questionable),[64] several American theologians submitted their critiques of the concept.

---

raise this question and bring a norm once again to the Holy See for review" (NCCB, Committee on the Liturgy, *Newsletter* [May 1994], 17).

Writing prior to the NCCB's 1993 vote, Robert Duggan, "The Age of Confirmation: A Flawed Proposal," 12–14, offered a scathing assessment of the bishops' pending request, arguing that "the proposal they are about to vote upon reflects neither filial reverence for the mind of Rome, nor theological acumen, nor even tested pastoral wisdom gained through long experience and careful reflection. Rather, it is the business-as-usual approach of trained legal minds, wiggling out of a painful pastoral bind" (13). Earlier in his article, Duggan had observed that "we are in the midst of a crisis of substantial proportions. Frankly, we are losing our credibility as teachers and as pastors when one of the foundational sacraments of the Christian life is the subject of such widespread confusion, misunderstanding and needless controversy" (12).

[62]For example, Dunning, *New Wine, New Wineskins,* 101–3; Downey, "Clothed in Christ," 73.

[63]Upton, *Next Generation,* 74–77.

[64]As an example, Upton, *Next Generation,* 73, citing the 1977 article of Paul Vanbergen, "Infants of *non satis credentes* Parents," refers to the 1970 "Togo letter" of the SCDF, which would later form the basis for *PA* 30 (see discussion in ch. 4). Writing ten years after *PA,* Upton asks essentially the question Vanbergen had posed in his note 1 (in her words: "By recommending that their names be

Gerard Austin, referring to the "1973 Scottsdale Statement," agreed that many theologians consider the infant catechumenate as pastorally advantageous. Austin saw "problems with this point of view," however, and thought the only situation in which a catechumenate might be helpful would be "when parents request baptism for their child but do not show adequate indication that the child would be raised in an atmosphere of faith." In the case of believing and practicing parents, Austin questioned whether there was "any real advantage in not baptizing the children in infancy."[65]

Austin's comment clarifies an aspect in the discussion of the child catechumenate not always understood at the parochial level. The infant-child catechumenate was envisaged by most as an alternative to the indiscriminate baptizing of infants. As Aidan Kavanagh had remarked, the enemy was not "baptism of infants, but indiscriminate baptism of anyone done for sentimental reasons."[66]

Mark Searle agreed that "a succession of rites and stages which are themselves sacramental in a broad sense" is appealing[67] but observed that discussions concerning the child catechumenate often failed to address several points. First, while many theologians legitimately referred to a catechumen as a *Christianus in fieri*, the application of the

---

inscribed is the [SCDF] suggesting that these infants be regarded as catechumens? This could be the first step in a theology that addresses the pastoral reality of the Church today"), apparently unaware that the SCDF in *PA* 31 clearly answered the question in the negative.

[65]Austin, *Rite of Confirmation*, 127: "If the parents are truly committed Christians, is there any real advantage in not baptizing the children in infancy? In such cases it would seem that infant baptism would signify both the notion of the solidarity of the believing family and the fact that it is God who takes the initiative." (For the "Scottsdale Statement," see our discussion of the fourth perspective in ch. 1.)

[66]Upton, *Next Generation*, 74–75, also makes this distinction: "Indiscriminate infant baptism persists because there is no other pastoral alternative. . . . With the possibility of a catechumenate, the decision of whether or not to have their child baptized could more realistically be returned to the parents."

From a different perspective, Miller, "Confirmation as Ecclesial Commissioning," 120, notes that the concept of the catechumenate "is the only proposal I know of which attempts to give some substance to the 'new' norm [of the *RCIA*]. However, there are weighty reasons for challenging this delay of Baptism, not the least of which would be the outcry from Christian parents themselves, in spite of any explanation that the catechumen is a 'Christian-in-process.'"

[67]Searle, "Infant Baptism Reconsidered," 29.

term to an infant or very young child was misleading, as the conditions for admission into the catechumenate laid down in *RCIA* 42 are those that an infant cannot meet.[68] In addition to observing that the question of *when* to initiate remained unanswered, Searle also faulted the one-sided understanding of sacramentality implied by the proposal as well as the "possible inconsistency in subjecting the helpless infant to the 'sacramentality' of enrollment in the catechumenate but refusing to submit it to the 'sacramentality' of the complete rite of initiation."[69]

While the catechumenate for infants was originally proposed as an alternative to infant baptism, Gail Ramshaw-Schmidt proposed alternative rites for *surrounding* the celebration of infant baptism. Her intention was to alleviate the ritual poverty of the *RBC*—a poverty only too apparent when the rite was compared with the richness and complexity of the adult ordo—and to more clearly situate the celebration of infant baptism in the appropriate domestic and ecclesial contexts.[70] The stages of Ramshaw-Schmidt's proposal parallel the four stages of

---

[68]Ibid., 30. Searle refers also to *PA* 30–31. Interestingly, the only writer apparently voicing these same objections to the infant-child catechumenate before *PA*, as we noted in chapter 2, was Paul Donlan, "Second Thoughts."

[69]Searle, "Infant Baptism Reconsidered," 30. In line with this, Osborne, *Christian Sacraments of Initiation*, 100, raised questions concerning the notion of the *adult* catechumenate: "This status of the catechumen 'in the Church' accords well with the practices of the early Church, which considered catechumens part of the ecclesial community and awarded them all the assistance which the Church might offer. However, this positioning of the catechumen 'in the Church' tempers the theological position that baptism makes one a member of the Church. Baptism welcomes one into the eucharistic community of the Church. In the preliminary section of the new rite, it does say that 'through baptism men and women are incorporated into Christ' (2), and again we read: 'Baptism is the sacrament by which men and women are incorporated into the Church' (4). Evidently, there is still some theological discussion necessary as to the way in which one can say that a catechumen is already part of the Church, and that baptism is the way in which one is incorporated into the Church. Some nuancing and clarification remains to be done."

[70]Gail Ramshaw-Schmidt, "Celebrating Baptism in Stages: A Proposal," 137: "[My] proposal affirms that the grace of God saves human children even before they as conscious adults reject sin and accept God. This proposal uses biblical images, besides the death and resurrection of Christ, which are particularly amenable to the baptism of infants, as well as offering home and church rituals before and after baptism which attend to the family context of infant baptism."

the adult faith-journey of the *RCIA*. Thus the first stage (precatechumenate) contains a "ritual before birth" and a "rite of baptismal intent." The second stage (catechumenate) entails a "ritual after birth" and a "rite of enrollment" (as well as an appropriate ritual in the tragic circumstances of miscarriage, stillbirth, or death after birth). A "prayer before baptism" and the sacramental rite of baptism itself parallels the third stage of the *RCIA* (purification and illumination), while stage four (mystagogy) suggests individual rites for the remembrance of one's baptism in the parish church and at the home of the family.[71]

The postconciliar discussion of infant baptism lacked neither literature nor complexity, and in the preceding chapters I have attempted a modest sampling of both. In the next chapter I conclude part 1—my report on the American postconciliar discussion of infant baptism— by reviewing the five perspectives that have guided our review of the literature of these past thirty years and by offering some observations concerning the current "shape of baptism."

---

[71]Ibid., 155: "It is hoped that these nine rituals surrounding the event of the Christian baptism for infants will, like the classic stages of precatechumenate, catechumenate, purification and illumination, and mystagogy, give an appropriate context to the sacramental entrance of infants into the Christian community."

Chapter 5

The Postconciliar Discussion of Infant Baptism: Conclusions and reflections

"What the value of baptizing infants might be is an extremely obscure question. But one must believe there is some value in it" (St. Augustine, 388).

"What the re-enunciation of [the principle of the catechumen as a *Christianus in fieri*] will do to the institution of infant baptism remains to be seen, but it seems likely that it will not leave it unaffected indefinitely" (Aidan Kavanagh, 1974).

"The baptismal waters have calmed since Aidan Kavanagh and others claimed that adult initiation is the "norm." . . . The conversion and growth of the adult envisioned in the RCIA is the norm, and anything done earlier should contribute to that growth" (James Dunning, 1981).

"If there is any reason for not admitting an infant to faith and baptismal life . . . , it may only be that the child's own God-given household is not faithful" (Mark Searle, 1987).

We began our study by reviewing the two schools of baptismal thought identified by Nathan Mitchell in 1975: the Mature Adulthood School (ch. 1) and the Environmentalist School (ch. 2). In chapter 3 we considered the Sacred Congregation for the Doctrine of the Faith's 1980 *Instruction on Infant Baptism,* which remains the sole major curial document on infant baptism since the promulgation of the 1969 *Rite of Baptism for Children.* And we resumed our review of the American literature in chapter 4 by examining the writings of the most recent decade.

Assessing the American postconciliar discussion of infant baptism, I offer the following conclusions and observations. I report first on the five perspectives that have guided our review of the literature.

THE FIVE PERSPECTIVES:
A REVIEW AND SUMMARY

The first perspective: The problem of indiscriminate baptism

"Christians are not born, they are made." Tertullian's words suggest well the approach to Christian initiation dominating the postconciliar era, an approach that departed significantly from the preconciliar practice of the sacrament. The conventional view of this preconciliar practice, in which the automatic baptism of infants was generally expected, accepted, and applauded, was frequently seen in the years following the council as encouraging "baptism on demand." The indiscriminate baptizing of an infant accompanied by the unexamined assumption that the child would be reared as a practicing Christian was deemed an act of ecclesial self-destruction—a "malign abnormality"—which did little to foster ecclesial communities capable of witnessing Christian ideals in and to a world disposed to pursue secular values. The language and images of the postconciliar literature lamented this too-ready surrender to societal standards as the depletion from Church bones of much-needed "calcium": the witness of mature adults committed to the gospel who, prior to being sacramentally initiated, had demonstrated their commitment to their faith by embarking upon a mutually demanding relationship with the community charged with overseeing their "conversion therapy."

The SCDF's 1980 *Instruction on Infant Baptism (Pastoralis Actio)*, issued eleven years after the publication of the *RBC*, addressed the indiscriminate baptizing of infants by maintaining that infants be baptized only when their future Christian education and formation could be reasonably predicted or guaranteed. About two years later the revised *Code of Canon Law* legislated the discernment of a "well-founded hope" for the child's future Catholic upbringing as a requirement for the licit baptism of an infant.

Many Catholic parents received an abrupt initiation into the academic discussion when, following the practice of previous generations, they routinely requested baptism for their newborn. Expecting to be summoned to the Church the following Sunday afternoon, they were instead called to account for their commitment to—and often, the actual, observable practice of—their faith.

The widespread criticism of indiscriminate infant baptism was often tempered, however, by what some feared might be a less-than-discriminate refusal of baptism. Several authors, sympathetic to the principles of ritual integrity and honesty, questioned whether the desire to build and maintain a Church strong in ecclesial and societal witness had led in some instances to pastoral decisions that exceeded the letter and spirit of well-intentioned requirements. Agreeing that calcium-enriched bones were needed to provide a sturdy framework for a countercultural Church, they feared that such bones might well support the strong but might also act as a barricade that would not foster—and perhaps would not even allow—the gradual conversion of Catholics whose faith be judged weak or marginal. The curial documents, American authors, and diocesan guidelines urged a sensitive and patient approach when dealing with parents who, while requesting baptism for their children, might not readily or easily reveal a well-developed understanding of the lifelong significance of the sacrament. The key word, as noted by authors and documents alike, was not the refusal of baptism, but its educational and formative *delay*.

Absent from most writings (including the SCDF's *Pastoralis Actio*) was excessive concern or preoccupation as regards the eternal fate of infants dying prior to baptism. While some authors suggested that enrolling an infant in the catechumenate would theologically address this issue and resolve parental concerns and anxieties (see our fifth perspective below), a more frequent suggestion (and one sanctioned by *PA* and the *Catechism of the Catholic Church*) encouraged the confident commendation of the infant's soul to the mercy of God.

The second perspective: The norm of baptism

Advanced first by Aidan Kavanagh in the early 1970s, the contention that the adult ordo presented the "definitive norm" for Christian initiation was referred to frequently throughout the postconciliar discussion. Although a precise interpretation of the term "norm" seems to remain elusive, it is clear that the adult ordo offered several ideals or guiding principles for an initiation theology of adults, adolescents, and infants. Among these was that baptism is initiation *by*, as well as *into*, a community; that initiation is a continuing process and not an act isolated in or exhausted by a specific sacramental moment; that there is an intrinsic unity among the three sacraments of initiation; that catechumens are considered "joined to the Church and part of the household of Christ"; and that the process of the sacramental initiation of candidates challenges and effects anew the baptismal promises of the community itself. These principles serve an understanding and appreciation of the sacramental initiation of Christians of *any* age. That the adult ordo offers the definitive norm of Christian initiation, however, is a concept some have found less convincing.

In the early 1980s, for example, several authors questioned the idea that the *RCIA* was "normative for all Christian initiation," and debated the legitimacy and advisability of considering any *one* form of baptism as the sacramental expression par excellence of Christian initiation. Readily acknowledging that the theology and rituals of the adult ordo had enriched the practice and understanding of Christian initiation, they believed that the adult ordo did not (and should not be expected to) bear the burden of expressing the full richness of the mystery liturgically, theologically, or pastorally. Mark Searle was one suggesting that the meaning of adult baptism, understood primarily with reference to the model of baptism as initiation into the death and resurrection of Christ, would be complemented and further completed by considering the meaning and unique character of the baptism of infants.

Much of the difficulty in discussing the concept of the "normative value" of the adult ordo lies in the term itself, for the word "norm" was used by many writers, many times, and in many ways. According to Aidan Kavanagh, the adult ordo's "definitive norm of initiation" referred not to the usual or more frequent rite through which Christians were initiated (which would, of course, be the *RBC*) but to the subjects (mature adult candidates), the process (the catechumenate), and the occasion (Paschal Vigil) of Christian initiation. Other writers, approaching the term from a broader perspective, considered the goal or end of the *RCIA* as the adult ordo's "norm": the formation and promotion of a Church of committed Christians actively witnessing their faith. In their view the norm of the adult ordo pointed to the lifelong conversion expected of all Christians, a conversion assisted by—but not *only* by—the methodology specific to the adult ordo. (The remark of James Dunning, cited at the beginning of this chapter, is one example of this approach.) Others avoided the word "norm" altogether, preferring to view the adult ordo as the "paradigm" or "model" through which one comes to adult faith. Such approaches to the term were characteristic of the most recent decade, as was the clearer acknowledgment that however the term "norm" be understood, the concept did not deny the legitimacy or integrity of infant baptism.

The theological or pastoral dismissal of infant baptism was never Kavanagh's intent, but it is clear that whatever the contributions the concept of the "normative value" afforded the adult ordo, such contributions were often at the expense of infant baptism: for the term "norm" was subject to misinterpretation and misrepresentation—and to pejorative connotations. Not the least of these was the unfortunate (and surely inevitable) insinuation that infant baptism, a "benign abnormality" even in the most favorable circumstances, best be considered by being abandoned. In response to this, numerous writers defended the theological significance and pastoral practice of the discriminate baptizing of infants from a variety of perspectives. Particularly creative assessments were offered by Nathan Mitchell and Mark Searle, who were among the first of American Catholic liturgists to explore the theological paradigm offered the adult Church by the baptism of an infant or child. We will consider their studies in greater detail in part 2 of our work.

The third perspective: The necessity of catechesis

The process of catechesis or "conversion therapy" around which the *RCIA* was structured was perhaps the most distinctive and attractive feature of the adult ordo. The catechumenate initiated candidates gradually into the sacramental and liturgical life of their own ecclesial community as much as it informed them of the doctrine and teaching of the universal Church. The liturgical rituals marking the progressive stages of the catechumenate, particularly when those rituals were witnessed by and celebrated with the broader community, offered vivid testimony that baptism was "*the* public event" in the Church. Caricatures juxtaposing the least attractive aspects of Sunday afternoon "jiffy infant baptisms" with the impressive features of the adult ordo could but persuade many to disdain the "instant confection of faith" mentality often attributed the act of infant baptism.

But that infant baptism also required catechesis (first, of parents) and that it clearly was directed toward the eventual adult commitment of the infant or child was evident throughout the postconciliar literature. Emphasizing that an infant was baptized in the faith of the domestic and ecclesial Church, many authors appealed to the expectation that the grace of faith conferred and symbolized by the celebration of the sacrament would be realized *in fact* as the child received guidance in and through those domestic and ecclesial environments.

Indeed, the strongest argument *against* the baptizing of infants was not based upon the inability of the child to profess his or her faith but, as Mark Searle had remarked, on the lack of desire or ability of the infant's parents to profess and share *theirs*. Most writers insisted that the grace-as-gift the sacrament symbolized and conferred *ex opere operato* at the time of the celebration must be nourished, supported, and continually effected anew by the subsequent *opus operantis* (response to the gift) of both parents and child. In a striking departure from the preconciliar ritual, the 1969 *RBC*'s mention of *quam primum* referred not to when the child was to be presented at the font but as to when the parents should present themselves to their pastor to arrange for the baptism of their child and, presumably, to discuss the faith requirements and expectations that would support the baptizing of this particular infant. The renewal of the baptismal promises of the infant's parents during the ritual celebration, then, was not simply an occasion for ritual participation but was the profession of and recommitment to their faith that legitimized *this* celebration of the sacrament, and in which and through which the "ultimate meaning of the sacrament would be fulfilled."

As the meaning and significance of infant baptism were developed (and in some cases, reoriented) throughout the postconciliar period, the influence of the adult ordo with its recurring themes of community involvement and conversion-as-process can be readily detected. Many writers stressed that infant baptism was a pledge on the part of the community initiating the infant, that the grace effected through the ritual celebration was and must be continually effected through the witness of parents and community, and that the sacrament of infant baptism constituted and challenged the Christian community as did the *RCIA* (albeit in a less dramatic and public form).

The traditional (and dogmatic) relationship between infant baptism and original sin was generally maintained throughout the postconciliar years but, in line with our observations above, usually with less emphasis on the "private" effects of that sin or on its automatic, once-and-for-all removal at a precise moment. Again, the emphasis was on baptism as a new life in faith initiated by the grace of Christ rather than on any "instant confection" of grace or faith. In explaining how baptism remitted original sin, then, many writers considered that baptism delivered the infant by inserting the child into a community committed to reversing the orientation and lingering effects of original sin in the lives of all of its members; others stressed that the removal of original sin through the grace of baptism signaled the beginning of Christian life and responsibility and not the fulfillment of the meaning of the sacrament. Some writers thought that original sin was not *the* reason to baptize an infant, and at least one maintained that the doctrine of original sin should no longer be considered a constitutive part in the theology of baptism. Several of the emendations of the 1973 *editio typica altera* of the *RBC*, however, as well as the 1980 instruction *Pastoralis Actio*, made explicit reference to the doctrine or reality of original sin, thus reaffirming the Church's doctrine on the necessity of baptism for salvation.

In addressing the fate of infants dying without benefit of baptism, few authors maintained the theological opinion of limbo as the inevitable outcome. Most counseled that such infants (and the attendant parental concerns) be entrusted to God's mercy, an approach supported by the SCDF's 1980 *Pastoralis Actio* and the more recent *Catechism of the Catholic Church*. While considered neither radical nor risky in the minds of the theologians, the recommendation remained for many parents an unacceptable ambiguity.

Of the five perspectives that have guided our review, the indispensability of pre- and postbaptismal catechesis as regards infant baptism is the one perspective in which there was unanimous agreement throughout the twenty-five years of the postconciliar period. *Pastoralis Actio* and the 1983 code gave further support and impetus to the importance of catechesis: the former by acknowledging that the Church "recognizes limits" to her practice of baptizing infants, the latter by conferring upon this reservation the weight of canonical authority.

The fourth perspective:
The unity of the initiation sacraments

The relationship among the sacraments of baptism, confirmation, and Eucharist—and, particularly, the question as to how the relationship of confirmation to baptism should be expressed liturgically—garnered considerable discussion throughout the twenty-five-year period we have surveyed. Many writers recommended that infants and children be baptized and confirmed (and communicated) within the same liturgical event; many others supported the generally prevailing practice of the Western Church in which confirmation was administered at various ages from seven years to late adolescence.

While the question of the liturgical expression of the unity of the initiation sacraments was not resolved, the influence of the adult ordo upon the discussion was clearly evident: virtually all authors understood confirmation as a sacrament related closely to baptism and the Eucharist and, as such, a sacrament that must always be considered, prepared for, and celebrated in such a way that its relationship to those sacraments be expressed clearly. Advocates of delayed confirmation, readily acknowledging the intrinsic relationship of confirmation to baptism, thought that neither the theological nor liturgical expression of the unity of the initiation sacraments need be interpreted in a way that would preclude what they considered pastorally advantageous or theologically well-founded reasons for a later reception of confirmation. Writers arguing for the sequential celebration of the initiation sacraments (confirmation precedes Eucharist) or for their simultaneous conferral (within the same liturgical celebration), however, held that theological and liturgical principles should determine rather than be determined by the pastoral practice. For the sake of this summary, it might be said that an author's response to the strategic question of why confirm, and to tactical questions such as what age to confirm, relied upon that author's theology of the sacrament—in other words, whether confirmation was considered primarily as a sacrament of initiation or primarily as a sacrament of formation and Christian development.

Discussion as regards "confirmation as initiation or formation" continues, as does the conferral of the sacrament at various ages and under diverse theologies throughout the United States. While many interpret the 1983 *Code of Canon Law* as calling for at least the sequential conferral of baptism-confirmation-Eucharist, the NCCB has allowed each bishop to determine the age for confirmation in his diocese. In the United States today confirmation is ordinarily conferred some years after baptism, usually after Eucharist and often not until mid- or late adolescence. In mid-1994 the NCCB received permission to allow confirmation to be conferred upon those between seven and eighteen years of age—thus in effect ruling out only the possibility of confirming infants and very young children as they are baptized.

The fifth perspective:
The catechumenate as a temporary alternative

A major contribution of the adult ordo to ecclesiology and initiation theology was the restoration of the order of catechumens. The catechumenate—a lengthy period in which the faith development of those seeking baptism was induced, supported, discerned, and guided—showed clearly that conversion is a journey ongoing and always unfinished and not a sudden burst of religious commitment.

What held the hearts of many Catholic parents and grandparents, however, was not the impressive process of adult conversion but simply the need to secure the salvation of their newborn. That the way to this salvation be "guaranteed" as soon as possible after birth by baptism continued to be for many families the primary motive for seeking the baptism of their children. Critics charged that such anxiety-laden approaches to the sacrament encouraged indiscriminate baptism, compromised ritual integrity, and contributed to the erosion of Christian witness to the world.

Seeking to alleviate parental concerns, preserve ritual integrity, and promote Christian witness, several authors proposed enrolling an infant into a catechumenate as a legitimate and preferred alternative to indiscriminate infant baptism: on the one hand, entrance into the Church through baptism would occur at a later date, following catechesis and the individual's free choice and mature commitment. On the other hand, as the catechumenate bestowed the right of Christian burial as one of its privileges, parents' speculations as to the "status" of their unbaptized sons and daughters would be resolved.

The suggestion enjoyed considerable momentum in the first full postconciliar decade and, as we observed in our review of the more recent decade, continued to prove attractive to many concerned about both future Church and fearful parents. The literature of this latter decade, however, also criticized the suggestion that a catechumenate for infants was an acceptable resolution to pastoral and theological difficulties. On the level of ordinary magisterial teaching, *Pastoralis Actio* clearly denied parents and pastors the option of delaying the baptism of an infant for reasons other than a manifest absence of a well-founded hope, and specifically cited "freedom of choice" as an unacceptable motive. The instruction also clarified that while infants or young children could be registered for a future catechumenate, this registration was *not* an enrollment or admittance into the catechumenate and therefore did not bequeath upon those so registered the privileges of that order.

Opposition to a "true" infant catechumenate as an alternative to baptism was not restricted only to the Roman document, however. Some writers, supporting the legitimacy of infant baptism when celebrated within the context of believing ecclesial and familial communities, thought that in such an environment there was no reason *not* to cele-brate sacramentally the initiation of infants. Others criticized what they considered to be a faulty transference of meaning from adult catechumenate to infant catechumenate, or the submission of an in-fant to one sacramental rite (catechumenate) while denying the infant entrance into another (water baptism).

While it is difficult to determine the influence of the curial docu-ment and the later criticism upon the idea of an infant catechumen-ate, it is clear that the adult ordo has influenced the postbaptismal years of those sacramentally initiated in infancy. Many religious edu-cators, catechists, and pastoral ministers welcomed the format and philosophy of the adult ordo as an effective structure through which to guide the spiritual and religious education of baptized children as they grow in age and in the knowledge and practice of their Chris-tian faith.

OBSERVATIONS AND REFLECTIONS: PREPARING A RESPONSE

Our survey of the postconciliar literature on infant baptism has been guided by the five perspectives we established in chapter 1. Having examined these perspectives in some detail we now conclude part 1, our report on the American discussion of infant baptism, with several observations.

The four citations introducing this chapter describe somewhat curtly the development and direction of the discussion. St. Augus-tine's admonition as to the necessity of believing in the value of in-fant baptism, "obscure though that question may be," seems an apt introduction to the literature of the postconciliar years. As discussion of infant baptism progressed throughout the quarter-century we have examined, Aidan Kavanagh quickly emerged as the most influential American writer concerning Christian initiation in general and the new adult ordo in particular. His strong endorsement and exposition of the *RCIA* and his serious questioning of the contemporary practice of infant baptism provided major reference points for the discus-sion—as well as an occasional lightning rod—throughout the post-conciliar years. Indeed, the five perspectives that have guided our study of the literature are evident in the earliest of Kavanagh's writ-ings.

We interrupted our review of the American literature by examining the *Instruction on Infant Baptism*, published by the SCDF in 1980.

Without designating that year as the turning point in the American discussion, it does seem that by 1980 the baptismal waters for both infants and adults had become, as James Dunning remarked, more tranquil. Pastoral imagination and writing in the immediate postconciliar years were focused on the *RCIA*, which not only restored to the Church an ancient order but also redefined the way in which baptism, the sacraments, and the Church were understood. The rite of infant baptism, celebrated within a few moments and removed from the kind of community participation and involvement that formed the very structure of the adult ordo, was often treated as the "mischievous kid brother" of the adult rite: sometimes disdained, occasionally ignored, frequently tolerated. That the SCDF found it necessary to publish its instruction is but one indication of the "infant baptism needs to be justified" ethos characteristic of the 1970s. As we noted in chapter 3, most of the contemporary challenges to infant baptism that the instruction addressed were associated with positions frequently held by writers commenting upon the vision of baptism encouraged by the adult ordo.

Throughout the 1980s, however, American writers seemed more intent in developing the theological significance and pastoral practice of infant baptism in its own right, and the phrase "corresponding practice" (coined by Paul Covino in his 1981 study of the discussion on infant baptism) seems to not only designate a third baptismal school of thought but also to accurately assess the baptismal reality at both parochial and literary levels of this more recent decade. Generally authors in the 1980s were content to explore the *value* of infant baptism—we note especially the contributions of Mark Searle—and less intent on playing one rite off against the other. One can even detect that a pact of "mutual aid" had been joined to the Church's demanding task of "conversion therapy," a pact in which the lessons offered by the ideals and principles, successes and failures of the *RCIA*, would benefit the understanding and practice of infant baptism.

Having surveyed twenty-five years of postconciliar writing on the baptism of infants, what can we say? We say, first, that *infant baptism is here to stay*. The confidence with which this statement is offered is not based solely upon the weight of ecclesial tradition or history, for many in the preceding pages argue effectively for the theological legitimacy of the practice. Even the words of those writers who might seem to hold an anti-infant-baptism stance reveal upon closer scrutiny that the "problem with infant baptism" is not infant baptism per se but an ecclesial and cultural heritage that has allowed (if not encouraged) many to approach the sacrament automatically or anxiously. The issue is not whether we should baptize infants; rather it is how we can foster an approach toward this sacrament of faith in which the parental fear of original sin is not the driving force and in which prebaptismal catechesis for parents and postbaptismal catechesis for parents and families are considered as necessary as they are valuable.

And, after examining twenty-five years of postconciliar writing, we say, second, that while infant baptism is here to stay, *our understanding of the sacrament has not stayed unchanged.* Challenges to the practice of baptizing infants certainly predate the Second Vatican Council, but spurred on in no small part by postconciliar efforts at renewal, the questioning of the practice stimulated perhaps unparalleled interest on a variety of levels of Church life: academic, liturgical, pastoral, catechetical, and parochial/familial.

As we discuss the reevaluation of infant baptism, a valuable perspective is offered by observing that such questioning has not been confined in these postconciliar years to what here is our major interest. The past quarter-century has witnessed a transformation of our understanding of other sacraments as well. In addition to confirmation—that "other sacrament of initiation" we have considered frequently in these pages—the sacraments of reconciliation and the anointing of the sick also have experienced marked development. And the vision of the adult ordo has certainly influenced our consideration of the sacraments of orders and of nonordained ministries as well as of the identity and mission of the Church herself. If we deem the confusion and criticism surrounding these matters fortunate (and in my view, it can not be considered otherwise), then we can readily agree with Aidan Kavanagh's description of the *RCIA* as a "pastorally explosive document": it has served and continues to serve the Church well.

A third observation concerns one "defense" of infant baptism seen frequently in these pages: the charge that the sacrament was often misunderstood because of excessive preoccupation with "what happens to the infant," a preoccupation which unfortunately all too often circumvents the sacrament's significance for parents, family, and the local and universal Church communities. Many authors saw infant baptism as having repercussions upon the community not unlike the challenge to the community and witness by the catechumens, upon which much of the value of the *RCIA* was based. This understanding, that infant and adult baptism are sacraments of the Church effecting the continuing initiation of the community *as well as* the initial entrance of the individual, can only be applauded as one indication that the theological ethos emerging from the council has discouraged a view of the sacraments as sacred acts able to be defined (and often, isolated) according to precise spaces, places, and times.

Hopefully this emphasis will continue, for it has offered a necessary balance or reorientation to a previous sacramental theology and practice that often seemed to have been unduly influenced by the notion of *opus operatum*. Utilizing the same Scholastic terminology, it appears that it is now the *opus operantis* that commands our attention.

But the method and goal of sacramental theology is not either/or. To speak of sacramentality or of specific sacraments is not to speak only of God's self-communication to humankind, nor is it to speak only of humankind's response. The sacraments symbolize and effect divine offer as they symbolize and elicit human response, and so any reflection of sacramentality in general or of "the seven" in particular must consider both the one who offers and those who respond. Sacramental theology explores the responsive word of humankind— a word that is always important—but it explores and encourages that human word with the full knowledge that it is God's word that is first and last.

In this respect, the sacrament of baptism offers a unique perspective, for in its different manifestations these dual aspects of grace (as gift from God, as accepted and responded to by humankind) are expressed. If it is our response to the word of God that is more readily witnessed in the initiation of adults, then it is the word of God as divine gift at God's initiative that confronts us more immediately as we baptize our infants. And if Tertullian's pointed reminder that Christians are not born, they are made, accurately describes that which is attempted through the process of the adult ordo, then it is the psalmist who portrays well a distinctive attribute of the baptism of infants:

"Before ever a word is on my tongue
you know it, O Lord, through and through.
. . . .
For it was you who created my being,
knit me together in my mother's womb.
. . . .
Your eyes saw all my actions,

they were all of them written in your book,
every one of my days was decreed,
before one of them came into being" (Psalm 138 [139]).

The practice of baptizing infants offers unique, sound theological perspectives that we have referred to throughout our survey of over seventy American postconciliar writers. As indicated above, in my opinion Nathan Mitchell and Mark Searle stand out among those considering the theological meaning of infant baptism: the former by his contribution toward a theology of childhood, in which children and the celebration of their baptism are an integral part in the sacramental dimension of the Church; the latter by his insistence that a more comprehensive approach to infant baptism would not only serve the Church and her practice per se but would also offer a necessary balance (and corrective) to an understanding of and approach to baptism that identifies itself too exclusively with the *RCIA*.

However the normative value of the *RCIA* is understood, this understanding need not—in fact, can not—dilute the theological significance of the sacrament of infant baptism. Theological pluralism, it would seem, would encourage the acknowledgment of the innate humbleness of any one rite or theology attempting to elucidate the mystery of Christian initiation. That the *RCIA* is the pastoral, theological, and liturgical norm for the Christian initiation of adults and adolescents is evident: adults and adolescents are those for whom this ordo was designed. And that the adult ordo poses ideals and principles even for the baptism of infants is also clear. Nor is there any question that the *RCIA* will continue to be a "pastorally explosive" document—a claim that need not extend, however, to its being pastorally or theologically exhaustive of baptismal theology or practice.

In his 1982 article in *Worship* (cited in ch. 4), Mark Searle warned about the theological and pastoral hazards of considering a single act or ritual of baptism as "capable of exhausting all that baptism means, all that is involved in the mystery of sharing the life of God in Christ." Observing that the Pauline exposition of baptism as participation in the Lord's death and resurrection, the primary model of the adult ordo, does not by itself serve infant baptism well, Searle referred to the "ancient Syrian baptismal liturgies [which] take the baptism of the Lord at the Jordan as their paradigm and offer a whole range of different motifs" as alternative models from which to approach the sacrament.

But the first of these motifs to which Searle refers can be attributed yet again to Paul. "Adoption," a New Testament metaphor found only in the Pauline corpus, vividly suggests and illustrates the extraordinary action of God that establishes Christians in a divine-human relationship.

The concept of adoption (in Paul's language, literally, the "making" or "placing of a son") directs our study in part 2. My hope is that our study of this concept will not only contribute to a baptismal theology particularly well-suited to the sacramental initiation of infants but will also benefit our understanding and appreciation of the relationship all Christians enjoy with their God: a relationship in which we rightly call God *Abba* only because God has called us sons and daughters "before ever a word was on our tongue."

PART TWO

RETURN TO GRACE

A Theology for Infant Baptism

An Overview of My Response

"The only thing that counts, and proves the presence of Divine Life in us, is total dedication to God, total dependence on Him. The small, helpless child at the font with new life in it, not the successful preacher in the pulpit, is the typical Christian; the last shall be first and the first last."[1]

"Far from barring children from the font, the chrism, and the altar, the Church should welcome their participation in these sacraments as a reminder both of the catholicity of the Church and of the fact that, no matter how informed or committed we might be as adults, when we take part in the sacramental liturgies of the Church we are taking part in more than we know."[2]

"Infant baptism is here to stay, yet our understanding of this sacrament has not stayed unchanged." So I observed in my concluding remarks in the previous chapter concerning the American Catholic postconciliar discussion of infant baptism. Thirty years of deliberation—by no means ended—have affirmed the legitimacy and value of infant baptism as they have also challenged our understanding of that practice.

Having reported the postconciliar discussion in part 1, I offer now my response to the "problem" of infant baptism. Two convictions support my response: first, that baptism is the "norm-al" means by which Christian families initiate their children into new life in Christ and the Church, and second, that the concept of adoption offers the Church a particularly appropriate paradigm from which to approach the sacramental initiation of infants and young children.

Chapter 6 serves as the door or bridge between the two parts of my work. In this transitional chapter, I discuss a theology of childhood, a topic referred to only briefly in chapter 4. As the sacramental initiation of infants and children is my primary concern, a consideration of the place and meaning of the child in the Church is essential in ordering the following theological reflections.

[1]Evelyn Underhill, *The Fruits of the Spirit,* 37.
[2]Searle, "Infant Baptism Reconsidered," 50.

In chapter 7 I approach the "norm of baptism" discussion from a new perspective, suggesting that our children—and the way we initiate them into our Christian community—offer a normative value to Christians young and old as regards their spiritual life and identity. The spirit of this thesis is reflected well by Evelyn Underhill's contention: "The small helpless child at the font with new life in it, not the successful preacher in the pulpit, is the typical Christian." In this chapter I also propose the concept of adoption as a paradigm helpful in approaching both the theology and the practice of baptizing infants and young children.

I conclude chapter 7 by reflecting upon the human act and experience of adoption and then explore the theological significance of adoption in chapter 8 by examining the use and significance of the term in the Pauline corpus. I believe there are a number of striking similarities between "human" and "theological" adoption and that these common elements suggest with particular clarity what it is Church and parents celebrate when they baptize infants and young children and so "claim them for Christ." I develop this line of thought in chapters 9 and 10, and in chapter 10 I conclude this work by responding to the five perspectives or position statements that guided the first part of this study "from my own perspective."

My primary interest is to suggest how an adoption-based baptismal theology can inform our understanding and appreciation of the sacramental initiation of infants and children. My hope is that what I offer will serve the adult Church as well. I realize such a hope may seem overly ambitious in a work concerned essentially with the baptizing of infants and young children. But I appeal to Mark Searle's wise reminder that "no matter how informed or committed we might be as adults, when we take part in the sacramental liturgies of the Church we are taking part in more than we know."

The Christian as the Once and Future Child: Who we are, to whom we belong

"Jesus' attitude toward children is perfectly clear. No one will enter the Kingdom of God, which has come close to us in Jesus, unless he makes a turnabout and returns to the mentality of his beginnings. 'Amen I say to you: Whoever does not receive the Kingdom of God like a child will not enter into it' (Mark 10:15)."[1]

"Adult faith and conversion lead to that childhood which consists in overcoming the last vestiges of resistance to the God who challenges us to lose ourselves in order to find ourselves. . . . The Christian who 'dies in the Lord' meets his childhood in a final act of complete surrender."[2]

Inquiring in 1975 as to what the theologians were saying about children, Nathan Mitchell offered an abrupt reply: not much. Acknowledging that a vast bibliography detailing psychological, intellectual, and liturgical aspects of childhood could be readily compiled, Mitchell noted a veritable vacuum when seeking a theological commentary on childhood.

Mitchell believed one factor contributing to this theological lacuna was the customary manner in which childhood and children are considered.[3] It is the future of the child rather than the child's

---

[1]Hans Urs von Balthasar, *Unless You Become Like This Child*, trans. Erasmo Leiva-Merikakis (San Francisco: Ignatius, 1991) 9.

[2]Mitchell, "Once and Future Child," 433. As we observed in chapter 2, Mitchell is among the first of the American Catholic writers to address the baptism of children from the perspective of a "theology of childhood." I acknowledge his kind permission to use his phrase for the title of this chapter.

[3]This period from birth and baptism until the traditional "age of reason at seven" is the "limbo" now being addressed vigorously by liturgists and catechists; a recent example is Duggan and Kelly, *Christian Initiation of Children*. Psychiatrist-author Robert Coles has written admirably on the spiritual dimensions of childhood.

present that ordinarily captures our imagination. Our inclination is to concentrate less on who the child is now, and more upon the mature, adult person the child will eventually become. Because we consider the future of the child as that which moves out of the past and leaves it irrevocably behind, Mitchell maintained it is usually difficult for us to "immediately see the value of childhood *in its own right*."[4]

THE MEANING OF CHILDHOOD:
AN ENDURING VALUE IN GOD'S EYES

If Mitchell's observation is correct—that it is often difficult to "immediately see the value of childhood in its own right"—such a dilemma was foreign to the One in whose name all Christians are baptized. For in the eyes and arms of the Lord children hold a blessed, even privileged, place. Each of the Synoptic Gospels relates that Jesus set a child among his disciples as he spoke of the kingdom,[5] the remembrance of which no doubt prompted Daniel Stevick's comment that "it is more than a debater's point to suggest that we have it on good authority that there is something normative in the life of the kingdom about a child."[6] In a similar vein, Mitchell contended that baptized children are "a significant dimension of the church's sacramental structure,"[7] while Mark Searle remarked that it is infants and children "who constantly bring the subversive message of the Gospel as salvation by obedience of faith to a Church constantly prone to place too much confidence in its intellectual re-

[4]Mitchell, "Once and Future Child," 423; emphasis in original. Describing our customary tendency to dismiss the significance of childhood, Mitchell continues: "Childhood, like mumps, measles, chicken-pox and whooping cough—is something we hope to grow out of. Being a child is preparatory, provisional, subordinate to the task of becoming a responsible adult. It is a necessary, but ephemeral stage of development, the human 'larva' directed toward adult maturation. The value we customarily assign to childhood is governed by our appreciation of its potential. Children are important not so much because they are children, but because they can become adults, productive, contributing members of the social body. Children are important for their becoming, for their future as fully socialized adult human beings."

[5]Matt 19:13-15; Mark 10:13-16; Luke 18:15-17. See also Matt 18:1-5; Mark 9:33-37; Luke 9:46-48 and 10:21-24.

[6]Daniel Stevick, "Christian Initiation: Post-Reformation to the Present Era," 106.

[7]Mitchell, "Once and Future Child," 433.

spectability."[8] Far from being considered simply a necessary but transient stage of human development, then, childhood not only has value in its own right but also suggests to us something about what it means to live in the hope of the kingdom.

That we ordinarily assign childhood only a provisional value is due to the way we ordinarily think of time: time passes, or it flies; time moves on into the future; time waits for no one. But our customary understanding of time, that of an inexorable march of seconds ticking by relentlessly, is incomplete. When considering the "time of humankind," an additional perspective is needed. Acknowledging that the earlier stages of an adult's life are "subordinate to and preparatory for what is still to come," Karl Rahner insists that

"[humans are not] pushed through the space-time dimension as though [they] were only in possession of the transient moment which is called the present. Man is a subject. He possesses himself. He is at all stages capable of taking himself as a whole. And for this reason, in spite of the continuous process of change and the alternation of action and passion in the time to which he is subject, he has before him his time *as a whole*. As his life advances he *retains* the past and goes forward into a future *that he has already worked out* beforehand. By the exercise of his freedom he makes the time allotted to him present as a whole, past and future together. . . . His future is the making present of his own past as freely lived."[9]

---

[8]Searle, "Infant Baptism Reconsidered," 41. French theologian Guy Bédouelle offers this perspective in a way that touches upon the foundation of the Church herself. In his "Reflection on the Place of the Child in the Church: 'Suffer the Little Children to Come Unto Me,'" 362, he remarks: "The 'blessing of childhood' . . . is reported especially in Luke with the greatest solemnity; Jesus utters it by the inspiration of the Holy Spirit in a truly sacerdotal prayer. That the context allows us to understand it as realized in the disciples of Christ (Luke 10:23-24) gives it an added intensity. The Lord's Church is first founded upon the very young and not on the wise and scholarly. The blessing answers in advance all adult arrogance, strengthened in recent years by a confusion between childhood and childishness. The appeal is to 'adult christianity' which claims to find its roots in Paul's exhortations (1 Cor 3:1-2) but would not be able to appropriate the look of privilege on the faces of the children in the Gospel."

[9]Karl Rahner, "Ideas for a Theology of Childhood," 34–35; emphasis in original. Acknowledging Rahner's influence upon his own work, Mitchell describes "Ideas" as "one of the few attempts I have seen in contemporary writing that aims to establish a sound theological basis for the Christian understanding of childhood." See "Once and Future Child," 424–28, for a helpful summary of Rahner's thought.

The idea that we embrace our time—*all* our time—is crucial to our reflection upon childhood, for as we have observed, we tend to see the time of childhood primarily as preparation for adult life. Because we have our time before us as a whole, however, we do not move completely and definitively away from childhood but rather move toward the eternity of our childhood. More specifically, we move toward the enduring and irrevocable value this childhood has in the sight of God.[10]

Childhood, then, is not something lost on a designated birthday or set aside the moment we conclude a given stage of human development. Nor is childhood, theologically considered, confined to those early years of life we eventually outgrow. Childhood is not that which we once were, but that which remains with us still: that which, in fact, we must reclaim and so bring to its full maturity.

This is the shrewd suggestion in Mitchell's depiction of the Christian as a "once and future child." The value and significance of childhood are not limited to its chronological progression into or its developmental founding of the life of the adult. The Christian adult, once a child, is called ultimately to become a child, a "future" child, a mature Christian child. As Christian adults continue to increase in wisdom, stature, and favor with God, their ideal is not to abandon the child they once were but to recover and reclaim the value of their "former" childhood by abandoning the pretenses of their present adulthood. The paradox inherent in a theology of childhood is that it is in their childhood that Christians see who they must become and remain before God as adults. Unless we become like children we shall not become the sons and daughters of God we are called to be.[11]

[10]Rahner, "Theology of Childhood," 35–36, remarks: "Childhood endures as that which is given and abiding, the time that has been accepted and lived through freely. Childhood does not constitute past time, time that has eroded away, but rather that which remains, that which is coming to meet us as an intrinsic element in the single and enduring completeness of the time of our existence considered as a unity, that which we call the eternity of man as saved and redeemed. We do not lose childhood as that which recedes ever further into our past, that which remains behind as we advance forward in time, but rather we go towards it as that which has been achieved in time and redeemed forever in time. We only *become* the children whom we *were* because we gather up time—and in this our childhood too—into our eternity" (emphasis in original).

[11]Stevick, "Christian Initiation," 106, echoes Mitchell's observation: "The adult is the odd one who must change and become like a child in order to enter [the kingdom]. A system which seems to say, 'Except you become as a grown-up, you

That childhood has value in its own right, and that this value is not simply preparation for adulthood, is evident also in Rahner's observation that "the grace of childhood is not merely the pledge of the grace of adulthood."[12] Because the child is the person, childhood enjoys the immediacy of a direct relationship with God, as do all other phases of life. But the unique value and importance of childhood are such that childhood "touches upon the absolute divinity of God not only as maturity, adulthood and the later phases of life touch upon this, but rather in a special way of its own."[13] This "special way," this unique character of childhood, is why the child may be considered a "sacrament of that radical openness to the future which is a characteristic posture of the Christian believer," and why baptized children are "a significant dimension of the church's sacramental structure."[14]

CHILDREN AND CHILDHOOD: WHOM ADULTS TEACH, FROM WHOM THEY MUST LEARN

Infant baptism presents a formidable challenge to the adult Church. As we reported the words of one author in chapter 2, the baptism of an infant is the Church's pledge "to demonstrate a faith so alive and dynamic that the child baptized may eventually find fulfillment in it."[15] But the challenge to visibly demonstrate its faith is only one way in which the baptism of infants challenges the adult ecclesial community. For the adult Church is called not only to live the gospel in such a way that her children will come to want to embrace that good news as their own; she is called also to reclaim her own childhood as a fundamental value of that gospel message. As the adult Church continues to meet the challenge of catechizing and forming her children (and adult catechumens) in the faith, she is confronted also with the more humbling challenge to remember that it is not only the adults who teach:

"Childhood has something essential to say to adults. 'Whoever receives one such child in my name receives me' [Mark 9:36]. 'Whoever

---

shall in no wise enter . . .' at least does not have all of the arguments in its favor."

[12]Rahner, "Theology of Childhood," 37.

[13]Ibid., 36.

[14]Mitchell, "Once and Future Child," 428, 433.

[15]Haggerty, "Adult Initiation and Infant Baptism," 159.

does not receive the kingdom of God like a child shall not enter it' (Mark 10:15). The kingdom is no carrot held before [the young child] as the prize of growing up for it is not a reward of adulthood at all. Both children and adults belong to God's kingdom *in the manner of childhood*, i.e., theirs is the kingdom by virtue of a grace not given by adulthood. Certainly possession of the kingdom, proclaimed in baptism, is not yet experienced in its fulness, but its fulness is not adulthood's gift. Adults await the fulfilment of the promise, too. Many, however, grow impatient with the childlike nature of Christian life; forgetting to await the kingdom they abandon the childlike character. The more they place their hopes in the achievement of adulthood, the less chance have they of entering the kingdom. 'For to such belong the kingdom of God' (Mark 10:14)."[16]

Rahner also sees the child and childhood as posing a challenge to the adult Church. While Stevick observed that "there is something normative in the life of the kingdom about a child," Rahner speaks of the child as "the prototype of those for whom the kingdom of heaven is," so much so that "for our existence to be sound and redeemed at all, childhood must be an intrinsic element in it."[17] Again, childhood is not something we grow out of because we mature or as we grow into the adult years but is the condition we seek to recover and to sustain the more mature we become in our faith in Jesus Christ. Childhood is "a basic condition which is always appropriate to a life that is lived aright."[18]

"Let the children come to me, . . . for to such belongs the kingdom of heaven" (Mark 10:14). We should not too casually point to the attractive yet amoral innocence of children as that which allows "those such as these" to serve as the prototype for the inheritors of the kingdom. Nor should we consider childhood as the symbol of the state of

[16]J.B.M. Frederick, "The Initiation Crisis in the Church of England," 151; emphasis in original.

[17]Rahner, "Theology of Childhood," 41, 47.

[18]Ibid., 47. Mitchell, "Once and Future Child," 427, remarks: "Development, then, has to mean something more than 'preparation for what's ahead.' It has to mean, as well, the comprehensive act by which *any* man at any state of his life embraces everything that he is, was and is becoming. We are fully adults only when we can meet and affirm our childhood as not only 'past history' but also 'present experience' and 'future becoming.' Adult maturity means allowing childhood to be released in us not as a fond or bitter memory but as a facet of what we are and hope to become" (emphasis in original).

pure and uncorrupted grace that sinful humankind must strive to reacquire. The individual history of a child does not appear sanitary-wrapped and vacuum-packed but emerges—and merges—into the already existing history of humankind: a history replete with grace *and* sin, with wavering loyalties, with divided hearts.[19]

This is not to condemn the child to the curse and darkness of original sin but is, rather, to introduce the child into that grace and light offered only in virtue of the saving redemption won for us by Christ. We readily acknowledge the doctrine and the reality of original sin because we know that the grace that redeems us is offered us as gift, both before we realize our need for it and after our feeble-but-proud efforts to earn it and keep it as our possession. Any understanding of children as blessed because they have not yet learned from their elders how to sin is absent from this theology of childhood—as is the subtle semi-Pelagianism that seems to bubble incessantly just beneath the surface of an adult Church that would seek to secure her salvation:

"Christianity's awareness of the guilt and tragedy which belong even to the beginning is . . . the necessary outcome of its awareness of the blessedness of grace and the redemption which overcomes this guilt and tragedy, and which comes both before and after it. For this is precisely the grace and redemption which the Christian experiences and to which he submits himself."[20]

THE ESSENCE OF CHILDHOOD:
A SACRAMENT FOR ALL CHRISTIANS

". . . the grace and redemption which Christians experience and to which they submit themselves." It is this submission to the grace and redemption wrought only through Jesus Christ and not an overly romanticized and inevitably abandoned infantile innocence that

---

[19]Mitchell, "Once and Future Child," 433: "[I]n the baptized child the church recognizes its 'original face' and its future destiny. This is not a sentimental recognition, but an intensely realistic one. The life of the child maps the total geography of the human pilgrimage. In the child the church sees a man in primordial confrontation with the history of grace and the history of sin and failure, for the child embraces all the infinitely complex experiences of human life. In the child the church recognizes both the luminosity and the darkness, the freedom for goodness and the freedom for destruction that sketch the magnificence of the human experiment."

[20]Rahner, "Theology of Childhood," 40; see pages 38–43 for a fuller development.

portrays the unique character of childhood and that again suggests, in Rahner's words, that "for our existence to be sound and redeemed at all, childhood must be an intrinsic element in it." This childhood as an inherent factor in our lives

"must take the form of trust, of openness, of expectation, of readiness to be controlled by another, of interior harmony with the unpredictable forces with which the individual finds himself confronted. It must manifest itself as freedom in contrast to that which is merely the outcome of a predetermining design, as receptivity, as hope which is still not disillusioned. This is the childhood that must be present and active as an effective force at the very roots of our being."[21]

"We are God's children now" (1 John 3:2). Rahner warns against understanding the phrase "child of God" as a mere figure of speech—as though the humanly understood concepts of child and childhood express a theological relationship in only a secondary, metaphorical fashion. Rather, it is through the theological application of the terms "child" and "childhood" that one comes to realize fully the richness and depth of the human concepts.[22] The childhood we have described above—a childhood manifested by trust, openness, expectation, and the willingness to submit to the control of another— exists in the physical, biological child only in a rudimentary and, hopefully, predictive way. But the childhood of the mature adult is a religious act, for this childhood speaks of orienting one's life to seek constantly "the boundlessness of God . . . without restraint or inhibition," and to know no resting place

"except that of total self-abandonment to the incomprehensible infinitude of the ineffable mystery. And it follows from this that it can be asserted truly and without reserve that man remains religious when

[21]Ibid., 47. See also Mitchell, "Once and Future Child," 432.

[22]See Rahner, "Theology of Childhood," 43–50, for a fuller development of this theme. Von Balthasar makes this point in an especially poignant way—and one that speaks well to the relationship between child and parents—throughout his chapter "The Human Child" in *Unless You Become Like This Child* (pp. 15–25). Observing that the "intuition of love" readily observable in an infant or young child relating to his parents "derives from a concrete encounter and thus does not at all communicate an abstract concept of being, this intuition is wholly unbounded and reaches to the Ultimate, to the Divine. This is why, for a child, his parents' concrete love is not at first separable from God."

he experiences the childhood which is an elemental factor in his nature, when he adopts this and maintains it as his basic attitude and outlook, and allows it to develop to the full and without limitation.

"Childhood is openness. Human childhood is infinite openness. The mature childhood of the adult is the attitude in which we bravely and trustfully maintain an infinite openness in all circumstances and despite the experiences of life which seem to invite us to close ourselves. Such openness, infinite and maintained in all circumstances, yet put into practice in the actual manner in which we live our lives, is the expression of man's religious existence."[23]

This openness is the essence of childhood, an openness made possible by and through the gift of God's grace: a gift accepted by us but sustained by God. It is this orientation toward God, this courageous submission to the ineffable mystery of the Father, that leads the adult man and woman to realize fully their enduring childhood before God. This is the "sacramental dimension" of childhood, the adult Christian understood as the "once and future child." In the child the adult Church sees her past and sees what she once was, and in the child the adult Church is not only reminded that life is a gift but is challenged to surrender more fully to the source and sustainer of that gift:

"The child, therefore, is a sacrament of that radical openness to the future which is a characteristic posture of the Christian believer precisely because the child reveals not only what we once were, but what we will be. Indeed, one could almost define Christianity itself as the state of childhood, the surrendering openness to God as the absolute future of man, the future that comes forward to meet men in unconditional love and acceptance.

"This perceptive permits us, I believe, to achieve a better grasp of the meaning of childhood for Christian faith and practice. The value of childhood does not consist primarily in being a provisional prelude to mature and adult faith. Rather, the significance of childhood lies in the youngster being met, embraced and loved—like every other individual by the God who continues to disclose and offer himself in creation, grace and covenant."[24]

[23]Rahner, "Theology of Childhood," 48–49.
[24]Mitchell, "Once and Future Child," 428, cited in part in our chapter 2. Rahner, "Theology of Childhood," 42, observes that this orientation toward God, this attitude that we strive to put into practice in our lives, is making the mystery of God, from whom all fatherhood in heaven and on earth derives its name (Eph

I do not claim the above discussion represents an extensive theology of childhood. Such a presentation would necessarily involve a host of areas relating to children, parents, and family life: the spiritual life of children and their psychosocial development, the evolving relationship of children with their parents and other family members, and children's quite natural identification of their human parents with the divine Father of us all, to name only a few. From our consideration here emerge the following major points that anchor our discussion throughout the remainder of this work:

1. While the developmental nature and aspects of childhood are neither denied nor ignored, the value of childhood does not depend upon what the child *will* become or upon what it is hoped the child *will* someday achieve or accomplish. Childhood has value in its own right because the child has value in his or her own right. As a person here and now, the child enjoys a direct and immediate relationship with God. This relationship is actual, not potential. It does not depend upon or point to a time in the future when the child personally will be able to "know" and respond to God but exists as he or she is now: as a child.

2. The child not only enjoys that direct relationship with God here and now, but that relationship is in many ways sacramental of the relationship to which God calls human beings of every age. This relationship is based on openness and trust and is characterized by hopeful expectation of the promises made and the willing submission to the One recognized as the giver and sustainer of life—as well as life's end.

3. While not abdicating the responsibilities, tasks, and duties obligatory to life in an adult world, adult Christians are called to turn away from the typical adult temptation of defining, mastering, and controlling the one relationship that defines them as *Christian* adults. Forsaking childish ways as they must, they allow the childlike qualities with which and through which they began to know the world to continue to direct and lead them to the God who was, is, and will be their Father. The Christian, through baptism, is a child of God: God's "once and future child."

To conclude our consideration here of a theology of childhood, we return to the "dispute about greatness" among the disciples of Jesus.

3:15), "the protection and defense of our lives. We are content to commit [ourselves] to the ineffable as sheltering and forgiving, to that which is unspeakably close to us with the closeness of love."

This dispute is recorded in each of the Synoptic Gospels, and in each it sets the stage for Jesus to embrace a child as an example—a proto-type—for the kingdom. We cite Matthew's rendition: "Truly, I say to you, unless you turn and become like children, you will never enter the kingdom of heaven" (18:3). To turn and become like children may well be *the* challenge of the Christian life: the full awareness of who we are—*and of whose we are*. That discovery is neither easy nor quick. It is crucial for our identity as Christians, however, for this discovery of to whom we belong is the ultimate fruit of our baptism: "For the baptism of any man is complete only when he surrenders himself back to God in ecstatic wonder through the act of death. The Chris-tian who 'dies in the Lord' meets his childhood in a final act of com-plete surrender."[25]

Mitchell believes Christianity can be defined as the state of child-hood, and von Balthasar maintains that unless we return to the men-tality of our beginnings we will not enter the kingdom of God. It would seem there is, indeed, something normative about childhood for the life of all believers. And maybe to turn and become like chil-dren *is* the ultimate challenge confronting Christians and their adult Church, for perhaps only then can we mature into the full awareness of who we are—and of whose we are.

As we continue to consider what lessons the adult Church might learn from her children, I return to the "norm of baptism" discus-sion—and suggest that perhaps this time the children should lead the way.

[25]Mitchell, "Once and Future Child," 433. Rahner, "Theology of Childhood," 43, offers a similar comment: "[T]he kingdom of heaven is for those who are children in this sense when, on the basis of this attitude of openness, and not without a certain *metanoia*, they become what they are—precisely children. Now this also implies, however paradoxical it may appear, that we do not really know what childhood means at the beginning of our lives until we know what that child-hood means which comes at the end of them; that childhood, namely, in which, by God-given repentance and conversion, we receive the kingdom of God and so become children." See also Bédouelle, "Place of the Child in the Church," 366–67.

Chapter 7

And a Little Child Shall Lead Them:
Baptismal norms and models

"If baptism is defined exclusively in terms of a paschal transitus 'from "shame" to "celebration," from the conviction of sin to the appropriation of one's complete forgiveness in Christ' (in Aidan Kavanagh's words), then it is indeed difficult to see what possible sense there could be in baptizing infants."[1]

"But besides the immediate liturgical sacramental dimension of infant baptism for the family and the local church, there is also the question of whether, when the sacraments of initiation are made accessible to small children, something important is not gained for the Church's own self-understanding. This is not the place to discuss whether and in what sense adult initiation might be said to be 'normative,' but even if this were to be admitted, it could not be used to disparage the practice of infant initiation as such, except at the cost of departing from the Catholic tradition or at least sacrificing significant elements of that tradition."[2]

We have seen that the "adult ordo as norm" thesis, proposed by Aidan Kavanagh in the early 1970s, generated considerable discussion among American authors. While many supported Kavanagh's formulation, the thesis was not entirely without its critics—nor was it consistently understood or expressed in the same way by those who promoted it. The claim that the adult ordo "sets forth the definitive statement of what the Roman Catholic Church's norm of baptism is henceforth to be" certainly underscored the importance of this "pastorally explosive document" to the Church. But the thesis' stated implication as regards infant baptism—that it was, even in the best of circumstances, a "benign abnormality"—was judged by some to be a thesis that even with the best of intentions was unfortunate.

[1]Mark Searle, "Response: RCIA and Infant Baptism," 329; the reference to Kavanagh is from his *Shape of Baptism*, 199.
[2]Mark Searle, "Infant Baptism Reconsidered," 50.

As regards my response to the "adult ordo as norm" thesis, I offer the following three statements, each of which has appeared or has been implied in our previous discussions. I collect them here to indicate the direction of our work in this and the following chapters:

1. That the *RCIA* is the pastoral, theological, and liturgical norm for the Christian initiation of adults and adolescents is evident; that the adult ordo poses ideals and principles even for the baptism of infants is also clear. Likewise, there is no question that the *RCIA* will continue to be a "pastorally explosive" document—a claim that need not extend, however, to its being pastorally or theologically exhaustive of baptismal theology or practice.

2. The baptizing of infants is, in the best of circumstances, not a benign abnormality but is the ordinary, proper, and "norm-al" means by which new members of our human family are sacramentally brought into new life with Christ and his Church.

3. Children are not the only ones who must learn and adults are not the only ones who can teach. There is something about the state of childhood that has a normative value for the Church and all her members, a normative value expressed liturgically when we baptize our infants.

My intention in this second part of my work is neither to denigrate the value and significance of the adult ordo nor to undermine the process of initiation that the ordo clearly sustains and guides. Rather, I hope to suggest and discuss an initiation theology that will assist us in answering the question posed by Mark Searle: "the question of whether, when the sacraments of initiation are made accessible to small children, something important is not gained for the Church's own self-understanding."

A NORM FOR BAPTISM?
LET THE CHILDREN LEAD THE WAY

Nathan Mitchell considered children a sacrament of that radical openness to God to which all Christians are called and challenged, and maintained that the baptism of infants is an integral part of the sacramental dimension of the Church. Infants and children are sacraments: models or paradigms for the life of the Christian individual and community and, indeed, for Christian identity. "The child is the prototype of those for whom the kingdom is," says Rahner, while Mitchell sees the Christian as God's "once and future child." To fully mature into our Christian identity as children of God so as to inherit the kingdom: *this* is normative (the standard according to which a thing is done) for the life of the Christian; *this* is the ultimate end to which any sacramental celebration of initiation is directed.

The sacramental initiation of infants and the process of adult initiation are complementary, then, for both express core values—normative values—for Christian initiation, Christian identity, and Christian life. Each in its own way speaks of the stuff of sacramental initiation and of the anticipated and desired effects of initiation: the faithful relationship of love among God, individual, and community as that community witnesses by its life the power of those relationships and so lives in the hope of the kingdom. To attribute to one ordo normative or near-premium status for every age, shape, and kind of Christian as regards initiation—let alone as regards Christian life and identity—seems to be moving yet another step toward defining the mystery of God rather than being drawn into it. Mark Searle is particularly adept at appraising the complementary relationship between adult and infant initiation:

"Adult baptism, the economy of the 'twice born,' tends to draw to itself the vocabulary of regeneration as opposed to generation; of brothers and sisters rather than sons and daughters; of voluntary decision rather than divine vocation; of change rather than faithfulness; of breaking with the past rather than growth towards the future; of death and resurrection rather than adoption and filiation. The language of infant initiation, on the other hand, is inclined to speak in terms of the womb rather than the tomb, of election rather than choice, of loyalty rather than commitment, of the preconscious operations of grace rather than of personal convictions, of nurturing the life of faith rather than of passing from unbelief to belief. In Jungian terms, a regime which attaches importance to infant initiation gives a larger role to the 'feminine' aspects of Christianity, while adult initiation displays the more 'masculine' elements of Christian imagery."[3]

In the adult ordo and in the *Rite of Baptism for Children* the Church sets forth her two primary expressions of sacramental initiation. These rites of initiation *of* the Church are rites of initiation *for* the Church. Both form the Church as they also inform her; both allow every Christian, no matter the particular sacramental expression and

[3]Ibid., 49–50.

effecting of that Christian's initiation, to be drawn further into the mystery of Christ and his Church. The images, models, and implications specific to each form suggest part of what it means to be initiated and to initiate. Neither sacramental expression in itself exhausts the significance of baptism, just as neither expression by itself should be expected to bear this burden. We might say that both children's ritual and the adult ordo (and the ritual of each of the sacraments, for that matter)[4] are normative as to meaning for the Christian individual and community in their own way: each informs and challenges our understanding of our past life outside of Christ, our present life in him, and our future life with him.

It is less helpful, I believe, to maintain that a specific ordo definitively states the Church's norm of baptism than it is to explore the unique contributions of adult ordo and children's ritual—for each is normative to and for a particular group—and to acknowledge the inevitable incompleteness of one when isolated from the other.[5] The adult ordo is rightly understood as presenting *a* norm for baptism: designed for and directed toward mature candidates, it presents the ordinary means through which adult men and women will be led to sacramental initiation into and full communion with the Church. And that this ordo poses ideals and principles even for the baptism of infants is, as I stated above, clear. But the adult ordo is an ordo for adults (*RCIA* 1) and therefore cannot be understood as offering "the

---

[4]Although it is beyond the scope of this work, I would encourage broadening our understanding and use of the term "norm" in such a way that we begin to apply the term to all the sacraments—or specifically, that we use the term in such a way that it encourages us to consider all the sacraments as normative for those who celebrate them. Christian initiation is about Christian life and identity, and certainly the adult ordo is normative for adults in that it suggests, challenges, and guides the conversion and witness of adults coming to faith. But should not the same be said of all the sacraments? Is there not something normative for all Christians, for example, in the sacrament of the anointing of the sick: the witness of the community's dependence upon God and the belief that one's Christian identity is of greater import than one's human inability to "contribute"? So, too, do we not find in the sacrament of orders a normative statement as to public ministry in the name of Christ and his Church, as well as our belief in transcendent fulfillment—just as in marriage we find a normative statement as to faithful and life-giving love through which is encountered the source of all life and love?

[5]Stevick outlines seven varieties or "Types of Baptismal Spirituality," 11–26. Among his conclusions: "None of the types described should be normative for the church. Indeed, several of them would be defective if they stood alone" (24).

definitive statement of what the Church's norm of baptism is henceforth to be" as long as the Church welcomes infants and young children as legitimate candidates for sacramental initiation. It is not only the adult ordo's process of initiation that will not translate favorably for the *RBC*, it is also its ethos and theological motif.

For example, the theological motif of baptism as participation in the death and resurrection of Christ guides and sustains the ethos and rites of the adult ordo. And there is no question that, as the initiatory process unfolds from evangelization to mystagogy, this motif serves the adult ordo well. But the model seems less forceful and clear when applied to the baptism of infants. Exactly what it means to participate in Christ's death and resurrection proves for many adults to be as enigmatic as it is arduous, and to speak of an infant's or child's participation in that death and resurrection in a way that is at once theologically and pastorally compelling is perhaps asking too much of model, pastors, and parents.

We will not find, nor do we need, a theology *(lex credendi)* or rite *(lex orandi)* of baptism applicable to all Christians in all circumstances. We do better to seek baptismal theologies and rituals that, by respecting the unique nature of individuals in their own initiatory circumstances, speak effectively and credibly in those circumstances to and for the Church.

Presbyterian minister Diane Karay has noted the irony that although the practice of infant initiation has been common from at least the time of Augustine, a theology oriented specifically toward that practice appears elusive. Her "Let the Children Lead the Way" develops the theme of spiritual rebirth and, as does Mitchell's "Once and Future Child," bids the adult Church to recall and to reclaim her eternal childhood before God.[6] Karay's work is one recent attempt to support the

---

[6]Diane Karay, "Let the Children Lead the Way: A Case for Baptizing Children," 346: "Church tradition contains baptismal imagery which refers to one of the great scriptural themes of baptism, the necessity for spiritual rebirth. Birth into the world and helpless infancy are one of the most elemental universal human experiences. To turn away from this powerful imagery is to turn away from the source of our being, to deny in some sense the magnitude of the growth required of us and our utter dependency upon God. I believe that the Christian church ignores this imagery at its peril. Neglect of this imagery strengthens the adultist illusion of having arrived and denigrates the Christlike graces inherent in childhood, graces like humility and utter trust which, once left behind in childhood, must be fought for with great tenacity to be regained."

initiation of infants and children with a theological model equal in richness and depth to that of baptism as participation in Christ's death and resurrection but one that responds more immediately to the actual circumstance of the sacramental initiation of the young.

Although the practice of infant initiation has been common from at least the time of Augustine, a theology oriented specifically toward that practice appears elusive. And as we have noted several times in these pages, it was Augustine himself who thought one must believe there is some value in infant baptism, even though that value might be "an extremely obscure question." In responding to this extremely obscure question, I suggest adoption as a theological model or paradigm that effectively addresses the unique value and significance of the sacrament of infant baptism.

BAPTISM AS ADOPTION:
THE CONSEQUENCES OF GOD'S GRACE

The redeeming powers of the waters of baptism are described variously in the opening paragraphs of the General Introduction that introduces the Church's rites of initiation. Through baptism "we are freed from the power of darkness and joined to Christ's death, burial, and resurrection" (1). This first sacrament "incorporates us into Christ and forms us into God's people" (2), for baptism is "the door to life and to the kingdom of God" (3) through which we are "incorporated into the Church and are built up together in the Spirit into a house where God lives" (4).

Perhaps the ultimate effect of the baptismal waters is described nowhere more succinctly, however, than in the words of St. Paul. Introducing the triumphant hymn that concludes chapter 8 of his Letter to the Romans, Paul leads his readers to consider: "If God is for us, who is against us?" (v. 31). Such is his confidence in God's saving action that after cataloging the powers that will not prevail over the one who believes, Paul concludes with the confident assertion that "nothing will be able to separate us from the love of God in Christ Jesus our Lord" (v. 39).

But what is it, exactly, that God has done? What is the grace offered those baptized into Christ Jesus? And how does one express the consequences of this grace in the lives of "God's beloved, who are called to be saints"?

To describe the effects of God's love in Christ Jesus and the new relationship God establishes with the believer through that love, Paul

132

requisitions the idea of adoption. That the word occurs only in the Pauline corpus—and there a mere five times[7]—belies its significance. For adoption brings us to "the very centre of the Christian message"[8] and, as "one of the chief constituent doctrines of the New Testament Theology," is the "climax of the redemptive process in its objective aspect, . . . the supreme illustration of grace, and the highest reach of glory for the redeemed."[9] Adoption is "the most comprehensive concept that Paul employed of man's restoration,"[10] and a "more vivid way of describing a man's new status 'in Christ' could hardly be conceived."[11] The concept of adoption describes the new relationship to God that baptized men and women enjoy "in a more comprehensive sense [than justification]": adoption is, furthermore, "the fruit, the consequence of the reconciling, redeeming appearance of Christ (Gal 4:5), it is the reconciliation accomplished by God himself, it is its realization."[12]

Such august claims for a one-word concept might seem at first a pedagogue's hyperbole, particularly as the mention of adoption in contemporary culture often invites pity and chagrin (and, occasionally, feeble attempts at humor) more than wonder or thanksgiving. But for Paul adoption *was* a word of wonder—as it was true reason for the Christian to be grateful. For adoption spoke of boundless grace, of the conquest of freedom over slavery, of promised inheritance and confident expectation. Through adoption, because of adoption, the Christian received the gift embracing and completing all given to those baptized in Christ Jesus: the gift of the Spirit, through whom God may be addressed as *Abba*, Father.

As is evident, the concept of adoption plays significantly in Paul's description of the effects of baptism. We will consider his exposition of the Christian's adoption by God in some detail in the following chapter. First, however, as regards a model informing a theology of baptism, I suggest some advantages the concept of adoption enjoys.

[7]Rom 8:15, 23; 9:4; Gal 4:5; Eph 1:5. The Greek word for "adoption," *huiothesia*, literally means the "making" or "placing of a son."

[8]M. Bernoulli, "Adoption," *Vocabulary of the Bible*.

[9]Thornton Whaling, "Adoption," *Princeton Theological Review* 21 (1923) 223.

[10]Daniel J. Theron, "'Adoption' in the Pauline Corpus," 14.

[11]L. H. Marshall, *The Challenge of New Testament Ethics* (New York: MacMillan, 1947) 259.

[12]Herman N. Ridderbos, *Paul: An Outline of His Theology*, trans. John Richard De Witt (Grand Rapids: Eerdmans, 1975) 199.

Adoption: A human word, a human experience

To speak of children's participation in the death and resurrection of Christ or of their spiritual rebirth as we celebrate their baptism is by no means out of place. The image of death and resurrection accurately predicts the road these young Christians must and will travel, just as rebirth properly describes the spiritual effects of the sacrament. These are not the only truths confronting us as we present our infants for baptism, however—nor do these models necessarily offer the images that address most effectively the mystery that draws family, community, and infant to the font.

One's experience in life can certainly lead one more deeply into the truth, and this is one reason why the models of death and resurrection and rebirth speak strongly and well to adult catechumens and the communities supporting them in their conversion. But the experience of death and resurrection may be particularly difficult to embrace when the baptismal waters are stirred not to initiate adults who have concluded the long and arduous journey of their catechumenate (and whose lives presumably have already seen their share of deaths and resurrections) but for those who have emerged only recently from their mother's womb and are far from embarking upon a conscious and determined faith journey of their own. While death and resurrection and spiritual rebirth are central to Christians' lives, perhaps these concepts are more often discussed in seminaries and seminars than they are experienced in the lives of many. These models speak volumes of theological truths, but they often seem to speak only to, or are only spoken by, theologians, liturgists, and "religious specialists." I suggest that the concept of adoption not only allows us a better understanding of what it is we do when we baptize our infants but also yields some gain for the Church's own self-understanding as well.

As is the case with the baptismal models of death and resurrection and spiritual rebirth, a theology of adoption enjoys both scriptural roots (as we shall see in the next chapter) and a regular place in the Church's understanding and explanation of the effects of baptism. The General Introduction to the Church's rites of initiation relates that through baptism Christians "receive the Spirit of filial adoption" (1), are brought "to the dignity of adopted children" (2), and are made "sharers in God's own life and his adopted children" (5). This is, of course, sound theology, a theology central to any exposition of the meaning of Christian baptism. But perhaps a unique advantage recommending adoption as a model or motif that helps us unravel the mystery of our baptism is that the concept speaks theological truth by suggesting first a reality and experience with which many are familiar.

We will examine Paul's use and the theology of adoption in the following chapter. But our theological interest should not lead us to dismiss too quickly the human understanding or experience of adoption. For adoption is a "human" word, a word that refers to or recalls what is for many people an actual experience. Neither abstract nor speculative, neither elusive nor foreign, adoption is a concept—an experience—many can claim as their own. Couples and individuals *have* adopted, daughters and sons *have been* adopted, and there are likely few people who do not know an adopter or the adoptee.[13] This is one advantage in constructing a theology of baptism based upon adoption: the concept is for many more immediately and naturally associated with actual experience than are the concepts of death and resurrection and spiritual rebirth.[14]

By considering the human experience of adoption prior to its theological exposition, we are following Paul's own methodology. For whatever the cultural or religious background from which Paul drew the metaphor, his theological teaching was strengthened by the familiarity with the concept his audience would have had. And so as we consider an adoption-based theology of infant baptism, we begin with the prospect that our familiarity with this human experience will assist our theological reflection.

A second advantage is that as it is ordinarily infants and young children who are the recipients of adoption, the concept informing our model is associated naturally with the very age group with whom we are concerned in this work. Furthermore, any theology of baptism is effective to the extent that it addresses both the immediate

[13]A 1992 newsletter of the National Committee for Adoption (Washington, D.C.) states: "About 25,000 American infants are adopted each year compared with the estimated 2 million couples and individuals who wish to adopt."

[14]Again, one could scarcely claim that an understanding of baptism based upon the models of "participation in Christ's death and resurrection" or "spiritual rebirth" is inadequate, and such is certainly not the claim here. I intend not to criticize these models but to suggest and support an additional (and traditional) model for the sacramental initiation of infants and young children that I believe addresses more directly and effectively the unique character and significance of that celebration.

effects and the continuing effects or fulfillment of the sacrament. Adoption offers clear terms and images both as to "what happens" to the infant or young child at the time of the celebration and as to the lasting privileges granted and the future responsibilities incurred.

A third advantage of an adoption-based initiation theology for infants may contribute also to our understanding and appreciation of the baptism of adolescents and adults. Adoption is a relational concept: it speaks immediately of family, of affiliation and relationship. One is not only adopted *by* a new family in which new relationships are *effected,* one is also adopted *into* a new family and so *affects* the relationships already formed.[15] Adoption readily lends itself, then, to our customary vocabulary of Christian initiation and identity: "children of God," "Our Father," "brothers and sisters in the Lord" and, perhaps, the family as the "domestic Church." And adoption not only effects these relationships but also describes *how* they are effected.

As mentioned above, adoption is for many families and individuals anything but an abstract idea or a theoretical construct. I offer now a brief reflection on the act and experience of human adoption. As will be evident, these reflections on the human perspective prepare us for and parallel the theological considerations we will explore in the following chapter.

Reflections on the human experience of adoption

In offering these reflections I proceed carefully and respectfully. Each act of adoption is unique, as are the relationships each adoption effects. My reflections here are what I consider "reasonably typical characteristics" of the human act and experience of adoption, and I offer them to suggest a clear and common focus for our subsequent discussion. Absent from these reflections are the myriad of legal, financial, medical-genetic, and psychological considerations that often make up the environment of adoption today. Although frequently a part of the reality and experience of adoption in society, these factors do not concern us.[16] The reflections offered here serve and reflect the

[15]This is obviously and certainly also the case when an infant is born "naturally" into a family. One point emphasized by our model, however, is that adoption as an extraordinary (out of the ordinary) act brings about that which would not have been realized through ordinary or natural means.

[16]That adoption is a "human word and experience" is reflected in my belief that at this point few of my readers will be neutral as regards the concept. It is unfor-

nature and purpose of this work: to explore the effectiveness of the concept as a theological model for infant baptism. I do not suggest that a theology of adoption will correspond exactly to society's practice, nor do I claim that Paul's exposition of the Christian's adoption by God parallels in every way our understanding or experience of adoption.[17] My interest is theological reflection and application, not technical blueprinting. That the theological implications underlying the following reflections of the human experience of adoption will be rather obvious in several instances, however, is yet another advantage to considering adoption as a model informing a theology of infant initiation.

The following reflections answer the question, "What in the human act and experience of adoption can assist us in our theological understanding of adoption and in our subsequent approach to the sacrament of infant baptism?"

1. *Adoption, the act by which one is made the child of another, is an act of extraordinary initiative and love.* Obviously all children are born and are brought into their family through the initiative of others. What is unique to adopted children, however, is that their membership in their (new) family is distinct from and independent of their natural birth. Birth is the ordinary and customary way by which one both begins to live and becomes the child of another. Ordinarily, birth gives life *and* family.

Adopted children, however, are not born as the sons or daughters of their parents. They become their parents' children—and they receive them as their parents—only through adoption. Family membership and affiliation for the adopted child is not natural. It is theirs neither by nature nor by right of birth but is initiated and made

---

tunate that the recent, more loudly proclaimed words about adoption revolve around the painful experiences of couples and children waging angry, convoluted legal battles as "to whom the child really belongs." Such publicity does not serve my thesis well. But it does serve as the humble reminder that while the human experience of adoption can assist us in our theological reflection, neither it nor our theological reflection is able to capture fully the wonders of God's adopting Christians as sons and daughters.

[17]One obvious difference is that adoption in the world of Paul ordinarily involved male adolescents or young male adults rather than infants or young children of either sex. Encyclopedias of religion or theology and exegetical commentaries on the Pauline texts will provide sufficient background for the general reader.

possible only through a separate and deliberate decision that this child will be made a member of this family. One "makes" a son or daughter because one desires a son or daughter—and because son or daughter needs a mother and father.

This is the extraordinary nature of the act of adoption. Apart from their adoption, these children would not enjoy nor could they claim that which belongs by nature and right of birth to "children by blood." Adopted children do not have parents or family, siblings or home; all these are given them.

2. *Adoption delivers a child from an unfortunate or tragic situation and into an advantageous or favorable situation.* The situations and circumstances that warrant (and in many instances compel) the removal of children from their original homes are legion, and are often of the nature that it is no exaggeration to describe the removal of the child as a "deliverance" (for example, parental neglect, abuse, or death; wars and famines). Furthermore, it is often the unfortunate situation or environment the child is in—and the utter helplessness and inability of the child to resolve the situation—that moves the parents to initiate the adoption.

Adopted from a given situation, children are adopted and brought into a new one. This new situation or environment is, most of all, a new life and, presumably, a better life: a life that supposes, if it does not also promote and reasonably promise, a future more fulfilling than would have been likely without the adoption. Referring again to the extraordinary act that adoption is, adopted children are not "rescued" because they have a father or mother; they are adopted so that they *will have* a father and mother and thus be rescued.

3. *Adopted children are identified and affiliated with—they are incorporated into—their new family.* This identification and incorporation includes but ideally extends beyond legal considerations such as place of residence, responsibilities of parents, or the (usual) assuming of the adopting family's surname. Adopted children become—they *are*—members of the family. Brothers and sisters in the family are their brothers and sisters, the elders of the home are their parents.[18]

---

[18]The point of this reflection is illustrated well by my own experience with adopted individuals, many of whom understand—but instinctively bristle at—the phrasing of the question "Do you know who your *real* parents are?"

4. The objective fact and act of the adoption is ordinarily irrevocable, but the adopted child's freedom of will always remains intact. Adoption brings children into a present and offers them a future marked by new directions and new hopes, but it does not coerce that future. While adoption effects deliverance from an unfortunate situation into one that is better, it does not guarantee that the full benefits of this new life will be realized or accepted. Adopted children are freed from their past—and as they grow into childhood, adolescence, and adulthood they remain free to refuse or reject the status, benefits, and obligations effected by their adoption.

5. While adopted children may have always known the fact of their adoption, they grow only gradually into the understanding and appreciation of what their adoption has meant—and continues to mean—to them. Reflection on the likely differences in their lives effected and influenced by their adoption will develop as they grow into adolescence and adulthood and according to their education and experience. Twenty- or forty-year-old adults reflecting upon (not "finding out about") their adoption as an infant or child will (hopefully) understand and appreciate the significance of their adoption with a greater clarity and depth than would be possible in their reflections at the age of ten or fifteen. And these reflections will be aided to a greater or lesser degree by the way in which their adoption is gradually and regularly explained to them by their parents.

In the preceding chapter we reviewed a theology of childhood that described the Christian as a once and future child and that considered the child the prototype of those to whom the kingdom belongs. In conjunction with this we observed something of a normative value for the life of the Church in the sacramental initiation of infants and young children.

In this chapter I expressed my belief that our customary understandings of baptism as participation in the death and resurrection of Christ or as spiritual rebirth may not always serve the baptism of infants and young children as well as they do the baptism of adults. Attempting to highlight the unique character of the sacramental initiation of the young, I introduced the concept of adoption. Suggesting several advantages to considering adoption a suitable concept from which to approach the baptism of infants and young children, I concluded by discussing several characteristics of the human act and experience of adoption.

I turn now to the Pauline letters to explore the theological significance of the concept of adoption: that gracious act by which God has made and claimed Christians as sons and daughters; that grace by and in which we enjoy our status as children of the God who is *Abba,* Father, of us all.

Chapter 8

God's Children by God's Choice:
Adoption in the Pauline corpus

"We may say, then, that the concept of adoption in the theology of Paul belongs to the history of salvation, inaugurated at the naming of Israel as God's son, and continued and perfected in the adoption of men and women into the family of God through the work of Christ and the Spirit."[1]

"We thus become children of God, not according to nature, for it is only too evident that we are born sinners and children of wrath, but by an adoption which, unlike human adoption, is not a legal fiction, but effects a profound transformation, a true assimilation with Christ, who is made the elder brother of an immense family."[2]

I remarked in the preceding chapter that although "adoption" (*huiothesia:* the making or placing of a son) occurs in the New Testament only in the Pauline corpus (and there a mere five times), the concept has considerable theological weight. To cite again the words of only one authority: a "more vivid way of describing a man's new status 'in Christ' could hardly be conceived."[3]

My presentation of Paul's exposition of the Christian's adoption by God is by no means exhaustive.[4] As it is in Romans that "adoption" occurs most frequently and in a more comprehensive and varied

---

[1]James I. Cook, "The Concept of Adoption in the Theology of Paul," 142.

[2]Francois Amiot, *The Key Concepts of St. Paul,* trans. John Dingle (New York: Herder, 1962) 158.

[3]Marshall, *Challenge of New Testament Ethics,* 259.

[4]Readers interested in further detail or in the more technical aspects of the scholarship surrounding Paul's use of adoption are directed to the bibliography. Most commentaries on the Pauline letters offer summaries of the scholarship and the significance of the concept. Among the more recent and accessible are Joseph A. Fitzmyer's *Romans,* Anchor Bible 33 (New York: Doubleday, 1993) and Frank J. Matera's *Galatians,* Sacra Pagina 9 (Collegeville: The Liturgical Press, Glazier, 1992).

sense, we will begin with and analyze that letter in some detail. After reviewing the Romans text, we will briefly consider the mention of adoption in Galatians and in the pseudo-Pauline Letter to the Ephesians. Our review is directed toward the premise of this second part of our work: that adoption serves as a particularly credible and helpful model from which to approach the baptism of infants and children.

PAUL'S LETTER TO THE ROMANS

"But now, apart from law, the righteousness of God has been disclosed, and is attested by the law and the prophets, the righteousness of God through faith in Jesus Christ for all who believe. For there is no distinction, since all have sinned and fall short of the glory of God; they are now justified by his grace as a gift, through the redemption that is in Christ Jesus" (3:21-24).

Paul could well boast of the prominence history has accorded his letter to "all God's beloved in Rome." "Scarcely an area of theological development has not been influenced by its teaching," as one exegete has remarked, adding that the contribution of Romans to Western Christian thinking is "inestimable."[5]

We consider the verses introducing this section a summary of the doctrinal section of the letter (chs. 1–11), which emphasizes that justification is gained not through observance of the Law but only through faith in Jesus Christ. "[A]ll have sinned. . . ; they are now justified by his grace as a gift, through the redemption that is in Christ Jesus." This justification affords Christians freedom from death and sin (5:12-21), from the self through union with Christ (6:1-23), and from the Law (7:1-25).[6]

"Freedom," "life," and "Spirit" are among the words commentators frequently use to describe the thought of Romans 8, the chapter in which we find two of the three occurrences of "adoption" in the letter. Two observations reflect the relationship among these three concepts and lead us to verses 14–17, Paul's first description in Romans of the Christian's adoption by God.

[5]Joseph A. Fitzmyer, "The Letter to the Romans," *The New Jerome Biblical Commentary* (Englewood Cliffs, N.J.: Prentice-Hall; Simon & Schuster, 1990) [12]; bracketed numbers refer to the paragraph numbers of his text.

[6]Fitzmyer, "Romans," *NJBC* [1–13], provides a helpful summary of the characteristics, nature, and structure of the letter, upon which we here rely.

142

1. *Christian life is lived in and by the power of the Spirit.* The Spirit orders the new life of the Christian, much as the word "spirit" governs chapter 8. This new life is "grounded in the act of salvation and [stands] in the sphere of the Spirit, in which the will of God is actually fulfilled as it could not be under the rule of the law."[7] Law remains a part of the Christian's new life, but "law" has been redefined: Christians now embrace the only true law "so that the just requirements of the law might be fulfilled in us" (v. 4). To embrace this true law is to embrace the freedom of the "law of the Spirit of life in Christ Jesus" (v. 2),[8] which enables the believer to "walk not according to the flesh but according to the Spirit" (v. 4).[9] The old Law, perverted by the weakness of the flesh, served only as the vehicle of condemnation; now the "law of the Spirit," effected by the power of God, is *the* instrument of salvation. Through the Spirit "God's commands have become God's enablings,"[10] and, as Paul will triumphantly conclude this chapter, "[nothing] will be able to separate us from the love of God in Christ Jesus our Lord" (v. 39).

2. *This new life is one of radical—though not autonomous—freedom.* Delivered from the slavery of the Law, Christians remain bound to the goal proposed by the Law. Christians *are* free but not "carelessly free." Their new life in the Spirit, given as gift, is given for purpose. Throughout this chapter Paul acknowledges this tension between promise and fulfillment, between grace as gift and grace as exacting a price. Christians remain debtors, but their debt is of those raised from the dead: the debt to "make use of the Spirit received."[11] Christian freedom is not autonomous freedom: it is freedom not in and to oneself but in and through Christ Jesus to the Spirit. Christians are

---

[7]Ernst Käsemann, *Commentary on Romans,* trans. Geoffrey W. Bromiley (Grand Rapids: Eerdmans, 1980) 215.

[8]Thomas W. Manson, "Romans," in *Peake's Commentary on the Bible,* eds. Matthew Black and H. H. Rowley (Camden, N.J.: Nelson, 1964) 946, describes the relationship of the three laws mentioned in these opening verses: "The matter can be put thus: Moses' law has right but not might; Sin's law has might but not right; the law of the Spirit has both right and might."

[9]Fitzmyer, "Romans," *NJBC* [82], describes "those who live according to the flesh" (v. 5) as those whose "motivation in life is a self-centered interest," and remarks that verses 5–13 develop the contrast between life in the flesh and life in the Spirit.

[10]F. F. Bruce, *Romans* (Grand Rapids: Eerdmans, 1985) 153.

[11]Fitzmyer, "Romans," *NJBC* [83].

obliged to change their obedience from the flesh to the Spirit, from the Law to God's graciousness, from addiction to self to craving for God. "Possessing the Spirit is at the same time a fresh obligation to be loyal to the Spirit."[12]

That Christian freedom obliges one "to make use of the Spirit received" is not to exchange one set of chains for another. The Spirit leads the Christian into a new relationship with God, a relationship marked by the status and privileges of *huiothesia*, of sonship.[13] Christians are no longer slaves, for they "have received a spirit of adoption."

"For all who are led by the Spirit of God are children of God. For you did not receive a spirit of slavery to fall back into fear, but you have received a spirit of adoption. When we cry, 'Abba! Father!' it is that very Spirit bearing witness with our spirit that we are children of God, and if children, then heirs, heirs of God and joint heirs with Christ—if, in fact, we suffer with him so that we may also be glorified with him" (vv. 14–17).

Paul's first mention of adoption in Romans proceeds directly from the "beneficial debt" of living in the Spirit. Those who live by the Spirit are those led by the Spirit: they are children of God.

That the Christian is led by the Spirit implies the diminishment of neither human obligation nor freedom.[14] To *act* as a child of God is the Christian's duty; to *be* a child of God is, first and always, the Christian's gift. The spirit of slavery inexorably leads humanity into the ever-churning fear and futility of self-justification. But this spirit of slavery is conquered by the Spirit of adoption, the act through which one receives full, restored sonship.

The human person is a child of God, of course, created and sustained even in life according to the flesh by the Father. But the dig-

[12]Emil Brunner, *The Letter to the Romans: A Commentary,* trans. H. A. Kennedy (Philadelphia: Westminster, 1959) 71.

[13]I cite Matera's remark in his *Galatians:* "[*Huiothesia* has] been translated as . . . 'sonship' in order to be faithful to the example the Apostle employs. Paul's thought here, however, is not gender exclusive" (151, n. on v. 6).

[14]"Led by the Spirit" (literally, "to be led") is one of many phrases in these verses that has received considerable exegetical attention. Most commentators consider the phrase as expressing both the Spirit's action and the Christian's co-operation with that action. Fitzmyer, *Romans,* Anchor Bible, remarks: "Being 'led by the Spirit' is Paul's way of expressing what later theologians would call prevenient grace, the initiative that God's favor takes in guiding Christian life" (499, n. on v. 14).

nity and status of sonship have been rejected and abandoned by those living according to the flesh. While the slave is destined to fall back into fear, the prodigal son falls only into the loving embrace of his Father, who restores him fully to the dwelling and privileges of the Father's house. Placed by God as son, the Christian's immediate privilege is to call God "Father."[15]

Although it is usually the Gospel of John to which the wry remark "a theology of prepositions" is attributed, such is also partly the case here. Many would consider the *NRSV* translation misleading at this point, and so we adopt the preferred translation which reads, "you have received a spirit of adoption by [or in] which we cry, 'Abba! Father!'"[16] Christians address God as Father through the guidance and gift of the Spirit: "[W]hen they address God by the same name as Jesus used [*Abba*], it is evident that the Spirit that animated Jesus has taken up residence in their lives."[17]

That Christians can address God as "Abba" is both the privilege and proof of their adoption. And that it is the gratuitous initiative of God that overcomes humankind's futile efforts for justification again is stressed: "[The Spirit] does not lead us to cry, 'I am God's child.' Rather, he leads us to call upon God as Father, to look away from ourselves to him who established the relationship."[18] Exegetical discussion over the word "abba" notwithstanding, it is clear that "abba" was the distinctive address used by Jesus to address his Father. Other than in Galatians 4, "abba" occurs only in Mark's account of Jesus at Gethsemane (14:36), and there as the "cry used by Jesus in the moment

---

[15]Franz J. Leenhardt, *The Epistle to the Romans,* trans. Harold Knight (Cleveland: World, 1957) 215, observes: "The first privilege of the adopted is to be able to call God Father. Although he is of course a son, the sinner has lost the dignity and status of sonship. He has to receive it afresh by a deliberate and gratuitous act of God which restores to life the dead son ('this my son was dead'). Adoption and resurrection overlap, for God manifests His pardoning grace by showing His power to call back into life what was dead and to create out of nothing. Thus He shows Himself to be the God of the promise (ch. 4:17, 25)." Leenhardt's pages 213–15 suggest the Lukan parable as a fine illustration of the consequences of adoption.

[16]Fitzmyer, "Romans," *NJBC* [84], noting that the phrase literally means "in which [or by which] we cry," translates it as "which enables us to cry." His point—and that of similar translations—is the power of the Spirit in the Christian's new life: it is "through the Spirit the Christian proclaims that God is Father."

[17]Bruce, *Romans,* 157.

[18]Everett F. Harrison, *Romans* (Grand Rapids: Zondervan, 1976) 93.

of his supreme earthly confidence in God . . ., [and which] became for Paul even in Gentile communities the mode of address distinctive of Christians."[19] Grammatical variations of particular translations cannot obscure the central point: it is the Spirit who "empowers the Christian's inmost conviction, as one exclaims of God, 'Father!' Without the Spirit the Christian would never be able to utter this cry."[20]

It is the Spirit in and by whom we cry "Abba," and it is the Spirit bearing witness with our spirit that we are children of God. "Bearing witness with" suggests more than that Christians "along with the Spirit" simply acknowledge a fact quite evident. That we *are* God's children is perhaps among the most difficult of truths for Christians to realize and accept. But the Spirit who effects our adoption establishes with us and for us the truth of our status.[21] Through adoption the Christian has two gifts, two dynamic powers: "the Spirit of sonship" and the "Spirit of the acknowledgement of sonship."[22] It is the Spirit in whom we cry "*Abba*, Father," and it is the Spirit who confirms the legitimacy of that appeal.

Led by the Spirit of God we are children of God, and it is the Spirit bearing witness with our spirit that we are God's children. Continuing to develop the consequences the Christian enjoys as a child of God, Paul describes the second privilege of the adopted Christian: "the wealth of his adoptive father is made available to him."[23] The Christian is not only a child of God but, precisely because of and through the Spirit of adoption, is also an heir.[24] To share in the inheritance of eternal life is the point, the divine motive, of the adoption:

[19]Fitzmyer, "Romans," *NJBC* [84].

[20]Fitzmyer, "The Letter to the Galatians," *NJBC* [26].

[21]Fitzmyer, "Romans," *NJBC* [85], explains that "Paul would not mean that an unregenerate person, without the influence of the Spirit, could come to the knowledge of adoptive sonship, so that the Spirit would just concur with the human spirit recognizing this. The preceding context makes it clear that the vital dynamism of the Spirit constitutes the sonship itself and bestows the power to recognize such a status. Now Paul goes further and stresses that the Spirit concurs with the Christian as one acknowledges or proclaims in prayer this special relation to the Father. Paul is going beyond Gal 4:6."

[22]Brunner, *Romans*, 72.

[23]Leenhardt, *Romans*, 216.

[24]Paul directly attributes adoption as the basis of Christian inheritance. See Werner Foerster, "kleronomos. . . ," *Theological Dictionary of the New Testament* (Kittel), trans. and ed. G. W. Bromiley (Grand Rapids: Eerdmans, 1964–) esp. 3:781–83.

"One may say in fact that the aim of adoption is to make someone a beneficiary of goods which otherwise he would have been deprived of. Right is here placed in the service of the heart's generosity. The metaphor borrowed from the juridical domain suits therefore the dispensation of grace. The idea of inheritance emphasizes the gratuity of the wealth received and its transcendence of ourselves: it comes from a source far beyond us and we count for nothing in attaining it."[25]

"The . . . inheritance comes from a source far beyond us and we count for nothing in attaining it." The Christian is a child of God not by nature but by God's choice, by adoption—not by self-acquired merit or title, but by grace. What Christians can claim (a share in God's inheritance) can be claimed only as gift; what Christians have been given (the status and privileges of sonship) have been given only through grace. The relationship Christians enjoy with God is enjoyed only through virtue of the adoption.[26]

We refer again to the tension between gift and response. What is freely offered must be freely and responsibly accepted. Even an inheritance set aside must be claimed. Paul again addresses this tension, observing yet another relationship brought about through God's act of adoption: Christians are "joint heirs with Christ—if, in fact, we suffer with him so that we may also be glorified with him." Led by the Spirit, Christians are led into the Father's house, yet they remain in a world led too easily by a spirit of slavery and that too eagerly follows the flesh. Adoption abolishes the former and formidable chasm between God and humankind—the isolation of a slave from a place at the master's table—but another distance remains: Christians *are* heirs but they have *not yet* received the full glory of the inheritance. Because they are joint heirs with Christ, their share in

[25]Leenhardt, *Romans*, 216. C. K. Barrett, *The Epistle to the Romans* (London: A & C Black, 1991) 154, remarks: "Of course the analogy [to legal practice] is imperfect. Ordinarily an heir enters upon his inheritance only at the death of the testator; but the language of inheriting can be adopted here because in the Old Testament the word 'inheritance' is regularly used of that which God gives to his people (especially the land of Israel)."

[26]Burton H. Throckmorton, *Adopted in Love: Contemporary Studies in Romans* (New York: Crossroad-Seabury, 1978) 75: "A Christian is related to God as a child. *This* relationship is not a *natural* relationship that a human being has with God simply by virtue of being born. It is not a birthright but a relationship that God *gives*, in Christ, to anyone who will receive it. Children of God are children by *adoption*: they have been bought with a price" (emphasis in original).

Christ's sufferings is the inescapable prelude to the full glory to be received.[27]

Paul considers this share in Christ's sufferings quite reasonable, for "the sufferings of this present time are not worth comparing with the glory about to be revealed to us" (v. 18). "Creation waits with eager longing" as well (v. 19), Paul observes: cursed by God because of Adam's sin (v. 20), it will not be a "mere spectator of humanity's triumphant glory and freedom,"[28] but will itself "be set free from its bondage to decay and will obtain the freedom of the glory of the children of God" (v. 21). Christians and creation groan together, but this groaning is sustained by their hope of the future revelation of the children of God. This future revelation eagerly awaited in hope is the context for the second mention in Romans of Christian adoption: "[A]nd not only the creation, but we ourselves, who have the first fruits of the Spirit, groan inwardly while we wait for adoption, the redemption of our bodies. For in hope we were saved. Now hope that is seen is not hope. For who hopes for what is seen? But if we hope for what we do not see, we wait for it with patience" (vv. 23–25).

The apparent contradiction posed by the anticipated adoption here to the adoption already received of verse 15 has led some to question the authenticity of the word in this text.[29] But the future orientation of adoption here is consistent with the eschatological character of the

---

[27]Käsemann, *Romans,* 229, observes: "In all Paul's theology participation in coming glory does not mean that the cross can be dodged. . . . [Paul] confronts [his readers] with the theology of the cross and reminds them that the Spirit who makes Christ present on earth is the very one who imposes on them a pilgrim theology."

[28]Fitzmyer, "Romans," *NJBC* [87].

[29]Bruce M. Metzger, *A Textual Commentary on the Greek New Testament* (London: United Bible Societies, 1975) 517, lists the chief manuscripts that omit the word and reports "adoption" as "a word which copyists doubtless found to be both clumsy in the context and dispensable, as well as seeming to contradict [v.] 15."

Fitzmyer, "Romans," *NJBC* [88], is one who considers the omission preferable (the text then reading: "as we wait for the redemption of our bodies"), since "Paul nowhere else speaks of such sonship as a form of eschatological redemption." He continues: "The Christian is already son of God (cf. 8:15), made so by the Spirit received. With such 'first fruits,' the Christian looks forward to the full harvest of glory, the redemption of the body. . . . If, however, 'sonship' is to be retained as the *lectio difficilior,* then Paul would be referring to a phase of it still to be revealed." The majority of exegetes consulted prefer the inclusion of the term.

second half of Romans 8 and is a natural piece of Paul's continuing depiction of Christian life as lived in tension between gift and acceptance, status and expectation, promise and fulfillment. The shift from an adoption received to one eagerly awaited betrays no theological contradiction but reflects well the human condition Paul had acknowledged earlier: "For I do not do the good I want, but the evil I do not want is what I do" (7:19).[30] Christians are heirs of God and joint heirs with Christ, but the ultimate bestowal of their inheritance—the full realization and manifestation of their status as children of God—lies in the future redemption of their bodies.[31]

Baptized in Christ Jesus, Christians enjoy the status and privileges of sonship: they are children of God and may confidently address him as *Abba*. The fulfillment of their adoption, the full transformation

[30]Käsemann, *Romans*, 237: "[T]here is no real contradiction, since Paul never regards the gift of salvation as an undisputed possession. He always characterizes it dialectically as now present and now future in order to balance its reality with its vulnerability on earth. Sonship will be unassailable and complete only in the [redemption of the body]." In an earlier section of his work, Käsemann—commenting upon the first occurrence of "adoption" in 8:15—had remarked: "Sonship is not always present . . . as though the Spirit were simply confirming it. . . . Imparted by baptism, it is expectation of and present participation in the [kingdom]" (p. 227).

[31]The phrase "redemption of our bodies" has merited the attention of exegetes. Bruce, *Romans*, 165, explains that "[it] is the resurrection, a theme on which Paul had recently enlarged in 2 Corinthians 4:7–5:10. The same hoped-for occasion is called 'the day of redemption' in Ephesians 4:30, where believers are said to be sealed with the Spirit in view of it." Matthew Black, *Romans* (Grand Rapids: Eerdmans, 1973) 117, believes that "[t]his can only mean our 'complete adoption,' i.e., transformation into 'sons of God'; and this is further defined as the 'deliverance' of our body." Barrett, *Romans*, 157, remarks, "Adoption is evidently (cf. v. 15) our final acceptance into God's family, and of this the redemption of our body must be a synonym."

Finally, C. E. B. Cranfield, *Romans: A Shorter Commentary* (Grand Rapids: Eerdmans, 1985) 199–200, addresses both the phrase and (indirectly) the inclusion of *huiothesia* in verse 23: "The clue to the right understanding of this is provided by v. 19 ('is waiting for the revelation of the sons of God'). We are already sons of God (vv. 14 and 16), but our sonship is not yet manifest. We have been adopted, but our adoption has yet to be publicly proclaimed. It is the final public manifestation of our adoption which is meant by 'our adoption' here (contrast the use of the word in v. 15). [The phrase 'the redemption of our bodies'] interprets 'our adoption.' The full manifestation of our adoption is identical with the resurrection of our bodies at the Parousia, our complete and final liberation from the effects of sin and death."

of their earthly life and the reception of eternal life that has been pledged, lies in the future. In 1 Corinthians 13:12, Paul writes, "For now we see in a mirror, dimly, but then we will see face to face. Now I know only in part; then I shall know fully, even as I have been fully known." The Christian now enjoys the first fruits of the Spirit, the mirror—the pledge and guarantee—through which can be dimly glimpsed all that awaits those adopted as God's children.

Paul continues to emphasize the Spirit's empowering leadership in the life of the Christian. The Spirit "helps us in our weakness" and intercedes for us (vv. 26–27), thereby enabling that which would otherwise amount to further and futile human claims to God's love. The implications of adoption support the key argument of Romans: Christians have no need to claim God's love, for God has claimed them in Christ Jesus as his own.

The ways and means of God is a theme that will recur in chapters 9–11. Here Paul declares that "all things work together for good for those who love God, who are called according to his purpose" (8:28). Manuscript inconsistencies complicate a precise interpretation, but Paul's principal argument remains intact: "God's purpose and plan are what is really behind all that happens to Christians, for he is really in control."[32] Concluding the chapter with a triumphant hymn of praise, Paul summarizes the power of God's loving initiative as manifested in the Christian's adoption. To his fellow Christians—adopted children, heirs of God, and joint heirs with Christ who now eagerly await the full manifestation of their adoption, the redemption of their bodies—to these and for these does Paul boast: "If God is for us, who is against us? . . . [Nothing] will be able to separate us from the love of God in Christ Jesus our Lord"(vv. 31, 39).[33]

Paul's tone changes dramatically as he begins chapter 9. Painfully aware that the Israelites, his "own people," his "kindred according to the flesh" (9:3) have turned from God's love in Christ Jesus, his grief transcends that caused by personal or familial ties. For the Israelites are, above all, God's people by choice: "They are Israelites, and to

[32]Fitzmyer, "Romans," *NJBC* [90].

[33]Käsemann, *Romans,* 246–52, thoroughly analyzes the relationship of verses 31–39 to Romans 8 and concludes: "Thus the conclusion, which emphatically at the end of v. 39 again refers to true salvation in liturgical predication of Christ, provides us not only with a summary of the preceding chapter but also with the sum of Paul's theology."

them belong the adoption, the glory, the covenants, the giving of the law, the worship, and the promises; to them belong the patriarchs, and from them, according to the flesh, comes the Messiah, who is over all, God blessed forever. Amen" (vv. 4–5).

Chapters 9–11 proceed directly from Paul's exposition of the good news to the Gentiles in chapters 5–8 and address the question inevitably arising in the minds of Jews and Gentiles alike: the apparent contradiction between God's promise to Israel and the actual history of salvation. We will not discuss Paul's argumentation in detail. His intention is to illustrate again the absolute sovereignty God enjoys in salvation history: that God deals with humankind, be it the Israelite nation or those baptized in Christ Jesus, not on the basis of rewarding those who seek righteousness under the law "but on that of justifying those standing in need of a salvation that can come to them only as pure grace. The principle of [Romans] 3:21-24 remains the norm."[34]

The relationship between Romans 1–8 and 9–11 are bound together by Paul's teaching about "the character and deeds of God who is the source of salvation, . . . who elected the Jews and now calls the Gentiles."[35] It is precisely the character and deeds of this God who elected the Jews and now calls the Gentiles that here concern us.

Among the points repeatedly emphasized in our discussion of Christian adoption in Romans 8 was the gratuitous act through which Christians are made children of God. God does for those whom God has chosen what they cannot do, what they cannot earn, for themselves. Christians are led by the Spirit and the Spirit testifies to the truth of their adoption. Through the Spirit Christians address God with the familiarity accorded only God's children, and the Spirit is the pledge, the guarantee of the full inheritance of their adoption, the redemption of their bodies.

Similarly, in Romans 9 the gratuitous and elective power of God is clear, as it has been clear throughout the history of the Israelites. "[T]o them belong the adoption" (v. 4), not because of their merits or achievements but because of the promise and the free choice of God. Sarah and Isaac (v. 9), Rebecca and Jacob (v. 10), Moses and Pharaoh (vv. 15, 17): all were called or used as the potter shapes the clay

---

[34]Brendan Byrne, 'Sons of God' - 'Seed of Abraham': A Study of the Idea of the Sonship of God of All Christians in Paul Against the Jewish Background, 134.

[35]Barrett, Romans, 164.

according to *his* design, "to make out of the same lump one object for special use and another for ordinary use" (v. 21) "so that God's purpose of election might continue, not by works but by his call" (v. 11). To the theme of Romans 3:21-24 may be added Paul's conclusion: "So it depends not on human will or exertion, but on God who shows mercy" (9:16)—a conclusion strikingly similar to Paul's commentary in 8:28: "We know that all things work together for good for those who love God, who are called according to his purpose."

God will be the ultimate victor in salvation history, for God's design and purpose—grace—will triumph over the sin and weakness of humankind. That not all Israelites have accepted their adoption has allowed the Gentiles to hear the gospel and receive their own salvation. And as "through [the Israelites'] stumbling salvation has come to the Gentiles," that salvation will "make Israel jealous" (11:11), a jealousy that will eventually lead to their deliverance—and to the fulfillment of God's plan, "for God has the power to graft them in again" (v. 23).[36] God's saving design will not fail: God's will *will* be done. Concluding chapter 11 and the doctrinal section of the letter, Paul can but marvel at the character and deeds of God, who, according to the divine purpose and design, calls all to be God's children: "O the depth of the riches and wisdom and knowledge of God! How unsearchable are his judgments and how inscrutable his ways! 'For who has known the mind of the Lord? Or who has been his counselor?' 'Or who has given a gift to him, to receive a gift in return?' For from him and through him and to him are all things. To him be the glory forever. Amen" (vv. 33–36).

PAUL'S LETTER TO THE GALATIANS

"We ourselves are Jews by birth and not Gentile sinners; yet we know that a person is justified not by the works of the law but through faith in Jesus Christ. And we have come to believe in Christ Jesus, so that we might be justified by faith in Christ, and not by doing the works of the law, because no one will be justified by the works of the law" (2:15-16).

---

[36]Paul was more successful as Apostle to the Gentiles than he would have been as gardener. Martin W. Schoenberg, "Huiothesia: The Adoptive Sonship of the Israelites," *American Ecclesiastical Review* 143 (1960) 272–73 (and n. 37), is one who observes that the meaning of Paul's analogy, while clear, is inaccurate.

Galatians, among the most passionate and personal of Paul's letters, is often described as the Magna Charta of Christian liberty. Written several years prior to the Letter to the Romans, it is "the first exposé of Paul's teaching about justification by grace through faith apart from deeds prescribed by the Law."[37] We will proceed directly to the mention of adoption in this letter.

The first part of chapter 4 supports the arguments Paul has posed earlier in the letter.[38] Proposing a legal analogy, Paul observes that in the eyes of the law a child is as a slave as regards powers of freedom and disposition (v. 1); although the legal owner of the estate, the child—and the de facto administration of the estate—are "under guardians and trustees until the date set by the father" (v. 2).[39]

And "so with us," Paul remarks, incorporating his point of "before faith came" (3:23-24) into the analogy: "while we were minors, we were enslaved to the elemental spirits of the world" (v. 3). Paul will refer again to these elemental spirits in verse 9 as he berates the Gentiles for their inclination to again submit to the slavery of "beings that by nature are not gods" (v. 8). Whether these elemental spirits represent elementary (and therefore imperfect) teachings now surpassed by the gospel or those powers and elements thought to control humanity, the point is clear: the condition of all humanity before faith came was one of slavery. "But now that faith has come, we are no longer subject to a disciplinarian" (3:25):

---

[37]Fitzmyer, "Galatians," *NJBC* [7].

[38]Byrne, *Sons of God*, 186, explains: "These seven verses do not really go beyond what is asserted in vv. 25, 26 and 29 (cf. [ch. 4] v. 7, which sums up each in turn), but provide the basis for what is there simply *asserted*: that is, that all—therefore specifically the Galatians—are no longer slaves, but are sons who can look forward to the inheritance. Since God willed to confer the inheritance as pure gift . . . , sonship was not a status to be earned, but something to be freely conferred at a later time, following a period of non-sonship, of slavery" (emphasis in original).

[39]To enter into a word study of these verses is to enter into a dense thicket of scholarship indeed. More to the point for our purposes is the observation by Hans Dieter Betz, *Galatians: A Commentary on Paul's Letter to the Churches in Galatia*, Hermeneia Commentaries, ed. Helmut Koester and others (Philadelphia: Fortress, 1979) 203 (and n. 12), that although Paul's comparison "must be taken *cum granu salis*," the point he wants to make is clear: "both, the minor and the slave, lack the capacity of self-determination."

"But when the fullness of time had come, God sent his Son, born of a woman, born under the law, in order to redeem those who were under the law, so that we might receive adoption as children. And because you are children, God has sent the Spirit of his Son into our hearts, crying, 'Abba! Father!' So you are no longer a slave but a child, and if a child, then also an heir, through God" (Gal 4:4-7).

The similarity of Galatians 4:4-7 to Romans 8:14-17 allows us to summarize without extensive repetition the main points concerning the Christian's adoption by God. The status and privileges of adoption are given solely through God's initiative. Adoption is received, not earned by merit. Furthermore, adoption was "*intended by God to be received.*"[40] It is the reason why God sent the Son: to fulfill the promise to Abraham and his descendants in faith (3:7) and to confer upon humanity as gift that sonship which is Christ's by nature. That we might receive adoption as children is "the positive aspect of redemption . . . the ultimate purpose of the Incarnation."[41]

As in Romans, adoption allows the distinctive cry by which Christians address God as *Abba!* Father!—and, as in Romans, grammar complicates the theology. The Greek conjunction introducing 4:6 is understood by many commentators in the causal sense (as reflected in the *NRSV* translation, "because you are children, [therefore] God has sent the Spirit of his Son"), with the understanding, then, that sonship precedes the gift of the Spirit; others, however, interpret the conjunction as a declaration (that you are children . . .), thereby preserving the parallel with Romans 8:15, in which the Spirit is the indicator of sonship. Either approach is grammatically possible; our interest is in the complementary rather than chronological relationship between sonship and Spirit. Paul intends a description of the Christian's new relationship to God, not a systematic treatise on the Trinity. Christians are children of God through the gift of adoption; the Spirit dwells within them and tes-

[40]Byrne, *Sons of God,* 184; emphasis mine.
[41]Donald Guthrie, *Galatians,* Century Bible (Camden, N.J.: Thomas Nelson & Sons, 1969) 120. Ronald Y. K. Fung, *The Epistle to the Galatians* (Grand Rapids: Eerdmans, 1988) 182–83, considers the clause "so that we might receive the adoption as sons" (*RSV* translation) as "expressing the purpose or intended result" of "to redeem those under the law."

tifies to the legitimacy of their cry. "God sent his Son to make sons,"[42] and has sent the Spirit of the Son into their hearts that they, with the Son, may cry "*Abba!* Father!"

The concluding verse in this section summarizes Paul's discussion of adoption, which in effect began in 3:26. As in Romans (and here, as a continuation of the legal metaphor with which he began ch. 4), Paul confirms the change in status, privileges, and consequences effected through their adoption by God. Christians are no longer slaves but children and, because children, also heirs. In contrast to 4:1, "you are no longer a slave but a child, and if a child then also an heir" (v. 7). Again, although not as explicit as in Romans (8:17, 23), the Christian's inheritance is both acquired *and* expected: even an inheritance promised and set aside must be claimed. That Christians "wait for adoption, the redemption of [their] bodies" (Rom 8:23) is, in one sense, the burden of Galatians 5 and 6, in which Paul's ethical exhortations to the Galatians bear a remarkable resemblance to those verses in Romans 8 preceding the first mention of adoption.[43]

The phrase "through God" concluding verse 7 is no afterthought for Paul but is the thought always foremost in his mind: the end of slavery, the freedom of God's children, the reception of the inheritance, the cry *Abba*—all of this is effected not by observance of the Law but only "through God."[44] God is "the source of the inheritance as well as the author of the adoption."[45]

THE LETTER TO THE EPHESIANS

"For by grace you have been saved through faith, and this is not your own doing; it is the gift of God—not the result of works, so that no one may boast" (2:8-9).

---

[42]James D. Hester, *Paul's Concept of Inheritance: A Contribution to the Understanding of Heilsgeschichte* (London: Oliver & Boyd, 1968) 64.

[43]For example, see Gal 5:16-18, 25; 6:8.

[44]Betz, *Galatians*, 212: "[These words] are a reminder of Paul's insistence since the beginning of the letter that the entire process of redemption is the work of God." (In his accompanying note Betz gives twenty-three references in Galatians to this point!)

Guthrie, *Galatians*, 121, remarks that "Paul means to draw emphatic attention to the fact that any inheritance is entirely due to the gracious action of God. He can never conceive of Christian experience apart from the essential part played by the divine initiative."

[45]Fung, *Galatians*, 186.

Some consider the Letter to the Ephesians the "queen of the epistles," while others consider it "the most impersonal letter Paul ever wrote."[46] The introductory hymn, a rambling Greek sentence divided into twelve verses in which occurs the fifth and final instance of adoption in the Pauline corpus, has had mixed reviews of its own. What is "Paul's Magnificat" to one is simply "the most monstrous sentence conglomeration . . . ever met in the Greek language" to another.[47] Having already examined adoption in some detail, I select several major points pertaining to the concept.

Paul begins by identifying himself as "an apostle of Christ Jesus by the will of God" (v. 1). This first of six references to God's will in the letter "underlines a dominant theme in [Ephesians]: God's eternal will and plan to create a community of all men in Christ."[48] The notion of God's will is joined to God's choice in verse 4, as the author writes that God "chose us in Christ before the foundation of the world to be holy and blameless before him in love." The will and choice of God are but two similarities the hymn bears to Romans 8.[49] The next occurrence of God's will follows the mention of adoption in verse 5: ". . . just as he chose us in Christ before the foundation of the world to be holy and blameless before him in love. He destined us for adoption as his children through Jesus Christ, according to the good pleasure of his will, to the praise of his glorious grace which he freely bestowed on us in the Beloved" (vv. 4–6).

As in Romans and Galatians, it is God's love as expressed through his action of placing us as his children—and not any merit or earnings of humanity—that effects our adoption. That God predestined

<hr />

[46]Paul J. Kobelski, "The Letter to the Ephesians," *NJBC* [11], is one of many believing that the letter's content, style, vocabulary, theology, and relationship to Colossians "[argue] for the Deutero-Pauline composition of this letter."

[47]As reported respectively by Martin W. Schoenberg, "St. Paul's Notion on the Adoptive Sonship of Christians," *Thomist* 28 (1964) 69, and Marcus Barth, *Ephesians*, Anchor Bible 34 (Garden City, N.Y.: Doubleday, 1974) 1:77.

[48]Joseph A. Grassi, "The Letter to the Ephesians," *JBC* [13]. Grassi observes that the phrase "will of God" "is not unusual in an introduction, but there are six references to God's will in Eph (1:1, 5, 9, 11; 5:17; 6:6), more than in any other epistle."

[49]Byrne, *Sons of God*, 126-27, notes "a striking reflection both in language and content of the sonship statements of Romans 8." Among the vocabulary similarities he observes are "choice," "predestination," *"huiothesia,"* "predestined us according to his will," and "the 'down payment' of the Spirit."

us in love "for adoption through Jesus Christ according to the good pleasure of his will" bears a striking resemblance to Romans 8:28-30.[50] Just as adoption can not be considered apart from God's love, neither can our adoption be thought of as independent from Christ: "God sent his Son to make sons."[51] As in Romans 8:15, 23, there is tension between the present and future aspects of adoption and redemption. Verse 7 speaks of the redemption we now have through Christ's blood, while verse 14 speaks of our acquiring possession of it in the future. This redemption, spoken of in Romans 8:23 as "the redemption of our bodies," is in verse 7 defined as the "forgiveness of our trespasses" (present), while in verse 14—as in Romans 8:23—the Holy Spirit is the guarantee or "pledge of our inheritance." While the NRSV translates verse 7 literally as "In him we have redemption through his blood, the forgiveness of our trespasses, . . ." one commentator renders the opening phrase as "we possess freedom," contending that it better emphasizes the "boastful assertiveness of each one of the key words used"; and as verse 7 is "a statement about the present rather than a remote past or future," it has "a triumphant ring."[52] The future orientation or result of God's act of adoption is also emphasized by the mention of the inheritance in verse 14.

The word "possession" in verse 14 has several nuances: "act of saving or preserving life," the act of "acquiring some good," or the "state of possession" itself.[53] As to these possible meanings, Marcus Barth offers an interesting perspective on the relationship between the adopting God and the people God claims:

[50]Barth, *Ephesians*, 105–9, warns against understanding "predestination" as an absolute determinism. Among the points he emphasizes is that the election by God requires response and that it is Christ who is the means or instrument of the election. Grassi, *JBC* [14], observes: "It is not a question of individual predestination but of a selected brotherhood of sons to be saved through Christ. Salvation comes to the believer in and through a community in Christ, not precluding individual salvation by God in some other manner."

[51]Barth, Ephesians, 82–83: "The election of men by God and his outgoing grace are inseparably connected with God's warm and personal relation to Jesus Christ. And election cannot be separated from love—or else another election is spoken of than the one discussed in the overture to Ephesians."

[52]Ibid., 83. Barth comments on "the presence of the future" on pages 115–19, citing numerous passages in Ephesians that "support realized eschatology *and* the future coming of salvation" (116; emphasis in original; see also nn. 239–43).

[53]So Barth, *Ephesians*, 97, who also provides the appropriate scriptural references.

"A decision for but one of these meanings appears unwarranted. However, if only *man's* enrichment were focused upon, the breadth of the contents of Eph 1:14 would be reduced. The reference in 1:14a to inheritance ('what we shall inherit') shows sufficiently that man will be enriched. Both verses, Eph 1:11 and 14, add to this a hint that God is gaining something for himself too: a people that praises his glory. In blunt terms: *God is not only spending, he is also earning. Man is not only a receptacle that must remain passive; he is also to live actively.*"[54]

The idea that God gains from adopting us as children and making us heirs may be inferred from our previous considerations of adoption in Romans and Galatians: the very idea of inheritance suggests, after all, that one does not set aside a treasure for one *not* loved. "God gains" when those whom he has called live in God's love, not under God's fear. Romans 8:28-30, cited above, also speaks of this. Here though, at least in Barth's commentary, it is clear that if the children God has made beneficiaries use their inheritance wisely, God benefits from the adoption as well. God sent the Son to make *more* sons: that God might see and love in us what God sees and loves in Christ.[55]

OBSERVATIONS FOR A THEOLOGY OF (INFANT) BAPTISM

We have considered the act of adoption, that act through which Christians become "God's children by God's choice." From our review of the Pauline texts I offer the following observations, which will accompany us in the following chapters.

1. Adoption speaks first of the initiative of God, and portrays the utter benevolence of grace in a particularly articulate way. The Israelites were chosen as God's people because of God's love for them, a love that preceded their response to that love. The letters to the Romans (3:21-24), Galatians (2:15-16), and Ephesians (2:8-9) emphasize that justification comes through faith in Christ Jesus: justification is the gift of God, not the result of works. Adoption is not earned by merit, but is received as gift; it is occasioned by grace, not acquired as reward. God bestows divine grace, chooses and elects—adopts and claims God's children—according to God's designs and purposes.

[54]Ibid.; emphasis at conclusion of citation mine.
[55]*Roman Missal*, Preface of Sundays in Ordinary Time VII.

"Christians are not born, they are made," and it is through adoption that God makes them sons and daughters—a status among others and a relationship with God to which they have no natural right or claim. The Christian becomes God's child only by virtue of God's gift, through God's act of adoption.

2. *Adoption is deliverance and liberation.* Adoption delivers Christians from a spirit of slavery to the law of sin and death and effects for them the freedom to walk according to the Spirit. To allow oneself to be led by the Spirit is not to exchange one set of chains for another, for through adoption the law of condemnation is overcome by the law of saving grace. While slaves are destined to fall back into fear, God's children fall only into God's loving embrace. Through adoption "God's commands become God's enablings."

3. *Through the Spirit, Christians address God as* "Abba." This cry is both their privilege as a children of God and the Spirit-testified truth that they are indeed God's children. And because they are God's children, Christians are also joint heirs with Christ.

Christians are not *similar* to God's children, they *are* God's children and so enjoy the full rights of their adoption: the inheritance of their adopting Father's wealth and a share in the sonship of their brother, Christ.

4. *Adoption is given as gift, and as gift it can be accepted or refused.* To act as a child of God is the Christian's duty; to be a child of God is, first and always, the Christian's gift. And so Christians are heirs, although they have not yet received the full inheritance, the redemption of their bodies. As gifts must be unwrapped, so even an inheritance set aside must be claimed.

5. *Adoption speaks of the enduring faithfulness of God's saving design.* The Spirit of adoption, the power and proof underlying Christian sonship, is also the pledge and promise of that sonship and its inheritance. Christians await the full reception and manifestation of their inheritance, the redemption of their bodies. They wait with longing and with confident hope, for it is the Spirit that bears witness to the truth of their adoption and the promise of their inheritance.

The grace given as gift through adoption is grace given also for purpose. Adoption is both gift and duty: it is the gift of the Spirit, it is the "duty to make use of the Spirit received." Again, even an inheritance set aside must be claimed.

The exegete Franz Leenhardt remarked that adoption is a term "pregnant with meaning." I now attempt to bring to fruition the insights of this and the preceding chapter as I discuss the concept of adoption as a paradigm well suited for our understanding and practice of the baptism of infants and young children.

Chapter 9

Return to Grace:
A theology for infant baptism

"Perhaps infant initiation ought to be seen less as a problem to be grappled with than as an opportunity to be grasped."[1]

"Jesus' attitude toward children is perfectly clear. No one will enter the Kingdom of God, which has come close to us in Jesus, unless he makes a turnabout and returns to the mentality of his beginnings."[2]

"Less a problem to be grappled with, more an opportunity to be grasped." I fully agree with Mark Searle's assessment of infant baptism, for I believe this sacrament—for most Christians their first sacrament—offers the Church a unique perspective regarding all her sacraments, as it also challenges her understanding of God's relationship with humankind. Infant baptism is neither problem nor abnormality but is opportunity and challenge: the opportunity for the Church to see herself, in Nathan Mitchell's words, as "God's once and future child"; the challenge for the Church, the sacrament of God's grace, to rediscover within herself the childlike qualities that clearly mark those to whom God's kingdom belongs. I hope my response in the next two chapters to the American postconciliar discussion of infant baptism contributes to the discussion, clarifies the opportunities, and suggests the challenge.

This chapter revolves around three assertions or considerations, each of which draws from our previous discussion of a theology of childhood, the human experience of adoption, and the Pauline teaching on adoption. The first consideration addresses what is both a characteristic unique to infant baptism and a common criticism of the practice: that the sacrament of faith is conferred upon one who is passive by nature and who, therefore, can neither profess that faith nor respond to the grace offered. Many authors counter this criticism

---

[1]Searle, "Infant Baptism Reconsidered," 50.
[2]von Balthasar, *Unless You Become Like This Child*, 9.

by reminding us that infants are baptized in the faith of their family and ecclesial community. This is certainly true, but there is yet another faith aspect in infant baptism that is often overlooked as the adult Church baptizes her infants—and as she celebrates her other sacraments as well: our belief and hope that in our lives God has not only the last word but also the first.

A second consideration deals with what is often understood at the parochial level as *the* effect of infant baptism: the remission of original sin. Both the difficulties in interpreting that doctrine and in understanding the relationship of original sin to (infant) baptism have received considerable comment in recent years and have occasioned among some an apparent ambivalence toward the teaching on original sin. Affirming the reality and the doctrine of original sin, Searle thought the context necessary for interpreting the doctrine was not always understood. I believe adoption offers a helpful image of this context, portraying as it does the radical difference between one's old life in original sin and the new life one is given through the action of God and the Church. Drawing from the theology of childhood we have considered, this second consideration attempts also to provide some insight and pastoral direction as regards the question of the fate of an infant dying prior to baptism.

A third consideration recalls the ideas that the child is the prototype of those for whom the kingdom is, and that it is in the child that the Christian community most clearly sees the future to which it is called. Developing the idea that it is in the Eternal Child Jesus that Christians find that which must orient their relationship with God, this consideration reminds us that the ultimate challenge of Christian life is to realize fully who we are and whose we are: God's "once and future child."

GOD'S WORD IS FIRST:
AN EXTRAORDINARY INITIATIVE

"Before ever a word is on my tongue
you know it, O Lord, through and through" (Ps 138[139]).

Postconciliar theology has endeavored mightily to move us beyond understanding infant baptism merely as something "done" to the infant. Aidan Kavanagh reminded us that baptism "does not confect faith on the spot and out of nothing," and he and many writers have emphasized that adults play an active and crucial part in the baptism of a passive infant. As we have already observed, the baptism of an infant does not presuppose faith "on the part of the infant recipient but faith on the part of the Christian community"; it "does not bind the infant to faith [but] binds the community to demonstrate a faith so alive and dynamic that the child baptized may eventually find fulfillment in it."[3] But while we must continue to promote the roles and responsibilities of adults, we should not overlook the simple fact that on the first level baptism *is* something infants receive—something "done to and for them." At the celebration of their baptism infants do nothing: they make no promises and profess no faith, and only in the most literal sense do they even "accept" that which is done on their behalf.

Charges of sacramental malpractice based upon this passive nature of infant baptism, however, are simply inappropriate. Far from being "a problem to be grappled with," the fact that the infant "does nothing" quietly proclaims the unique significance of infant baptism— and proclaims a fundamental truth spoken by all our Christian sacraments. Infant baptism is, indeed, "an opportunity to be grasped." For the very nature and circumstances of infant baptism point first to that which underlies and precedes, that which alone makes possible and gives meaning to, any sacramental celebration: that God takes the initiative in the divine-human relationship and that it is God's offering of grace that precedes, sustains, and perseveres beyond every response on our part.

This consideration of God's initiative does not exhaust the theology or celebration of the sacraments, nor does it suggest that sacramental grace is fruitful *ex opere operato* (a claim totally foreign to that teaching). It is to give due consideration, first consideration, to the source and end of theology, sacraments, and liturgy: God's initiative, God's graciousness, God's action and grace. Infant baptism, the first sacrament for most Catholics, signals the first truth about all our sacraments, a truth we often seem to forget as we enter our church to celebrate our adult liturgies or as we leave and go about the business of our adult lives. Infant baptism reminds us that "in the beginning there was God," that this God knew us in the womb, and that even in the case of adults who have come to the faith, it is God who speaks the first word to us and for us: "All sacramental encounter is based on prior and consequent divine initiative, 'an invitation of universal

---

[3]Haggerty, "Adult Initiation and Infant Baptism," 159, cited also in our chapter 2.

and limitless love, the words of a Father calling all his children and wishing them to have the greatest of blessings.'"[4]

This dimension is a reminder and, occasionally, a needed corrective to one of the "stumbling blocks" Mark Searle identified in *some* approaches to the *RCIA*: "the identification of the biblical doctrine of justification by faith with a conscious, once-for-all, 'adult' commitment to Christ as requisite both for salvation and membership in the Church."[5] The adult ordo clearly charges the community with the "conversion therapy" of its catechumens. Also clear is the catechumens' legitimate expectation that the community witnesses for them an active and vibrant faith. As we observed in chapter 1, an adult catechumen responding affirmatively to the question "Do you believe?" testifies that the Church has already been at work in her mission of evangelization by living out in the world what she professes liturgically in her churches. Christians are not born, they are made, and the adult ordo clearly approaches faith as a communal journey, a journey requiring of those seeking the sacrament of faith a mature commitment.

But a subtle truth underlying this process of coming to faith is that even adults do not come to faith through their efforts alone. Just as infants are brought to the font, adults, too, are brought to the faith. Or, more accurately, the faith is brought to them long before they recognize their need for it or are able to accept the demands it will make upon their lives. In light of the commendable postconciliar emphasis on baptism as a sacrament of *faith*, and notwithstanding the splendid reinforcement given this emphasis by the adult ordo, we must not lose sight of the fact that faith, before all else, is gift. "Our" faith is our always inadequate, always wavering response to the perfect love offered us by God. And our hope is our humble realization and acknowledgment that God deems our ability to respond to this great gift of less importance than God's desire to offer it. Karl Rahner has observed that God speaks to an adult "as to a colleague or a partner," but that even though God speaks to the mature "in order to be answered, . . . it is He who inspires the answer." God always "speaks the first word," Rahner insists. "Everywhere and on every occasion when a man meets his God he finds Him because God has first sought him."[6]

---

[4]Irwin, "Important Questions," 12; the citation within Irwin's material is from *Pastoralis Actio*, no. 10.

[5]Searle, "Response: RCIA and Infant Baptism," 328.

[6]Karl Rahner, *Holy Baptism*, 6.

Infant baptism confronts us with the priority of God's word and work, and both the Pauline concept and the human experience of adoption emphasize the priority of this word and work that is so characteristic a feature of the baptism of an infant. Adoption speaks first of the initiative of another: "God sent his Son to make sons," to do for us what we could not accomplish for ourselves. All that humankind attempts to accomplish through its observance of the law— to recover from its many lapses, to reform its ways, to be reconciled in its relationship with God—all of this is accomplished not through human efforts but only at God's initiative and through God's gracious act of adoption. Conversion is the turning around of one's life and the profession of one's faith. But it is also standing still and remaining quiet long enough so that one may realize where one already is and where one already belongs, *because one has already been claimed:* claimed for the Father, claimed by the Father's grace and love, claimed as a member of the Father's family. For those adults baptized as infants, the grace of their continuing conversion as adults is their constant return to the grace first offered them in baptism, the grace to know who they are and whose they are: God's children, God's "once and future children."

We should feel neither theological embarrassment nor sacramental discomfort as we consider the "passivity" of our infants at their baptism—nor should we feign their participation by having adults answer "on their behalf," as did the preconciliar rite.[7] As the Church baptizes her infants, it is the adults who should be silent! It is the strong and the wise, the committed and the mature, the experienced and the competent, who should feel the loss for words. For in infant

---

[7]That the child was "spoken for" in the preconciliar rite is evident in the questions addressed directly to the infant, questions the sponsors would answer on the child's behalf. I addressed the differences between pre- and postconciliar rites passim in part 1; see also my article, "Infant Baptism Reclaimed: Forgotten Truths About Infant Baptism," 36–46. Commenting upon the English translation of the postconciliar rite, Searle, *Christening,* 47–48, observes that the ICEL translation of *RBC* 2 is "inaccurate and slightly misleading," as it adds the phrase (here italicized): "[Children] are baptized in the faith of the Church. This faith is proclaimed *for them* by their parents and godparents, who represent both the local Church and the whole society of saints and believers." *([parvuli . . .] utpote qui in fide ipsius Ecclesiae baptizentur, quae a parentibus et patrinis ceterisque adstantibus proclamatur. Ab his enim repraesentatur tum Ecclesia loci tum universa societas sanctorum atque fidelium.)*

baptism—as in the initiation of our adults, the forgiving of our sins, and the anointing of our sick—it is *God's* word that effects, transforms, reconciles, and comforts. In infant baptism we "do" sacramentally to and for the infant what God has done and continues to do for us throughout all the ages and stages of our once and future childhood: we offer grace as gift.

That our response to and cooperation with this grace—that our "unwrapping the gift"—is essential is brought out well enough in our celebration of subsequent sacraments, as it is also by numerous indications in the *RBC* itself (nos. 3, 5.5, 63, 64). But that our infants cannot respond to what is taking place at their baptism, even that they are largely unaware as to what is taking place, challenges the adult Church to remember that God does not wait until we are willing and able to hear the word of grace spoken before it is offered us (as God's sending of the Word clearly indicates). While we are dependent upon that Word, God's free offering is not conditioned by our ability to respond. Even as adults turn to God in their times of need, they turn not to summon God from the heavens, to pull God into their lives. They turn themselves so that they might see the One whom the younger son saw when he "came to himself": his Father already at the door, patiently yet anxiously awaiting his return. As God has always anticipated our needs,

"the distance in time between His mighty life-giving Word and our living response to it is of no significance. What happens in the baptism of a child? Simply, what is always happening for our salvation is here more clearly revealed: God anticipates our need, His mercy enfolds us before we call upon it. He has already visited us so that we may knock on His door, He has already found us so that we may seek Him. So God already acts within this child in order that, once he has become aware of his own spiritual being, and aware of love, God may already be there as the heaven which arches over this dawn of a new life."[8]

Infant baptism is itself a symbol, a sacrament, of the notion that family life is grace and gift. Every conception and birth is an ordinary, natural reminder of this. But the extraordinary nature of adoption reminds us of just how extraordinary these ordinary manifestations of life and grace are. Whether made a son or daughter of another through adoption or brought into a family naturally through

[8]Rahner, *Holy Baptism*, 7.

birth, every Christian child is adopted: made a Christian child of a Christian family not automatically or by right of birth but only through the conscious decision and the loving initiative of others. The implication here, to which we will return below, is that parents are the first "sacraments" their infants and children receive. They effect their child's first encounters with God and grace, for it is through them that the infant or child is first brought into the Church, as it is from them that the child first learns what faith is.

As we suggest that adoption symbolizes one aspect of marriage and family life, there is one distinction between God's act and the human experience of adoption upon which we do well to reflect. While God's motives are pure, human motives seldom are. Some parents adopt because, due to medical or physiological reasons, they would not otherwise be able to have a child. Or an individual may adopt because, single and desiring to remain so, he or she yearns for the challenges and the relationships that are part of parenthood. It would be unaccountably brash to describe such reasons as altogether selfish, but it is clear that human adoption may be motivated by reasons that are not entirely selfless.

These less-than-perfect motives do not deny the child the benefits of adoption, nor should they be ignored or disguised as we attempt to relate the theological teaching and the human experience one to the other. Although it is usually the similarities the human experience of adoption bears to the Pauline teaching that assists and supports our understanding of a theology of adoption, here it is the discrepancy between the two that instructs us. This is particularly true if we consider what Paul's understanding of human adoption would have been.

In Paul's time and culture, for example, one often adopted to satisfy one's own needs or desires. "Making a son" through adoption would assure that the family's continuity, cult, property, and possessions would be maintained and protected. That the adopted son would benefit from being brought into and "made" a member of the family was acknowledged but was relatively unimportant, more "a peripheral matter that [had] no role in the motivation of the adopter."[9] When one compares this thoroughly human motive of

[9]Cook, "Concept of Adoption," 140. Cook's article provides a concise overview of several of the more technical aspects of adoption and of Paul's appropriation of the term.

adoption with Paul's use of adoption as a theological confession—it is that in which Paul is interested—there is a striking difference. As one scholar has pointed out, "Yahweh does not adopt Israel to meet a need within himself, nor because Israel was an impressive people. . . . Israel, not Yahweh, is portrayed as the chief, if not the sole beneficiary in the relationship, and his adoption of her is an act of his love and grace. And that which was true for Israel (Rom 9:4), Paul applied equally to his Christian readers (8:15, 23; Gal 4:5; Eph 1:5)."[10]

In what clearer way can God's love for us be expressed than through the notion that God adopts us as sons and daughters? And in what clearer way can the Christian family and community symbolize and sacramentally effect this loving initiative of God than by taking the initiative and adopting this *human* child as their *Christian* child? Every human child brought to the font becomes an adopted child. Brought to the font at the initiative of others—an initiative distinct from that which brought the child into the world—the child is claimed for Christ and as a Christian member of and by the family of Christians.

Mark Searle challenged us to see infant baptism not as "a problem to be grappled with" but as "an opportunity to be grasped." I modify his words slightly, and suggest that infant baptism is an opportunity to be *received*. For infants do not grasp the grace of their baptism, just as we adults do not call God's grace upon ourselves no matter how mature our faith, determined our conversion, or meaningful our liturgies may be. Rather than promoting unhelpful caricatures of *ex opere operato* (caricatures not without some basis in both past *and* present sacramental celebrations), our considering infant baptism as the adoption of the infant by God, Church, and family may not only assist us in recovering the humble wisdom of that teaching but may hold us accountable to it.[11]

In no other sacrament is God's initiative manifested as clearly and unmistakably as in the baptizing of infants. And this divine initiative

[10] Ibid.

[11] Irwin, "Important Questions," 12: "In its classical formulation the *ex opere operato doctrine* [is] important in the Catholic sacramental tradition, not for what it may have led to in a minimalism of sacramental theology and practice, but rather for what it means about the priority of God's grace and divine initiative in worship."

is, furthermore, itself sacramentalized and becomes a "visible word" (to use Augustine's phrase), as parents, having brought the child into the world, make with the community a separate and deliberate decision to claim the child for Christ (*RBC* 41). Our understanding that the fruitfulness of our adult sacraments relies not upon our passive presence but on our active participation and response needs to be coupled with the reminder that the sacraments are, first, God's *gift* to us. As words are spoken, water is poured, hands are imposed, and oil is smeared, let us remember that these words and actions sacramentally express and effect the love and grace of the God who "knows every word before it is on our lips, and who has recorded all of our actions before one of them has come into being" (Ps 138 [139]).

CHOSEN FROM THE BEGINNING:
DELIVERANCE AND FREEDOM, LIFE AND IDENTITY

"For all who are led by the Spirit of God are children of God. For you did not receive a spirit of slavery to fall back into fear, but you have received a spirit of adoption. When we cry, 'Abba! Father!' it is that very Spirit bearing witness with our spirit that we are children of God, and if children, then heirs, heirs of God and joint heirs with Christ" (Rom 8:14-17).

The General Introduction introducing the Church's rites of initiation tells us that baptism "rescues us from the power of darkness, and brings us to the dignity of adopted children" (no. 2) and that this first sacrament "washes away every stain of sin, both original and personal, and makes us sharers in God's own life and his adopted children" (no. 5).

Even had the concept not been mentioned explicitly in these citations, adoption illustrates well the transformation, freedom, and status enjoyed by those who have been made children of God. To be adopted is to be rescued and freed. Adoption removes the child from an unfortunate environment (an environment that in some cases is decidedly evil) and delivers the child into an environment that, by contrast, can only be reckoned as free and freeing. This transformation of one's original condition and the freedom it brings about is, in the case of infants, first a deliverance from original sin.

The relationship between baptism and original sin has been addressed by many authors, as we have seen. Their discussion may be summarized by the following statements: (1) many do not consider original sin as the sole (or even primary) motive for baptizing infants; (2) the removal of original sin signals the beginning of one's life in Christ and his Church and is not the final measure of the sacrament's success; (3) points one and two have not entirely alleviated the concerns of the many parents who remain anxious and uncertain about their child's relationship with God prior to baptism.

Concern for the fate of unbaptized infants often makes it difficult to understand infant baptism as the grateful response of family and Church to the initiative God takes in offering the child a share in God's own life. But while efforts to dispel frantic approaches to the font are to be supported, there is no need for a calm or even altogether festive pouring of the baptismal waters to dilute the doctrine or the reality of original sin. As Mark Searle has suggested, even minimal contact with Christians will confirm that the doctrine of original sin is "one of the most obvious truths of the Christian faith."[12]

But the *relationship* of infant baptism to original sin needs to be freed from considering the font an ecclesial emergency room as much as our infants need to be sacramentally freed from the sin. It is obvious that a child in danger of death should be baptized without delay: in such tragic and painful circumstances, baptism is the Christian's instinctive appeal to the God who is at the beginning and the end of all life. While such an "emergency baptism" may be thought of by distraught parents as spiritual insurance, it is perhaps more proper to consider baptism in these circumstances as spiritual *assurance:* the Church's confident expression that God "destined us for adoption as his children through Jesus Christ" (Eph 1:5), and that "nothing, not even death, will be able to separate us from the love of God in Christ Jesus our Lord" (Rom 8:39).

Emergency baptism, however, is not the norm—"the standard according to which a thing is done"—for our infants. We do not baptize our children to purchase for them what has already been bought at great price and yet is offered to all as gift. As we discussed above, infant baptism points first to the God who has always taken the initiative with us and on our behalf. Parental anxieties as to the fate of the unbaptized are understandable and pastoral assurances are necessary—and it is here that a theology of adoption and childhood can be helpful.

---

[12]Searle, *Christening*, 53, cited also in our chapter 2.

A theology of childhood reminds us that infants and children are definitely not "in limbo" as regards their relationship with God. When we baptize an infant we are sacramentally effecting, expressing, and celebrating the adoption of that infant as a child of God. But that sacramental action of family and Church is a response to the gift and grace God has already offered us. If God "created my being and knit me together in my mother's womb"; if God "destined us for adoption as his children through Jesus Christ"; if "God sent his Son to make sons," then the encounter at the font is not the first time God and child are introduced to each other.

The "point" of infant baptism—it is the point of adoption, of taking the initiative on behalf of another—is that neither God, nor Church, nor parents, keep the child "in limbo" until some future time when the child is able or willing to respond to the love already present and presented. Parents love their infants because of who they are *now*, not because of who they might eventually become. And if the precautions many parents today take even as the child is being "knit together in the mother's womb" is any indication, they love their child "*before* now": before the child from their flesh becomes their child in the world.

If it is possible for human parents to offer this generous love even *before* the birth of their child, must we not attribute it as well to the Father whose love everywhere and at all times seeks us out first? God loves the child as he or she is *now:* as child, as one whose "every action is already written in his book and whose every day is decreed before one of them [comes] into being." God encounters the child as *both of them* are *now:* as loving Father, as little child. Although he writes of infants already baptized, Rahner's observation that "a child too can be baptized" even though "underage and incapable of directing his life" would seem to proclaim the victory of God's initiative over the limitations of human chronology: "God deals directly with [the infant]. And because He always forestalls our needs, the distance in time between His mighty life-giving Word and our living response to it is of no significance."[13]

What happens to an infant who dies unbaptized? As we continue to speculate, theological proof and certitude will likely continue to elude us. But in addressing the question of the eternal fate of unbaptized infants, let us recall what it is we celebrate in infant baptism—and let us recall what is present even prior to that celebration.

[13]Rahner, *Holy Baptism,* 7.

We celebrate in infant baptism our belief that the infant is adopted by God as God's child. Parents and Church profess publicly their hope that the child will realize this adoption as gift, as they profess also their desire and commitment to nurture and promote that realization. It is that desire, that faith, that provides the "serious assurance that after baptism [the child] will be given a Catholic upbringing" (PA 15; CIC 868, §1,2°) and so justifies the baptism of this particular infant. And if God's grace is active in the faith and desire of believing parents (as it clearly is), then that grace is already offered to and has *already begun to claim* their infant. Infant baptism is a beginning. But much has already been expressed, much has already taken place, before this beginning:

"The Church is ready to baptize their child, . . . because the parents' desire to have the child baptized is a likely sign that the Spirit has, as it were, earmarked this child: the child is chosen by God. . . .

"The [proper] desire of Christian parents to have their child baptized is already the beginning of the child's grace of baptism. The same Spirit who acts in the pouring of the water is already active in the hearts of the parents, for both the desire and the water mark only the initial stages in the transformation of this child into an adult believer, a mature, Spirit-filled disciple of the Lord."[14]

Unbaptized children die not, therefore, unaffected by or strangers to God's grace. Grace has already entered their lives through the conscious and deliberate decision of their parents—a decision made *in* faith, a decision made *for* faith—a decision that in ordinary circumstances would have been effected and expressed through the sacramental words and actions of their child's baptism. Augustine's battle against the Pelagian denial of the necessity of grace (a heresy not confined to the distant past) and the Church's teaching on the necessity of baptism for salvation do not speak against parents who, as is evident by their very desire to have their child baptized, have no quarrel with either grace or baptism. The Church may not explicitly "guarantee" in so many words that an infant whose baptism was sought but not sacramentally celebrated enjoys the fullness of eternal life. But this reflects more her obligation to emphasize that it is the redemptive work of Christ alone—that which has been done for us by

[14]Searle, *Christening*, 49. See also the writings of Kiesling, cited in our discussion of the third perspective in chapter 2.

another—that effects salvation for all. Church teaching was not developed as a direct response to the extraordinary situation in which infants are deprived of baptism against the graced desire of their parents and through the fault of no one. The action of God—and we have stressed repeatedly that the concept of adoption speaks of the initiative God takes—is certainly able to overcome the various so-called acts of God that might tragically intervene between the moment of a child's conception in the womb and the scheduled moment of sacramental initiation in the Church.

As we minister to worried parents, we do so with the humble acknowledgment that we have yet to master the mind of the Lord or be appointed God's counselor. But our assurances need not appeal to the generally bewildering opinion of limbo, nor must they rely upon complex theories that suggest that an infant at the moment of death "might attain to the use of reason" and so "arrive to spiritual maturity and be enabled to make a choice for God."[15] In the pastoral setting it seems more plausible and altogether responsive for us to remind parents that their infant has enjoyed a relationship with God from the beginning—that, again, the encounter at the font is not the first time God and child are introduced to each other. This is so because their child comes from their marriage (itself a sign and cause of God's grace for them and for the Church), and their desire to have their child baptized is not only their personal response to God's offer of grace to their child, but a response that certainly renders them as instruments—ministers—of that grace. Finally, we may suggest that the embracing grasp of God's mercy and love is seen more often and more convincingly in the history of salvation than is even the partial exclusion from that love and mercy of those of whom Jesus remarked, "Let the children come to me . . . for to such belongs the kingdom of God" (Mark 10:14).[16]

[15]As, for example, Brockett, *Theology of Baptism*, 84, reporting the views of Ladislaus Boros. I cannot here do justice to Boros' well-ordered argument, but whether his systematic reflections would soothe the souls of concerned parents is arguable. My point is that theologically credible pastoral assurances can be offered without recourse to complex theological constructs. For a summary of my remarks in this regard, see my article, "Infant Baptism Reclaimed," 36–39.

[16]We again cite no. 1261 of the *Catechism of the Catholic Church:* "Indeed, the great mercy of God who desires that all men should be saved, and Jesus' tenderness toward children which caused him to say: 'Let the children come to me, do not hinder them,' allow us to hope that there is a way of salvation for children who have died without Baptism."

The above discussion emphasizes that the primary motive for baptizing our infants should be our hope and thanksgiving of who our children become through baptism and not our fear of what might be denied them should they die unbaptized. Through baptism—the sacramental accepting, effecting, and celebrating of God's grace—the sons and daughters of our flesh become sons and daughters of God and are brought into new life in Christ and his Church. We baptize our children because we hope that as the grace of their baptism continues to unfold, they will mature as adult sons and daughters of God, ever learning how to walk according to the Spirit as they eagerly await their full inheritance, the redemption of their bodies (Rom 8:23).

The effects of baptism include the sacramental overcoming of the power of original sin. The link between infant baptism and original sin, however, is not theological speculation as to how God can receive an unbaptized infant but the pastoral application of how the Christian community can receive an infant in such a way that the infant will learn from the beginning the community's ways and means of overcoming the effects of original sin that linger stubbornly in the lives of all. Baptism is the pledge and promise that infants are delivered from original sin—not by slow trickles of water, but by the flood of grace that rushes forth as one is transformed and deliberately brought into the family of God and the Church.

Mark Searle has remarked that "the concept of original sin is derived by way of contrast to the prior concept of the new life of Christ made available in baptism, and is thus to be understood in contrast to the life of the Spirit lived in the communion of the Church."[17] Paul's theology of adoption addresses this concept well. Freed from the spirit of slavery, Christians need no longer fall back into fear and approach God as slaves. Christians have received a "spirit of adoption" and are, therefore, children of God. Through their adoption a new future as one of God's children and as a member of God's family is offered them. Led by God's Spirit, they can put aside their slavish ways and, through the Spirit, address God with the heartfelt, childlike "*Abba!* Father!"

Reflecting upon the human experience of adoption reinforces and paints a vivid picture of this theological truth. Standing alone and lonely, the child is rescued from an unfortunate situation so as to

[17]Searle, "Infant Baptism Reconsidered," 37.

grow in and into an environment that is more beneficial—more graced. Adopted and thus "made" the child of another, she is not merely brought out of her isolation and servitude but is brought into the *home* of her parents. She is not shown the room for guests, for guest she is not. Truly a member of the family, she does not address her parents with the polite titles of Mr. or Mrs. but calls to them with the affectionate words "father" and "mother"—names that define for her and for them whose child she has become and to whom she now belongs.

This is what adoption frees one for: a future, a family, a father and mother—and to be the child of another. Because of the gift of adoption, the adopted child will know the terms and, more importantly, will come to know the relationships of "father" and "mother," of "son" and "daughter," not as theoretical concepts but as the actual and tangible relationships they are meant to be and are meant to effect. One biblical commentator[18] has taken care to link the theological significance of adoption with its human counterpart. I present his words in parallel columns to emphasize his comparison:

"To be adopted as a 'child' by a 'Father' is to be incorporated into a new relationship in which the ultimate meaning of life is revealed, in which life is transformed and recreated. If a lost and lonely child is adopted by a family, then because of belonging in a family, all is not lost if he or she fails in an undertaking. One may accept the failure as a failure and transcend it, because of a more significant relationship one has to parents who love one. The child is enabled to accept himself or herself *with* the failure, because he or she, *with* the failure, has been accepted by others in love. And if a child

"So, also, with the Christian. The Christian as an adopted child is incorporated into a new community, the church, in which God is known as Father. In this community, if the children are indeed children, sorrows are transcended and joys are heightened—life is re-created. The whole community has been adopted by God, called into being by his Spirit, whom all children share alike. All the members of the community were lonely and forsaken and lost until God adopted them into the household of faith. Now they need no longer seek acceptance, for they are already accepted,

[18]Throckmorton, *Adopted in Love*, 75–76; emphasis in original.

who has been adopted *succeeds* in some enterprise, the joy will not be emptied by loneliness but will be increased in the home when it is shared in love."

else they would not be children. Now they need no longer prove themselves, for they are loved *before* they succeed—or fail. The church is the community of the redeemed. This does not mean that its members are morally perfect; it means that they have been given life and have found themselves because they have been found by God."

Through baptism the infant is adopted by God and is brought into God's family. While the Church maintains that "she knows no other way apart from baptism for ensuring children's entry into eternal happiness" (*PA* 13), she also teaches that deliverance from original sin is only the beginning of the meaning of the sacrament: "To fulfill the true meaning of the sacrament, children must later be formed in the faith in which they have been baptized" (*RBC* 3). The meaning of infant baptism is fulfilled in this life not when infants are delivered from limbo but as they are continually liberated from the original, personal, and collective sin that often seems to prevail in our society. This is what baptism frees our children for: to be adopted by and into a home and Church that will form them in the Word of God so that, throughout their lives, that Word may always find a home within them. Adoption frees our children to know God as their Father *from the beginning*, and to address their Father with that cry distinctive both of Jesus and of those who bear his name: those who now belong to God because they belong to God's family of sons and daughters on earth. Because of their adoption they may pray with us, and they pray with the words the Lord himself has taught us (*RBC* 68). Mark Searle has commented shrewdly on the power of the waters of baptism and the transformation of the Christian's condition and status it effects:

"A newly baptized infant is not merely one who is delivered from sin and from the threat of damnation, but one claimed by the irrescindable Word of God to be an adopted child of God, a living member of Christ, a temple of the Holy Spirit. The child in baptism enters into a new set of relationships with God, with the Church, and—we have argued—with its own family. In this instance, at least, water is thicker than blood!"[19]

The Church's waters of baptism *are* thicker than human blood, for they claim our infants as God's own children, inject them with the life-giving blood of Christ, and instill in them the Holy Spirit. The Spirit of adoption given through baptism leads them into a new relationship with the Father and with all whom God has claimed as sons and daughters. Baptism, adoption, the making of Christian children: these sacramental, divine, and human acts literally change the scene.

Who is to say whether this scene will stay changed—or better, whether the grace of this scene will continue to develop and unfold? The most immediate answer is, of course, the infant's parents (in later years the children themselves, as they grow in, and because of, their changed environment and condition). Addressing the parents' role in the unfolding of their child's baptismal grace, I turn again to the concept of adoption.

I remarked earlier that much of what can be said of the human experience of adoption applies also to those who are parents and children by blood. The concept of adoption does not suggest new truths about baptism or parenthood as much as it allows and encourages us to see the "old" or "ordinary" truths in a new and stronger light. By highlighting the bond between parents and child brought about through the special act of another, adoption reminds us of how extraordinary these "ordinary" relationships really are.

While human identity—flesh, bone, blood, and genes—is derived, literally, from one's parents, the same can not be said either literally or figuratively about one's Christian identity. Christopher Kiesling had remarked a generation ago that for a child to belong to a committed Christian community was *not* natural but was, rather, "grace, a gift from God."[20] More recently, Mark Searle spoke much the same and, as had Kiesling, spoke also in the context of the parental and ecclesial responsibilities associated with the baptizing of an infant:

"Christian identity is precisely *not* inherited from Christian parents, . . . the 'accident' of being born into a practicing Christian household is rather an indication of the child's vocation, which it is the duty of the Church to affirm, ratify, and nurture. Consequently whenever a

---

[19]Searle, "Infant Baptism Reconsidered," 45, cited also in our chapter 4.
[20]Kiesling, "Infant Baptism," 621, cited also in our chapter 2.

child is presented for baptism it will be the responsibility of the local community to discern whether this child is certainly called to the life of faith by looking at the faith life of the family. More positively, those with pastoral responsibilities will take seriously the ecclesial character of the family as a household of faith and seek to raise the community's awareness of the sacramentality of the family."[21]

As we celebrate the sacrament of baptism, we neither instantly confect faith nor do we hastily administer an antidote for original sin—which is not to deny that the gift of faith is offered and sin is taken away at that moment. But "that moment" already has a history behind it: the history of a community of faith and of a husband and wife, the fruit of whose mutual love and support "begins again to be continued" through the baptism of their infant. And standing even before that human history is the history of salvation. God does not wait for us to respond before claiming us: "He destined us for adoption as his children through Jesus Christ, according to the good pleasure of his will" (Eph 1:5). "God sent his Son to make sons."[22]

While grace is given and sin is removed—while the environment is changed from one of slavery to one of freedom, from the "kingdom of darkness" to the "kingdom of light" (*RBC* 49-A)—Christians do not fully realize their sacramental adoption through baptism instantly or easily. "Christian identity is precisely not inherited from Christian parents," but must be planned for, nurtured, supported, and effected daily. In the case of an adopted child the child belongs to this family and is the son or daughter of these parents not by nature's process or the right of birth but only through their initiative. It is the task of the adopting parents to continue that initiative so that the gift given through adoption might continue to be unwrapped.

The baptism of a couple's infant (particularly the baptism of their first infant) is not only the sacramental adoption and "making" of a new Christian but also the effecting of *Christian* parents. While the baptism of an infant is not something done primarily for the parents, infant baptism—justified by a well-founded hope that the child will be raised in the faith—confers upon husband and wife the ministry of Christian parenthood.[23]

[21]Searle, "Infant Baptism Reconsidered," 47.

[22]Hester, *Paul's Concept of Inheritance,* 64, cited in our chapter 8.

[23]I repeat here Searle's sensitive comment in "Infant Baptism Reconsidered," 53 n. 44: "The reference to the sacrament of marriage is not intended to preclude the

Understanding Christian parenthood as gift and as ministry is expressed poignantly by Hans Urs von Balthasar's observation that "for a child, his parents' concrete love is not at first separable from God."[24] Many a young child does believe his parents are omnipotent, omniscient, and omnipresent (particularly!) and, in fact, for many children their parents *are* God. These remarks should not lead us merely to chuckle condescendingly at a child's naive misappraisal of his elders but should remind us that parents are for their children the first sacraments, the first encounters with the grace of God they will experience.

This is the gift of Christian parenthood for the child sacramentally adopted through baptism; this is the ministry of Christian parenthood that effects the home as the domestic Church. Parents do not claim God's place in the life of their children but, having adopted them into the domestic Church through baptism, they offer their children—as they claim for themselves—their vocation as *Christian* parents. Bringing their child to the font, these Christian parents themselves symbolize God's initiative as God adopts these little ones as sons and daughters. It is the parents who must teach them the ways and means of the Christian family into which they have been brought and so allow the grace of their children's sacramental adoption to unfold: "Baptism calls explicitly into consciousness of the parents and the Christian community what God would do for this child if they cooperate with him. . . . The benefit for the child in being baptized is his gaining Christian parents *explicitly conscious of their responsibility and pledged to fulfilling it,* and thus an open channel, so to speak, for the grace of God extended to him."[25]

A child is not adopted so that she may go her own way, just as parents do not adopt and then simply wait to see which way their child will go. If parents are unwilling to accept the defining adjective in the phrase "Christian parenthood," then there appears to be little reason to support a request for Christian initiation. Original sin is remitted through the waters, but perhaps we have not emphasized enough the

---

possibility that single parent families or irregular marriages might not de facto be microchurches in virtue of the quality of the faith life and public witness of such families, but merely to underline the sacramental and ecclesial dimension formally established by a marriage witnessed by the Church."

[24]von Balthasar, *Unless You Become Like This Child,* 18.

[25]Kiesling, "Infant Baptism," 622; emphasis in original; cited also in our chapter 2.

lingering effects of that sin. If there is a state of limbo that needs to be addressed in our baptismal catechesis, it is not a hypothetical limbo between earth and heaven but the spiritual limbo existing in quite tangible form in far too many homes today.

"Christian identity is precisely not inherited from Christian parents." Effected first through the sacramental adoption of baptism, God's grace is effected anew each day as parents claim their rightful place as sacraments in the eyes and souls of their children. Christian parents and the Christian community are sacraments, effective signs, of God's own initiative, for they have claimed their children for Christ: they have professed their faith at their children's baptism so that their adopted children might benefit from that which is not theirs by blood, but which is given them only through the loving action of others.

REALIZING THE GIFT:
PROMISE AND FULFILLMENT,
DEPENDENCE AND THANKSGIVING

"For by grace you have been saved through faith, and this is not your own doing; it is the gift of God—not the result of works, so that no one may boast" (Eph 2:8-9).

The distinction between the pledge of the inheritance given through baptism and its full *possession* by the Christian is the tension between the two adoptions of Romans 8. This tension reminds us that our adoption as God's children is both gift and the duty to "unwrap the gift" so that it might be used. "Christians are not born, they are made." And Christians are made, the adult ordo forcefully reminds us, as they continually turn toward and surrender to their faith in the hope that "all who are buried with Christ in the death of baptism [may] rise also with him to newness of life" (*RCIA* 222).

But about surrender to God and dying in the Lord, children are not the only ones who must learn and adults are not the only ones who can teach:

"Then they came to Capernaum; and when he was in the house he asked them, 'What were you arguing about on the way?' But they were silent, for on the way they had argued with one another who was the greatest. He sat down, called the twelve, and said to them, 'Whoever wants to be first must be last of all and servant of all.' Then he took a child and put it among them; and taking it in his arms, he said to them, 'Whoever welcomes one such child in my name welcomes me, and whoever welcomes me welcomes not me but the one who sent me'" (Mark 9:33-37).

"People were bringing little children to him in order that he might touch them; and the disciples spoke sternly to them. But when Jesus saw this, he was indignant and said to them, 'Let the little children come to me; do not stop them; for it is to such as these that the kingdom of God belongs. Truly I tell you, whoever does not receive the kingdom of God as a little child will never enter it'" (Mark 10:13-15).

"Whoever does not receive the kingdom of God as a little child will never enter it." But how does a child receive the kingdom of God?

A child receives the kingdom in the way a child receives everything: in the manner of a child. Children recognize that what they may call theirs is theirs only as gift and whatever they have comes from their depending upon, their receiving from, another. This dependence upon both the gift and the giver is the condition of childhood. The child is the constant receiver: always dependent upon, always receptive to, the love offered by another.

Adults will acknowledge that they, too, depend upon others. But the condition of adulthood seems to urge the quick dismissal of any suggestion of vulnerability, such as the notions of dependence or receptivity would imply. The adult approach to life is, characteristically, the "making of one's own life" by one's own resources, efforts, and powers. What is unique to the child's way of relating to others and to the world, however, is the child's willingness to receive and to depend, a willingness seen readily in the ease with which the child turns to father or mother for food and warmth, shelter and love. Children know of no other approach to life than this, for their relationship with giving parents—and their own identity as dependent receivers—is what has defined them in their own eyes from the beginning:

"When Jesus holds up the child to us as the prototype of those for whom the kingdom of heaven is . . . [what is implied in this saying is] that we can be like children in being receivers and as such carefree in relation to God, those who *know* that they have nothing of themselves on which to base any claim to his help, and yet who trust that his kindness and protection will be extended to them and so will bestow what they need upon them. And thus without glorifying children or failing to recognize the radical insufficiency of their natures Jesus does see in children those whom he can receive lovingly into his heart. This is what he means when he says 'Of such is the kingdom of heaven'" (Matt 19:14).[26]

Von Balthasar has suggested that when Jesus placed a child in the midst of his disciples—thus placing the child also in the midst of an argument as to who among them was the greatest—he instinctively interrupted a typical adult approach to life. For it was Jesus' tenacious clinging to his Father's side, his preoccupation with his identity as God's Son, that perhaps best characterize his earthly life. Resisting the human inclination to define himself by title or defend himself with achievement,[27] Jesus is "the Eternal Child." He never forgot who he was because he always remembered to whom he belonged. And that Jesus "can define himself by speaking about 'my Father,'" von Balthasar observes, "shows to what extent he remains a child even as an adult,"[28] even "at the highest point of his maturity and responsibility with regard to his mission" as the treasured words, "*Abba*, Father," come from his lips.[29] The child is "the prototype of those for

[26]Rahner, "Theology of Childhood," 41; emphasis in original.

[27]One need only recall Jesus' rebuke of the young man: "Why do you call me good? No one is good but God alone" (Mark 10:18). The passage immediately follows Jesus' blessing of the children, cited above in our text.

[28]von Balthasar, *Unless You Become Like This Child*, 33; we provide here the context of the citation: "For Jesus, however, the ground that permeates and unifies everything in his life remains always identical with the concrete and personal reality of the Father, so that he can define himself by speaking about 'my Father.' Precisely this shows to what extent he remains a child even as an adult, and why this permanent characteristic gave him such a unique understanding of childhood and made him exalt so highly the condition of being a child."

[29]Ibid., 41; we again provide the context for the citation, which further supports Mitchell's description of the Christian as God's "once and future child": "What is called for is not at all a form of infantilism, but a repetition of the eternal Son's loving readiness to obey the 'command' *(mandatum)* of the Father: we must persevere, together with Christ, in fleeing to the Father, in entrusting ourselves to the Father, in imploring and thanking the Father. The model for all of this is Christ at the highest point of his maturity and responsibility with regard to his mission. And the more we identify ourselves with the mission entrusted to us, in the manner of the eternal Son, the more thoroughly do we become sons and daughters of the Heavenly Father: the whole Sermon on the Mount testifies to this. In the figures of the great saints the truth is crystal clear: Christian childlikeness and Chris-

whom the kingdom of heaven is," and the Child Jesus is the prototype of God's "once and future children," those who "have been re-
born in baptism" and "are now called children of God, for so indeed
they are" (RBC 68).

Von Balthasar discusses four "essential traits of the man who lives
this childhood in God as an adult," traits "most evident in Christ
himself, since he retained all the traits of the child of God even as he
was entrusted with the difficult, superhuman task of leading the
whole world back home to God."[30] I will not elaborate here upon
three of these traits, each of which encourages further discussion of a
theology of childhood: that Jesus' actions and words "reveal that he
abides in looking up to the Father with eternal childlike amazement,"
that "the childlike attitude of Christian life keeps alive . . . the inti-
mate character of the Church as mystery," and that it is the child's
sense of time that allows the "once and future child" to "find God in
all things, just as Christ found the Father in all things." I comment
only upon the fourth, the trait that seems to describe best "the mentality of our beginnings" to which we must return (as von Balthasar
put it) so as to enter the kingdom of God. This trait, which von
Balthasar considers "the quintessence of Jesus' stance toward the
Father," is thanksgiving.

I offer here no manual for giving thanks but simply reflect upon
the child's fundamental attitude and approach to life. This attitude
and approach comes naturally to children, but it must infiltrate and
govern the awareness of all who, baptized as infants or adults, are to
attain their ultimate destiny as God's "once and future children." Re-
calling a comment from our earlier discussion of a theology of childhood, to turn and become like children may well be *the* challenge of
the Christian life. And this coming to the full awareness of who we
are, and of whose we are, is a discovery made neither easily nor
quickly. But the discovery is crucial to and for our identity as Christians, for the realization of to whom we belong is the ultimate fruit of
our baptism.

Our decisive task as Christians is to *realize*—the word means both
"to be aware of" and "to attain"—who we became through our

---

tian maturity are not in tension with one another. Even at an advanced age, the
saints enjoy a marvelous youthfulness" (40–41).

[30]Ibid., 44; see von Balthasar's pages 44–55 for the full discussion. The summary citations that follow in our text are found on pages 44, 51, and 54.

adoption by God and who we are called to remain: children of God, adopted sons or daughters of the Father, God's heirs, joint heirs with Christ. To be a child of God is, as I have said often, the Christian's gift. But what does it mean to be a child of God? What does it mean to be a child?

"To be a child means to owe one's existence to another, and even in our adult life we never quite reach the point where we no longer have to give thanks for being the person we are. This means that we never quite outgrow our condition of children, nor do we therefore ever outgrow the obligation to give thanks for ourselves or to continue to ask for our being. Individual men, cultures and institutions may forget this. Only the Christian religion, which in its essence is communicated by the eternal child of God, keeps alive in its believers the lifelong awareness of their being children, and therefore of having to ask and give thanks for things. *Jesus does not insist on this childlike 'say please,' 'say thank you,' because otherwise the gifts would be refused, but in order that they may be recognized as gifts.* 'Ask and it shall be given to you; seek and you shall find; knock and it shall be opened to you' (Matt 7:7), and this with such certainty that 'even as you ask you can already give thanks for what you have received' (Mark 11:24)."[31]

Adopted as sons and daughters by God, Christians are children of God and co-heirs with Christ their brother. Their status as God's children is given as gift but also given for purpose: having been baptized into Christ's death and resurrection, they are to "become more perfectly like [God's] Son" (*RBC* 223; *RCIA* 222-B). And I suggest that Christians become more perfectly like God's Son to the extent their lives are governed and marked by this trait of thanksgiving. For in the action of giving thanks Christians return to that quality and experience intrinsic to the condition of childhood: the dependence upon another who is greater than they, and the willingness to receive from One who anticipates and provides for their needs.

This orientation of thanksgiving that should mark the life of the Christian, the essential attitude through which Jesus always approached his Father, must not be dismissed as a polite yet otherwise banal mien of religious etiquette. For it is precisely when we give thanks that we realize—that we are aware of and so attain—our iden-

---

[31]Ibid., 49–50; emphasis mine.

tity as God's sons and daughters. We give thanks for this great gift. We need to give thanks not "because otherwise the gifts would be refused, but in order that they may be recognized as gifts."

As the adult Church continues her laudable and often successful efforts at making Christians, it is no small temptation for her to forget—or simply not to remember—that it is grace that makes all possible, that it is grace that both calls us to and leads us through our journey of faith, and that, as is illustrated memorably in Francis Thompson's *Hound of Heaven,* it is Grace who has been pursuing us "with unhurrying chase, and unperturbéd pace," even before we knew enough to take our first hesitant steps.

"Christians are not born, they are made." Tertullian's adage applies to all Christians, be they baptized as adults or infants. But as the adult Church challenges her infants baptized at the initiative and in the faith of others to "accept for themselves the faith in which they have been baptized," so must she humbly submit herself to the challenge presented her by her infants at the font. Infant baptism challenges the adult Church "to be what we proclaim," thus binding the community "to demonstrate a faith so alive and dynamic that the child baptized may eventually find fulfillment in it."[32] The Church accepts this challenge as she fosters and supports the future conversion of infants—first, by guiding Christian spouses in their vocation as *Christian* parents and, subsequently, by her ministry to the young child, growing adolescent, and mature adult.

But the challenge presented the Church by infant baptism is not to be understood only in terms of what the Church must "do" to and for the infant. For in her infants the adult Church is confronted not only with her obligation to minister but also with her own need to receive. As she baptizes her infants, the Church does more than simply initiate her future adults; she confronts her own childhood at the font and thus recalls her own dependence upon, and receptivity to, God and God's gifts. An infant has no choice but to submit passively to what God offers and to what Church and family sacramentally effect and express. An infant has no other hope. But that infant, years later and now an adult member of an adult Church, must learn again to surrender, this time willingly, and return to the grace that eternally precedes, always sustains, and remains forever the goal of us all:

[32]Keating, "Baptism Sets Our Boundaries" 102, and, again, Haggerty, "Adult Initiation and Infant Baptism," 159, cited first in our chapter 2.

"Children are introduced into the baptismal community because they reveal what that community's ultimate destiny and goal is. . . . Adult faith and conversion lead to that childhood which consists in overcoming the last vestiges of resistance to the God who challenges us to lose ourselves in order to find ourselves. . . . The Christian who "dies in the Lord" meets his childhood in a final act of complete surrender."[33]

"Let the children come to me, . . . for it is to such as these that the kingdom of God belongs." In our discussion of a theology of childhood in chapter 6, I reported Karl Rahner's observation that it was not the obvious yet largely amoral innocence of the child that supported the notion of the sacramental dimension of childhood but rather the openness of childhood: the courageous submission to the ineffable mystery of the Father, which leads the mature man and woman to realize fully their childhood before God. For the adult Christian this submission can be none other than the constant return to the grace offered as gift. Christians most fully live up to the name they bear when they acknowledge their dependence on God, the source and end of their life, and so remember who they are and to whom they belong: God's sons and daughters, dependent children, children who turn with ease to their Father so that they might receive. I repeat Nathan Mitchell's keen insight that the condition of childhood is the fundamental attitude toward God required of all Christians: "The child, therefore, is a sacrament of that radical openness to the future which is a characteristic posture of the Christian believer precisely because the child reveals not only what we once were, but what we will be. Indeed, one could almost define Christianity itself as the state of childhood, the surrendering openness to God as the absolute future of man, the future that comes forward to meet men in unconditional love and acceptance."[34]

If in the face of a child we see what it means to freely receive and willingly depend, it is in the face of the child made a son or daughter and brought into a family through adoption that we recall the extraordinary nature of our new life in Christ and his Church. In that face the Church is again challenged to remember. For *the* sin of the adopted child of any age is to forget that he or she was adopted, to forget that he or she *is* adopted. To forget this is to forget, to not re-

[33]Mitchell, "Once and Future Child," 432–33, cited also in our chapter 6.
[34]Ibid., 428.

member, that who one is and what one has is due solely to an extraordinary act undertaken at the initiative of another. Applying this to the Christian, *the* sin is to forget that we are God's sons or daughters, that we are God's heirs and joint heirs with Christ, and that we enjoy this identity and inheritance only because God offered us a Father's love prior to our response—and indeed, without considering first whether any response would be forthcoming.

Humankind evidently finds it difficult to believe in or accept such a gracious gift even from the divine, a difficulty painfully experienced by the hard-working, successful-in-his-duties older brother in the parable of the Prodigal Son. We may wonder whether *he* eventually returned to his true self (and thus also to his father's home), but we continue his struggle each time we forget that the approach to our Father's house is paved not with the proof of our good works but with our willingness to receive from him and depend upon him. Dependence, receptivity, thanksgiving: these are the postures that mark the true Christian life, for they are humble and honest assessments of a son's or daughter's relationship to their Father—a relationship initiated and sustained through the Father's love. Our willingness to depend, the humble freedom with which we receive, our remembering to give thanks: these conditions of childhood tell us who we are; they tell us to whom we belong.

Baptism "makes us" the people of God—God's adopted sons and daughters—because baptism makes a Church that, through her celebration of her sacraments, remembers and celebrates her dependence upon God. It is, therefore, not merely an etymologist's delight that the climax of sacramental initiation into the body of Christ on earth is also that body's most regular and public profession of their faith and their identity. *Eucharistia:* giving thanks, expressing our dependence, returning ourselves to the One who has given us as gift that which could only be acquired through gift—the status and freedom of God's adopted sons and daughters.

Aidan Kavanagh has written eloquently of the ministry catechumens offer the Church. Their corporate witness reminds the Church that she who moderates the "conversion therapy" of others is always herself in need of conversion. If the Church must accept the ministry her catechumens offer (a ministry "the church forgoes at her own peril," as Kavanagh has observed), she also risks losing her identity when she does not remember to return to the grace and constantly rediscover herself as God's "once and future child." For in the adopting of infant and child, in the extraordinary making of a Christian son or daughter, we see ourselves no longer as the older brother but as the Father's younger son: the child for whom the Father's love knew no bounds from the beginning, the child whose Father gave generously the inheritance promised——the child whose Father waited patiently at the door for his return.

I have remarked that the adopted child of any age remains always free to ignore or refuse, to reject or simply to forget the gift given through adoption. I also observe once again that while adopted children may know of their adoption from the beginning, they grow only gradually into the understanding and appreciation of what their adoption has meant and continues to mean to them. This growing understanding and appreciation, this too, is conversion. And although it lacks the drama and public process that accompany one's passage through the adult catechumenate, it is in its proper way impressive and instructive. For this ordinary, daily Christian conversion admonishes us to remember that grace builds upon nature, that a gift is given before it can be used, and that, put most simply, God has known us before we have known God.

Far from being a "benign abnormality" at best, infant baptism is at the least an "opportunity to be grasped." And an opportunity we do well to receive. It is the opportunity for the adult Church to see her destiny, to reclaim her identity, and to return to the grace that is offered Christians of all ages to bring them to their final age: the age at which they die in the Lord and thus, understanding and attaining, they realize "in a final act of complete surrender" their identity as God's "once and future child." At this baptism of an infant "we can see ourselves in this child and in his destiny and say to ourselves: 'You too began your life in this way. Did you continue so? Has the promise of this day been fulfilled in you? Has this day's sowing produced a harvest?'"[35]

---

[35]Rahner, *Holy Baptism*, 39.

Chapter 10

An Opportunity Grasped?
Reflections, perspectives, hopes

"What the value of baptizing infants might be is an extremely obscure question. But one must believe there is some value in it" (St.
Augustine).

"Perhaps infant initiation ought to be seen less as a problem to be
grappled with than as an opportunity to be grasped" (Mark Searle).

The above citations have served as mutual foils throughout this
work. Augustine's cryptic comment about the "extremely obscure
question" of the value of baptizing infants describes well the ethos
surrounding the understanding and practice of infant baptism in the
postconciliar era. As I remarked in chapter 5 (which concluded part 1
and my report of the American discussion), infant baptism seems
here to stay, but our understanding of the practice has certainly not
stayed unchanged these past thirty years.

The postconciliar assessment of the necessity, theology, and pastoral practice of infant baptism was influenced greatly by the *Rite of
Christian Initiation of Adults*, promulgated first in 1972. In chapter 1 I
reviewed the authors making up the Mature Adulthood School, who
considered the *RCIA* the "most explosive pastoral document" since
the conciliar documents themselves.

A full recital of the contributions the *RCIA* and its promoters have
made to postconciliar sacramental theology and ecclesiology could
only be impressive. Suffice it to say that the adult ordo's vision of
Church and its emphasis on initiation as process challenged any former understanding of infant baptism as an instant removal of sin, an
instant confection of faith, or the instant making of a Catholic. All
representatives of the Mature Adulthood School might not have agreed
with Augustine that the value of infant baptism was an "extremely
obscure question," but most did find the value of the adult ordo expressed well by an earlier African theologian—and Tertullian's adage
that "Christians are not born, they are made" was invoked regularly

to support the involved process of adult baptism in the postconciliar Church. One prominent refrain in the discussion was Aidan Kavanagh's thesis that the adult ordo presents "the definitive statement of what the Roman Catholic Church's norm of baptism is henceforth to be."

While the value of infant baptism might have been obscure to some, many writers labored to explain and clarify its significance. The Environmentalist School, first considered in chapter 2, agreed with Tertullian's premise—but thought the baptism of infants demanded mature adult faith no less than did that of adults. The 1969 *Rite of Baptism for Children* did not offer the impressive menu of rites characteristic of the adult ordo, but it did emphasize that baptism is but a beginning, that it is the faith of the domestic and ecclesial communities that justifies the baptism of a particular infant, and that only as those initiated as infants or young children "accept for themselves the faith in which they have been baptized" is the ultimate meaning of the sacrament fulfilled. According to Environmentalists, Tertullian's precept did not speak against infant baptism (although Tertullian himself argued against baptizing both infants and young adults) but served to emphasize the responsibilities incurred by parents, family, and ecclesial community as they brought their infants to the font.

In chapter 3 I examined what continues to be the only major curial document addressing infant baptism since the 1969 *RBC:* the SCDF's 1980 *Instruction on Infant Baptism.* In its appraisal of some fifteen years of postconciliar discussion, *Pastoralis Actio* reaffirmed the validity, legitimacy, and necessity of baptizing infants but also recognized that only a well-founded hope that the infant would be raised in the Catholic faith justified baptism in a given situation. Acknowledging that the absence of this hope would allow the baptism of a particular infant to be deferred, the instruction maintained that only the complete absence of this hope allowed such a deferral and emphasized that such a delay was neither preferable nor normal.

I first reported Mark Searle's comment that infant baptism presented the Church "an opportunity to be grasped" in chapter 4. In that chapter, entitled "Infant Baptism Reclaimed," I noted that Searle was one of several who thought no one rite or expression of baptism could exhaust the meaning and mystery of Christian initiation and that he stressed the complementary nature of infant and adult baptism. Comparisons may be as unwarranted as they are unwanted, but I think it accurate to say that through the course of the postconciliar discussion Mark Searle became the emissary for the baptizing of infants much as Aidan Kavanagh had become for the initiation of adults. While Kavanagh certainly is the most influential writer in the United States as regards the adult ordo, it was Searle who consistently argued that infant baptism need not undergo the kind of theological biopsy that, having already assumed an abnormality was present, could only hope for a diagnosis of "benign." Personal tributes in a work of this nature may be deemed inappropriate—but as one sound conclusion from my study, those of us attempting to contribute to the responsible discussion of either the adult ordo or the infant rite do indeed build upon the sturdy foundations these two scholars have established.

In chapter 5 I summarized the American postconciliar discussion of infant baptism by reviewing the five perspectives that guided my examination of the literature throughout part 1. In that chapter I concluded my report on the postconciliar discussion and suggested the orientation of part 2: that if it is our mature and committed response to the word of God that is witnessed most clearly and readily through the process of the sacramental initiation of adults, then it is the gift of God's word—a gift offered us entirely at God's initiative—that most immediately confronts us in infant baptism. Agreeing that Tertullian's "made, not born" reflected the adult ordo's rationale and ethos of conversion, I suggested the words of the psalmist portrayed a distinctive attribute of the baptism of infants:

"Before ever a word is on my tongue
you know it, O Lord, through and through.
. . . .
For it was you who created my being,
knit me together in my mother's womb.
. . . .
Your eyes saw all my actions,
they were all of them written in your book,
every one of my days was decreed,
before one of them came into being."

The *assumption* underlying part 2 of this work was that the baptism of infants is "normal." The *acknowledgment* was that part of the "problem" of infant baptism is that our understanding of and approach to the sacrament often are not informed by a theological model that speaks as directly and effectively to its unique significance as "death and resurrection" or "spiritual rebirth" speak to the adult ordo. My *ambition* in part 2 was to suggest a model that would allow us to "grasp the opportunity" presented by infant baptism—an opportunity that would benefit both our understanding of the unique character of the baptism of infants and of the grace that precedes the making of every Christian. I proposed the concept of adoption as a model able to address assumption, acknowledgment, and ambition.

ADOPTION AND INFANT BAPTISM: AN OPPORTUNITY TO BE GRASPED, A GIFT TO BE REALIZED

I began my response to the American postconciliar discussion in chapter 6 by outlining a theology of childhood. Observing that children enjoy a direct and immediate relationship with God because of who they are now (and not because of their future identity), I agreed with Nathan Mitchell that the relationship between child and God—a relationship based upon openness and trust and characterized by hopeful expectation and willing submission—is sacramental of and paradigmatic for the relationship to which God calls human beings of every age. Mitchell believes baptized children are "a significant dimension of the church's sacramental structure," and Evelyn Underhill contends that the typical Christian is not the successful preacher but the "small, helpless child at the font with new life in it." Seen in this light—and referring to Mitchell's portrait of the Christian as God's "once and future child"—it is clear that the baptized child confronts the Church with her own vocation, destiny, and hope.

Discussing the "norm of baptism" thesis in chapter 7, I suggested that infant baptism (and all the sacraments) were normative as to meaning for Christian life and identity. I then proposed adoption as a concept-theological model that could inform our understanding of the unique significance of the baptism of infants and young children. After reflecting upon the human act and experience of adoption, I reviewed in chapter 8 Paul's exposition of the Christian's adoption by God. While Paul was not writing about the baptism of infants in his letters to the first-century Churches (and while adoption in today's world is not identical to the practice of his times), the human experience and the theological teaching on adoption coincide in ways that can promote our understanding of what the Church does when she sacramentally initiates her infants and young children.

Three assertions or considerations shaped my essay on a theology for infant baptism in chapter 9. The first of these addressed what is both a unique characteristic and a frequent criticism of infant baptism: the conferral of the sacrament of faith upon one who can neither profess that faith nor respond to the grace offered. A second consideration addressed the immediate effects and the desired fulfillment of infant baptism, particularly as regards the relationship between the sacrament and original sin, and between the infant and the Christian community who sacramentally adopts the child. In the final consideration I developed further the ideas that the child is "the prototype of those for whom the kingdom is," and that the Christian community most clearly realizes—becomes aware of and attains—its origin, identity, and destiny when it returns to the condition of childhood.

No one image or theological model can fully express the meaning and mystery of our incorporation into Christ and his Church. But I believe the human experience of and the theological teaching on adoption speak clearly and credibly about infant baptism and so offer an effective paradigm for our understanding of and approach to the sacrament. My suggesting adoption as an initiation motif was both the major orientation of part 2 and its major conclusion. Among the aspects of baptism that adoption addresses are the following: the action of God and the Christian community in the initiating and effecting of the baptism, the immediate and enduring effects of the sacrament, the desired fulfillment of the meaning of the sacrament, and the freedom and responsibility of those baptized in realizing the full benefits of their baptism.

I have suggested that one advantage an initiation theology based upon the concept of adoption enjoys is the similarity between the human experience of adoption and its theological counterpart. Following the lead of the exegete whose comparison of human and divine adoption I presented in the preceding chapter, I offer the following chart, which attempts to illustrate the correspondence between the human experience of adoption and the Pauline teaching.[1]

[1]The chart is adapted from the reflections and observations found at the conclusion of chapters 7 and 8 and is arranged to reflect the three main points discussed in chapter 9. In presenting this chart I intend neither to stretch the relationship between human and divine adoption nor to abuse the Pauline understanding of the term. The categories and correlations are best approached reflectively rather than rigidly. My suggestion is that the elements proper to the theological significance and to the human experience of adoption are more complementary than contradictory and that reflection upon one assists our understanding and appreciation of the other.

I offer no additional commentary in presenting the chart (such has been the task of the previous chapters), but allow it to speak for itself. Better, I invite my readers to reflect upon and further develop the chart, for its intent is catechetical. While I leave it to those who enjoy more expertise and experience in that area than I to evaluate the chart's usefulness, I believe it no overwhelming task for even a young child to think about adoption—about what it is and what it means—and to distinguish between the "ordinary" and "extraordinary" ways one becomes a member of a family. My hope is that in the hands of a competent catechist the chart will be a useful tool for furthering their students' understanding and appreciation of what parents, families, and Church do as they bring their infants to the font—and what God has done for each one of us who, through our adoption by God, bear the name of God's Son.

1. God's Word Is First: An extraordinary initiative.

All children are born and are brought into their family through the initiative of others. What is unique to adopted children, however, is that their membership in their (new) family is distinct from and independent of their natural birth. One "makes" a son or daughter because a son or daughter is desired and because the child needs to have a mother or father, and not because the child has already proved itself worthy. One is adopted because one is in some way desired, one is loved—and this, prior to any exhibition of one's own merits or abilities to return that love.

The theological concept of adoption speaks first of the initiative of God. The Israelites were chosen as God's people because of God's love for them, a love that preceded their response to that love. The letters to the Romans (3:21-24), Galatians (2:15-16), and Ephesians (2:8-9) emphasize that justification comes through faith in Christ Jesus: justification is the gift of God, not the result of works. Adoption is not earned by merit, but is received as gift; it is occasioned by grace, not acquired as reward.

This is the extraordinary nature of adoption. Family membership and affiliation for the adopted child is not "natural" but is initi-

Adoption portrays the utter benevolence of grace, then, in a particularly articulate way. "Christians are not born, they

ated and made possible deliberate decision. Adopted children do not "have" parents or family, siblings or home; all these are "given" them.

are made." God bestows grace, God chooses and elects God's people—God adopts and claims God's children—according to God's designs and purposes.

2. *Chosen from the Beginning: Deliverance and freedom, life and identity.*

Human adoption delivers the child from an unfortunate situation, the examples of which in today's society are legion. Adopted *from* a given situation, children are adopted and *brought into* a new one. This new environment is a new life and, presumably, a "better" life: one that presumes, if it does not also reasonably promise, a future more fulfilling than that thought likely in the "original life."

God's adoption of Christians is for them deliverance and liberation. Christians are delivered from a spirit of slavery to the law of sin and death, and enjoy the freedom to walk according to the Spirit. Adoption overcomes the law of condemnation and introduces the Christian to the law of saving grace. "God's commands become God's enablings."

Adopted children are identified and affiliated with—they are incorporated into—their new family. Adoption affords parents where before there were none; it makes a child—and makes a parent for this child—not by nature but by extraordinary claim.

"Christians are not born, they are made," and it is through adoption that God makes them sons and daughters—a status among others and a relationship with God to which they have no natural right or claim. The Christian becomes God's child only by virtue of God's gift, through God's act of adoption.

This identification and incorporation includes but goes beyond legal considerations such as place of residence, responsibilities of guardians, and the assumption of the family's name. The adopted child becomes—*is*—a member of the family. Other

Through the Spirit Christians address God as *Abba,* the cry that is both their privilege as a child of God and the Spirit-testified truth that they are indeed God's children. And because they are God's children, they are joint heirs with Christ.

children in the family *are* his brothers and sisters; the parents who adopted him *are* his parents.

While human adoption is a legal fiction, the relationships it forges and the benefits it offers admit of no pretense. The adopted child *is* a member of the family and thus shares in the material and spiritual riches of the family.

Conferring upon Christians the status of God's sons and daughters, adoption pledges them the inheritance of the kingdom. Christians are not *similar* to God's children, they *are* God's children and so enjoy the full rights of their adoption: the inheritance of the adopting Father's wealth and a share in the sonship of their brother, Christ.

3. Realizing the Gift: Promise and fulfillment, dependence and thanksgiving.

The objective fact and act of adoption is ordinarily irrevocable, but the adopted child's freedom of will remains intact. Adoption brings children into a present and offers them a future marked by new directions and hopes, but it does not coerce that future. While adoption offers benefits, it does not guarantee that these benefits will be realized or accepted. The child, freed from the past, remains free to refuse or reject the status, benefits, and obligations effected by the adoption.

Christians submit to the leadership of the Spirit, who testifies to the truth of their adoption. The Spirit of adoption, the power and proof underlying Christian sonship, is also the pledge and promise of that sonship and its inheritance. Adoption liberates from the spirit of slavery and liberates for the Spirit of sonship. This is grace given as gift, but given also for purpose. Christian sonship is both gift and duty: it is the gift of the Spirit, it is the duty "to make use of the Spirit received."

While adopted children may always have known the fact of their adoption, they only gradually understand what their adoption means—an understanding that

God's adoption of Christians speaks of the enduring faithfulness of God's saving design. Christians await the full reception and manifestation of their

will develop as they grow and according to their education and experience. Older adults reflecting upon their adoption will understand and appreciate its significance with a greater clarity and depth than would be possible in their reflections at an earlier age.

inheritance, the redemption of their bodies. They wait with longing and with confident hope, for the Spirit bears witness to the truth of their adoption and the promise of their inheritance.

A final remark concerning my reflections upon the human act and experience of adoption is in order. Much of what I have said concerning the act of adoption, the adopted child, and the adopting parents may and can be said of those who are parents and children of one another by blood. But reflection upon the extraordinary nature of the act of adoption can strengthen our understanding and appreciation of the relationship between parents and children by blood as well—a relationship no less wondrous because it is "ordinary." Adoption can serve also as a model or paradigm for parenthood and for family life, then, as well as for the sacramental initiation of infants and young children.

I conclude this work with a second set of observations. Drawing from my words and from those of the many authors upon whom I have relied for my discussion of childhood, adoption, and infant baptism, I respond now to the five perspectives, or "position statements," that guided my report on the American Catholic postconciliar discussion of infant baptism in part 1.

THE FIVE PERSPECTIVES OF PART ONE: A RESPONSE "FROM MY OWN PERSPECTIVE"

I agree with virtually all the American writers whose views I reported in part 1 as regards two of the five perspectives: that the indiscriminate baptizing of infants is unacceptable, and that catechesis is as necessary and indispensable a part of the sacrament of infant baptism as it is of the sacramental initiation of adults. After commenting on these two perspectives, I will outline my disagreement with the suggestion of the child catechumenate, my position as regards the unity of the initiation sacraments, and my disagreement with the "adult ordo as norm" thesis.

Perspective: The necessity of catechesis

My hope is that further reflection upon the human experience of adoption (adoption itself being a "sacrament" not only of baptism but also of family life) might emphasize the responsibilities of parents, family, and Church in guiding those baptized as infants to eventually "accept for themselves the faith in which they have been baptized." As is true with every child and with every family—but as is emphasized with particular clarity through the extraordinary act of adoption—a child is brought into a family through the initiative of others. And as it is the family that makes possible and secures the adoption, so must the family form, educate, and support the one whom they have adopted. The child, though adopted and so considered a full member of the family from the beginning, grows only gradually and only with the family's assistance in learning the ways and means of those who have claimed him as one of their own.

As many have suggested, infant baptism commits parents and community to the child's education and formation in the faith. But this promise is not one made only during the sacramental celebration of baptism. The *Rite of Baptism for Children* does well in asking parents to begin preparing for the baptism of their child "as soon as possible, if need be even before the child is born" (*RBC* 8.2)—a welcome reinterpretation of the traditional *quam primum* requirement, which in the preconciliar ritual addressed the interval between birth and baptism. But I hold that preparation for their infant's baptism should begin even as the man and woman begin to consider seriously committing themselves to each other as husband and wife.

This does not mean that babies should be forthcoming within a year of every Christian marriage! It does mean that the family we consider to be the domestic Church begins not with the baby but with the marriage. Catechesis for infant baptism begins with catechesis for marriage, for it is in the home of that marriage that an infant will first encounter the word of God and the grace of sacramental adoption. Christian identity, given the child through baptism, is discovered and accepted by the child through the deliberate choice for faith made first by the parents.

The commitment to Christian marriage is, in my mind, the commitment to have one's children baptized as infants. While not every marriage will be blessed with children, the vocation of Christian marriage also ordinarily implies—confers—the vocation of *Christian* parenthood. A child is not brought into a family and then left alone. "Christian identity is precisely *not* inherited from Christian parents," as Searle observed. Christian adoption—the making of a Christian through baptism—requires not that the child have a family in which he will find "company" but one in which and from whom he will learn and live his identity as a Christian.

I also think that encouraging parents to assume responsibility for catechizing their sons and daughters includes encouraging parents to assume the responsibility for leading—indeed, developing—the family's life of prayer. If Christians are to be different from the world at large precisely because they are Christians, this difference should be reflected as much in a Christian family's religious behavior as in their religious beliefs and teachings. And the *lex orandi* of the domestic Church need not be exhausted by prayers before and after meals or upon awakening and retiring but can be expanded to address the full *lex credendi* of family life. Available resources supporting this notion include the *Book of Blessings* and *Catholic Household Blessings and Prayers*.[2] In addition to offering orders of blessings appropriate for use prior to and after an infant's birth and baptism, these volumes offer several orders designed specifically for family life: for example, the "Blessing of Children," the "Blessing of Sons and Daughters," and "Blessings for Special Occasions" such as a birthday or name day. Many of these blessings are offered with the hope that parents will "bestow this blessing of the Lord on their own children," and the *Book of Blessings* makes specific mention that spouses "exercise this ministry [of blessing] in virtue of their office [as parents]."[3] Encouraging the more frequent use of these resources reminds all once again that a sacramental encounter with God's grace is not restricted to that which happens only in church, that the family is the domestic Church, and that Christian parenthood is Christian ministry.

Perspective: The indiscriminate baptizing of infants

My agreement that this practice is unacceptable is accompanied by my puzzlement as to how frequent truly indiscriminate baptism is and by my concern (shared with others) that excessive standards of external conduct not be levied against parents who request baptism for their infants. My concern here does not compromise the seriousness with which I have spoken above as regards the vocation of Christian parenthood. If it is the faith of the family and ecclesial

[2]*Book of Blessings* (English translation of *De Benedictionibus*) (ICEL, 1987); additional blessings for use in the U.S., *Catholic Household Blessings and Prayers* (USCC, 1988).

[3]*Blessings*, par. 174; "General Introduction," 18-d.

community that justifies the baptism of a particular infant, that faith must in some way be able to be discerned.

It is true that parents will bring their infants to the font for reasons other than the theologically ideal. But I think it imperative that their approach to that font be recognized for what at least in part it is: their return to the font of *their* baptism—their return in some way to the grace and Christian identity offered them a generation or more ago. Every parental request ought not be granted automatically and without due pastoral consideration. But I urge that apparent "soft requests" for infant baptism be seized upon for what they are: an opportunity for the Church—better, her obligation—to shoulder the one or two who have wandered from the hundred we count as the registered and well-bred flock. And a little child shall lead them? God's vision is better than ours, and God's graced adoption of a couple's child can be (and often has been) an invitation, challenge, and opportunity for the parents to return to the grace of their own adoption.

For this reason, while I strongly object to depicting the baptism of a child of believing parents as a "benign abnormality," and while I disagree in principle with the truly indiscriminate baptizing of infants, I am not completely at ease with designating the baptism of a child of parents whose faith be judged marginal, somewhat superstitious, or even practically nonexistent, a "malign abnormality." Just as the true meaning of baptism is not fulfilled as the family sings the concluding hymn and leaves the church, so is the power of God's grace not exhausted nor is it necessarily wasted when baptism is conferred upon one whose parents' faith is questionable. Allowing marginal Catholics into the community will likely result in a community that is less strong than it could be and less committed than it might be. But such is an inherent part of community life, whether that community be familial, ecclesial, religious, or social. A community receives power from its stronger members but it is called to be grace to all, and the gift of being strong is accompanied most always by the cross of carrying the weak. While the desire to safeguard the quality of the community is understandable, a land built for heroes can become a land in which only heroes can live.

I do not encourage indiscriminate infant baptism, but I do recall the pledge made by the Church as she confers the sacrament: a pledge of continuing ministry to parents, family, and child. When a request for indiscriminate baptism is made, such a request speaks more about what the Church must do *now* than it does about what parents have as yet been unable to do. And a little child just might indeed lead them: for the household in which as the child grows, grow not also the parents, is, I think, rare. Children are not the only ones who must learn, and adults are not the only ones who can teach.

I find the proverbial straddling of the fence as regards the indiscriminate baptizing of infants unfortunate and uncomfortable. Yet to invoke (actually, to mutilate) another cliche, I am reluctant to throw out baby and baptismal water because of the parents. Although the *RBC* and *Pastoralis Actio* both speak of a "well-founded hope" and the *Code of Canon Law* mandates it, the documents are not particularly helpful to pastors or associates in defining exactly what constitutes that well-founded hope—or, more to the point, what implies its absence. Again, one principle (suggested often in the literature) is that the parents' request to have their child baptized is in some way a manifestation of some faith on their part. If their expressed desire for their infant's baptism is that they want to save the child from limbo (the concept may be dismissed by some, but the parents' concern must by honored by all), an obvious point from which the pastor or minister may begin their instruction is by inquiring why this is important to the parents and what the parents seek as regards the Church's help in the future. (What is often forgotten in the discussion at this point is the obvious fact that their child is important enough for them to ask something for her from the Church.) Another principle is that delaying an infant's baptism so as to prepare or educate the child's parents makes no sense whatsoever unless the delay is *in fact* educational. If acceding to the parents' request to have their child baptized would in a particular case be truly an indiscriminate baptism, then that baptism should be delayed. But this is not a solution to the problem: it means that the Church's pilgrimage with parents and family has only begun.

Perspective: The infant or child catechumenate

I do not support the suggestion that an infant or child catechumenate provides a suitable and temporary alternative to infant baptism and am in general agreement with those who also oppose the notion (see ch. 4). At the most basic level, considering a child as one in the order of catechumens would require redefining our understanding of what both order and catechumen signify. The *RCIA* has successfully recovered the significance and promoted the restoration of both, and adding yet another defined "church within the Church" would, solely on the practical level, seem likely to add to the difficulties many parishes experience in their implementation of the adult ordo. While there is certainly room for an order of catechumens for children in the Church, such an order is not what our Church needs.

What *is* needed is that we form and instruct our children in the ways and means of their faith, not as catechumens who approach us to continue their conversion under the Church's direction and support but because *we* have sacramentally effected, expressed, and celebrated their adoption by God by adopting them into our body and claiming them for Christ. Infants and children learn the ways and means of their family not so that one day they can finally be received into that family but because they are already a member of that family. An adult order of catechumens is necessary: adults choose to enter the Church because they recognize their need for God's grace and they acknowledge where grace has led them. Infants and young children can neither choose nor acknowledge; they go only where they are led and can only follow those who lead them—precisely the value and significance of the practice of adoption, parenthood in general, and Christian parenthood in particular.

Some maintain that given the significance of baptism, individuals should be baptized only when they are fully able to make such a momentous decision for themselves. In that case I think the logical response is that we must then withhold baptism for quite some time indeed. For if the ability to make momentous decisions is the requirement for baptism, do we hold that this ability is attained at age seven? Or seventeen? Or—exactly when? Asking the question is not to encourage baptism at twenty-one or at age eighteen, the two magic moments of maturity mandated by secular society. It is to appeal again to the belief that our sacramental celebrations are first and above all else celebrations of *God's* word—a belief seen perhaps most clearly, as I have suggested, in the sacrament of infant baptism. If the argument is that people should decide for themselves whether they want to be baptized, I answer that the daily task of Christians baptized at whatever age is precisely that: to decide for themselves each and every day whether they want to live as baptized Christians are called to live. Children are not asked if they want to be adopted; they are adopted because they need to be and because they are loved— loved to the extent that a particular family wishes to bring them into the family as a full member.

While I am more sympathetic with those who hold that baptism should not be celebrated until children are old enough to retain some memory of their baptism, I also approach this view from a different perspective. I agree that such a memory can strengthen and support those children as they grow and mature. But, again, the unfolding knowledge and awareness that one has been adopted loses no significance because one does not remember the actual act of adoption. There is much to recommend the suggestion that Christians would benefit from being able to remember their baptism, just as they benefit from "seeing" that memory time and again through the Church's annual initiation of her catechumens at Easter. Of great benefit also is the adult seeing the baptism of an infant and reflecting—with gratitude and humility—that on some day now long past, others whom she did not yet know initiated her because of how important she was to them. Moreover, there is much that could be taught about Christian identity in the child learning to appreciate what has been done on her behalf. As von Balthasar remarked, we teach our children to say "thank you" not because future gifts might not be forthcoming but because otherwise our children might not learn to recognize them as gifts.

What might be of even greater import is that we raise our children in such a way that they have no memory of *not* being baptized: in other words, that their education, their formation, and their life within the family has been such that their baptism "has always been with them." A sudden explosion of grace radically changed the nature of Paul's approach to life and the Christian Church. But God's grace also builds upon nature quietly, calmly, and without fanfare. That is no less impressive—and remains for the Church just as challenging a prospect.

To summarize, the notion of a catechumenate for infants or children seems to me an unfortunate avenue from which to approach the initiation of the children of believing parents. Even when the suggestion is made so as to resolve "the limbo question," I hold that more appropriate pastoral and theological assurances are available and ought to be offered (see ch. 9). Finally, to the charge that indiscriminate baptism exists because there are no alternatives to water baptism, I counter that the best alternative available is alluded to often in the literature and is mandated by the *RBC:* catechesis of, and ministry to, the parents.

Perspective: The unity of the initiation sacraments

The current norm for the age of confirmation in the United States is from "about the age of seven until age eighteen." The decree from the Congregation for Bishops approved this norm for a five-year period (ending July 1, 1999) "in order that the bishops, with the lapse of time and the addition of new perspectives, may again raise this question and bring a norm once again to the Holy See for review." My remarks here are a modest attempt to contribute to a new perspective—for I believe a theology of baptism based upon the concept of adoption suggests an answer to the tactical question of what age to confirm because it suggests the context in which the strategic questions of "What is it we are doing when we confirm?" and "Why do we confirm?" might be addressed.[4]

Neither the baptism of an infant nor the adoption of a child guarantees that the freedom and deliverance effected "automatically" by these acts will ultimately be fruitful. Baptism and adoption deliver one from the present condition of slavery and into a situation in which a new life marked by freedom is possible, but they do not guarantee that the freedom and benefits offered by that new life will be appropriated. That the true meaning of baptism is fulfilled only when children "ultimately accept for themselves the faith in which they have been baptized" has been, as we have seen, both a refrain and a concern of the discussion throughout the postconciliar years.

But while infant baptism commits the domestic and ecclesial communities to attend to the child's future growth in faith, the sacrament affects the child *now*. Baptism establishes a relationship between child and God and between child and communities *now*. We emphasize—rightly—the obligations and responsibilities incurred by parents and community as they baptize their children and hold that some of these responsibilities are assumed even prior to the child's birth. But as much as these obligations are oriented toward the child's future, they have as their ground the truth spoken *now*, at the moment of baptism. The fulfillment of the sacrament lies in the future, but that fu-

---

[4]Again, I take care to abuse neither the Pauline teaching on nor the human experience of adoption. Paul was certainly not addressing the question of initiation unity in his letters, and I know of nothing in the human experience of adoption corresponding to a solemn "confirmation" (or first Eucharist), particularly when confirmation is considered as a commissioning for service, as the mature acceptance of the responsibilities one inherited at baptism, or as a "confirmation of the faith of adolescents."

ture has already begun because family and Church act on the child's behalf *now*. Through baptism the infant or child is incorporated into Christ and into the Church, and these immediate and lasting effects (the *res et sacramentum*, in Scholastic terminology) rely neither upon the infant's ability to understand them nor his later acceptance of them. And as I have said, these effects are, first, gifts: gifts given by God at God's initiative, gifts sacramentalized—made visible—by and through the Church as she "claims the child for Christ" through the adoption of baptism.

Reflecting upon the human experience of adoption, I suggested that although a child grows into the awareness of and appreciation for her adoption only gradually, she is "made" a full member of the family as she is adopted. Once the papers are signed, sealed, and delivered—in the case of baptism, once the child is marked, sealed, and claimed as a member of Christ and his Church—the child enters fully into the life of her new family.

That infants and young children must be led to assume responsibility for the course of their lives is as central to the meaning of parenthood as it is to the ultimate meaning of baptism. Parental responsibility for their young is in large part the imposing of their own decisions upon their child because it is those decisions that make a future possible for the child. And although adolescents and adults always remain free to reject their parents or parental values and decisions, no family considers their children partial or part-time members until that time when the children accept their identity within the family or confirm the values in which their family has formed them. Even though they may not bear the full responsibilities or enjoy the adult privileges of the mature members of the family, children become full members of the family as they are adopted.

Adoption does not admit, then, of degrees of belonging to the family. One is not "a little bit adopted." The child's awareness, understanding, appreciation, and acceptance of the adoption will mature as he matures physically, but once adopted, he *is* a member of that family. And as adoption does not admit of degrees of belonging, neither does it admit of degrees of receiving the benefits of belonging. The family's love, acceptance, talents, experience, background, gifts: all of these and more may be considered the benefits of family life. But the family does not treat the child as one who must earn or merit these benefits. They withhold none of these from him, but introduce him gradually and consistently to the family's ways and means. That children may not be capable of fully understanding the full significance of these ways, means, and benefits is less important than that they are members of the family and so enjoy immediate and direct access to them.

As God adopts this child as God's own, then, and as the child's domestic and ecclesial families sacramentally effect, express, and celebrate the divine adoption through baptism, the child deserves to be treated as he or she is now: as those who enjoy a direct and immediate relationship with God, just as they now enjoy such a relationship with their family and Church. I do not think our children need qualify for confirmation and Eucharist by virtue of age, demonstrable faith decision, or personal request. Having been brought into the family, they should be graced from the beginning with the full sacramental expression of who they have become and now are: adopted sons and daughters of God and members of Christ's body. The significance of infant baptism, illustrated clearly through the human experience of adoption, is not that children recognize *now* what is happening to them but that they will be brought up within a family where they will continue to recognize what has been done for them—and why that has been done. At the loving initiative of others they have been made Christian sons and daughters of this Christian mother and father and have been placed into a Christian family as full members of the family. Baptism, confirmation, and Eucharist entail, as do all the sacraments, responsibilities and obligations: "we are debtors" (Rom 8:12), and our debt is to cooperate with the grace offered. But these sacraments of initiation (and the other sacraments as well) are first and foremost gifts. If baptism, confirmation, and Eucharist are required for full Christian initiation (*CIC* 842, §2), I think it sensible and credible to confer those sacraments as the person (in our case, an infant or child) is brought into the family as a full member of that family.

I realize that the spiritual and familial ethos surrounding the celebration of first Communion (and the conferral of confirmation) is powerful and has figured significantly in the Catholic coming of age of most every twentieth-century Christian baptized as an infant. The suggestion that infants or young children be confirmed and communicated at their baptism is made with the recognition that the significance of these milestones in the lives of individual Catholics and their families may well be altered. I do not deny the importance of these milestones, but I think the potential of our catechetical programs and the talents of our catechists, religious educators, and liturgists would be better utilized were we to move away from what many have called the carrot-on-a-stick approach and instead consistently emphasize the nature of baptism, confirmation, and Eucharist as initiation into the family of God and the Church and, as many have suggested, develop alternative liturgical rites that mark stages of human growth, maturity, or accomplishment.[5] In line with this, we need to rethink our approach to the various resources—sacramental and otherwise—we have at present.

For example, a well-prepared, solemn, and communal celebration of the sacrament of reconciliation (not "first confession")—one informed, perhaps, by the theology of Luke's parable of the Prodigal Son, with its emphasis on the Father waiting for his son to come to himself and return home—may speak more to confirming adolescents in the faith and grace of their baptism than would confirmation celebrated as a sacrament of maturity. (Remember in this regard that the early Church often described her penitential discipline as a second baptism.) Confirmation depends not upon human maturity or adolescence but belongs to those incorporated into the body of Christ and his Church. The sacrament of reconciliation, which implies in its preparation and celebration a serious and mature appraisal of one's relationship with God, Church, neighbor, and self, would seem a more appropriate sacrament of mature Catholic adulthood than confirmation—and a more regular one as well. And I suggest that a renewed emphasis on this sacrament (be the emphasis on communal or individual celebrations) would assist many parishes in their efforts to promote that fundamental idea expressed so well by the adult ordo: that conversion is a lifelong process continually supported by and effected within the ecclesial community.

That much of this would require a reevaluation of our approach to the sacraments is obvious. That such a reevaluation might encourage the greater use of available liturgical resources and the development of new ones—that perhaps it might foster the notion that Christian

---

[5]I do not intend these remarks to suggest what would be an obviously false and unjust dichotomy of "either-or." I recognize that the catechetical programs of many parishes and dioceses embrace far more than sacramental preparation, as I recognize also that, given the situation in many parishes, simply preparing children for the sacraments is often a major task in itself. As I offer these remarks, I commend wholeheartedly the catechists and pastoral workers who, although from various perspectives and theologies, are working admirably toward the same goal: that those brought into the Church as infants "may ultimately accept for themselves the faith in which they have been baptized."

parenthood is a vocation within and for the Church and so open ways in which Christian husband and wife can minister to their baptized children as Christian mother and father—is splendid.

Perspective: The norm of baptism

I disagree with the thesis that the adult ordo presents "the definitive statement of what the Roman Catholic Church's norm of baptism is henceforth to be." If we accept Kavanagh's definition of "norm" as the "standard according to which a thing is done," I think the thesis inaccurate—for, according to the adult ordo, the adult ordo is an ordo for adults. I also consider the choice of the term "norm" unfortunate, as it suggests that anything other than the norm is abnormal. Such nomenclature may work well when comparing things of the same kind, but as Mark Searle has remarked, "Baptism at the age of seventeen is not the same as baptism at the age of seventy or at the age of seven years or seven weeks." Moreover, to ascribe the term "abnormal" to the outpouring of God's grace upon one not yet able to respond seems to place more emphasis on the adult ordo and less on God's grace. Far from being abnormal, God's adoption of an infant through the Church's celebration of infant baptism is a paradigmatic expression of what occurs in the celebration of any sacrament.

I readily agree that the adult ordo has contributed several principles essential for our understanding and practice of the sacramental initiation of a Christian of any age. The more important of these principles, however, are also found in the *Rite of Baptism for Children*: the necessity of catechesis, conversion as a lifelong journey, and the future acceptance of one's baptismal faith as the fulfillment of the true meaning of sacramental initiation. That the 1969 rite of infant baptism is derived from and has its roots in the adult rite is clear and again confirms the tremendous impact the adult ordo has had upon our postconciliar understanding and practice of the sacraments. The adult ordo obviously suggests standards for the practice of baptizing infants because it suggests standards for understanding and fostering the significance of Christian initiation. It does not, however, suggest the abnormality of a practice it clearly influences but for whom it was not designed.

While I disagree with the "adult ordo as norm" thesis as it was originally expressed, I support the thesis in a modified form. I agree with Kavanagh, for example, that the adult ordo is the "most explosive pastoral [postconciliar] document," and that it has greatly influenced the manner in which we approach all sacramental and liturgical celebrations (see my concluding comments in ch. 5). As regards sacramental initiation in particular, I think the adult ordo is the "standard according to which [baptism] is done" for adults (as is the *RBC* for infants and young children) and that, therefore, adults are initiated outside of the *RCIA* only for serious reasons. For adults seeking baptism, the adult ordo is the norm; for parents and their baptized children, it is *a* paradigm for Christian growth and formation; for, to, and by the Church at large it is Christian witness, ministry, and life at its best.

Furthermore, I believe—I hope—the adult ordo *does* present the norm ("the standard according to which a thing is done") for all future schemata or revisions of liturgical rites. The principles it espouses as regards the active participation of the community, the ongoing nature of conversion, the understanding of baptism as entrance into the Church's ministry, and from a different perspective, the rite itself—with its well-prepared, theologically informed commentary as well as the massive amount of supporting and explanatory literature it has encouraged—will hopefully be the norm kept in mind as Vatican congregations, episcopal conferences, and diocesan liturgical commissions revise our current rituals and create new ones.

In conjunction with this, one looks forward to the forthcoming revision of the 1969 *RBC* under the possible title *Christian Initiation of Children.* I have reviewed a copy of the "Consultation on Revision of the Rites for the *Christian Initiation of Children*," prepared by ICEL. My copy is an unofficial draft, and so I refrain from making specific comments. But it is clear that the revision—in content and in structure—will reflect much of what we have learned about infant baptism these past three decades.

Concerning this project—and this is a hope, not a prediction—a revised English edition of the *RBC* would seem an appropriate place to find *Pastoralis Actio:* a document that supports and supplements the various introductions in the *RBC* and that remains the sole document on infant baptism issued by the hierarchy since the publication of the *RBC* itself a quarter-century ago.[6]

---

[6]The Canadian Bishops recently published the first Canadian edition of the *Rite of Baptism for Children* (Ottawa: Canadian Conference of Catholic Bishops, 1989), and the instruction *Pastoralis Actio* is included as one of the ritual's four appendices. This new edition presents the approved English translation of the 1973 *editio typica altera* (footnotes designate the original 1969 reading) but curiously does not reflect the changes mandated by the 1983 *CIC.* For the rationale underlying the

And as the recently published *Book of Blessings* offers a variety of orders to precede and follow an infant's birth and baptism, the inclusion of some of these orders in a new edition of the *RBC* would seem proper and wise. That these orders could be found in a new *Christian Initiation of Children* might both encourage their use and support the notion that parental responsibility and ecclesial involvement in the sacramental initiation of infants neither begins nor ends at the font.

A final comment concerns the language of the *RBC* and other liturgical rituals. ICEL translates the Latin *adoptio* into "adoption" apparently only with reluctance, preferring to offer the terms "sonship" (as in the 1969 *RBC*, no. 68) or, as indicated in another text in the draft of the current revision, "children."[7] I respectfully suggest that what I have attempted to offer in this work supports the richness and, therefore, encourages the more frequent use in future texts of the concept of adoption.

---

new ritual and a description of its features, see *National Bulletin on Liturgy* 120, "Baptism for Children" (Ottawa: Canadian Conference of Catholic Bishops, March 1990) esp. 3–8.

[7]That the corresponding section of the draft revision of the 1969 *RBC*'s no. 68 offers the word "adoption" may represent the laudable desire to avoid exclusive language rather than an appreciation of the concept. A comparison of the *Missale Romanum* with the Sacramentary reveals that of the more than thirty occurrences of the various forms of *adoptio* in the Latin text, the word is rendered as "adoption" only six times in the English translation.

Concluding Remarks:
A few last words

"Christians are not born, they are made." To an adult Church eager and willing to embrace the gospel and its demands, infant baptism presents an especially rigorous challenge as regards the making of Christians. For infant baptism calls the Church to task. It calls her catechists and religious educators, her pastors and ministers, her young and old, and her weak and strong. It calls all these and, especially, it calls her Christian spouses and parents to return to the grace of their own baptism so as to allow the Word of God—the first and enduring Word in their lives—to be spoken strongly and clearly to others.

I entitled chapter 4, which reviewed the American literature from 1980 to the present, "Infant Baptism Reclaimed." But I am corrected by Paul's comment in his Letter to the Galatians (4:9; emphasis mine): "Now, however, that you have come to know God, *or rather to be known by God*, how can you turn back again to the weak and beggarly elemental spirits? How can you want to be enslaved to them again?"

Perhaps it is not so much that we have reclaimed infant baptism as it is that our reflection on infant baptism can reclaim us. For infant baptism reminds us that we, too, have been claimed by grace, and that ours is the task to return to the grace that sought and found us—or that has been stalking us these many years—"before ever a word was on our tongue." Baptism is a sacrament of faith, but even as that faith is professed by adults as they progress through the long and arduous journey of the catechumenate, their profession of faith is a response: a return to the grace offered freely and at the initiative of God. To that which we have been given, to that we must return. God's word is always first in our lives: "Every one of my days was decreed before one of them came into being" (Ps 138 [139]). Christians are they who readily acknowledge this—and who profess their hope that it will also be the last.

Adult conversion is and will forever remain impressive. It is the blood and seed of the Church and the "calcium in her bones" that support, nourish, and give life to those who seek the gospel as their guide. But the slow, steady, and often subtle building of grace upon nature—also witnessed throughout the many ages of the Church—is no less impressive or life-giving. The adult ordo reminds us that the end of the catechumenate is not the end at all but is yet another of many beginnings in turning away from ourselves and returning to the God who is the author of all grace and the *Abba* of us all. Neither the Rite of Baptism for Children nor the *Rite of Christian Initiation of Adults* guarantees that once a Christian has been made, he or she will live as such. They do guarantee, however, that, whenever we abandon our adult pretenses and return to the mentality of our beginnings—whenever we, God's "once and future children," remember who we are and to whom we belong—grace, the word spoken first in our lives, will also be the word spoken last.

As humans count words we have, as is often our wont, used many. My hope is that at least a few of these many words might offer a better understanding of and appreciation for what remains for most Catholics their "first sacrament," the sacrament through which God adopts us as God's children and makes us joint heirs with God's Word. And of these many words—so many of them about infants and young children—I acknowledge the irony. For it is from these little ones that many words are seldom encouraged. "Children should be seen and not heard," our adult wisdom proffers.

And so let our children be seen. But as we bring them to the font, let us allow them to lead the way. For as we approach that font to baptize our infants it is we, the adult Church, who should remain silent. It is we—the strong, the committed, the mature—who should feel the loss for words as those waters of adoption are stirred. For in infant baptism, as in the celebration of all our sacraments, it is *God's* word that effects, transforms, reconciles, consecrates, and comforts. At these times we do well to be silent and listen, so that *God's* word may be heard.

"We have said enough. May God say His own Word to this child, the Word of His love, His grace and His eternal faithfulness. He is faithful who begins the good work in this child—He will bring it to perfection. We will let God say His Word. May the life of this child, and our own lives also, be our answer, through God's grace. Amen."[1]

---

[1]Rahner, *Holy Baptism*, 40.

Bibliography

The bibliography consists of three sections. Section I includes the literature of the American postconciliar discussion of infant baptism cited or referred to throughout this work. Section II lists the literature cited in the discussion of a theology of childhood in part 2. Section III offers a number of ordinarily accessible references for readers interested in studying further the Pauline teaching on huiothesia (adoption), as well as several more technical works (marked with an asterisk).

I. THE POSTCONCILIAR DISCUSSION OF INFANT BAPTISM

Allen, William F. "Baptism of Infants." *Priest* (March 1973) 18–24.

America. "When to Baptize . . . When to Dismiss." No author listed. (September 21, 1974) 123–24.

Austin, Gerard. *The Rite of Confirmation: Anointing with the Spirit.* New York: Pueblo, 1985.

Balhoff, Michael J. "Age for Confirmation: Canonical Evidence." *Jurist* 45.2 (1985) 549–87.

"Baptizing Children." *National Bulletin on Liturgy 73.* Ottawa: Canadian Conference of Catholic Bishops (March–April 1980).

"Baptism for Children." *National Bulletin on Liturgy 120.* Ottawa: Canadian Conference of Catholic Bishops (March 1990).

Braxton, Edward. "Adult Initiation and Infant Baptism." In *Becoming a Catholic Christian,* ed. William J. Reedy, 305–15. New York: Sadlier, 1979.

Brockett, Lorna. *The Theology of Baptism.* Theology Today 25, gen. ed. Edward Yarnold. Hales Corners, Wis.: Clergy Book Service, 1971.

Brusselmans, Christiane. "Christian Parents and Infant Baptism." *Louvain Studies* 2 (1968) 29–48.

Buckley, Francis J. "The Right to the Sacraments of Initiation." *Origins* (November 9, 1978) 329–36.

_____. "What Age for Confirmation?" *Theological Studies* 27 (1966) 655– 66.

Challancin, James. "Infant Baptism: More Difficult Requirements?" *Homiletic and Pastoral Review* (February 1977) 61–68.

Champlin, Joseph M. *The Marginal Catholic: Challenge, Don't Crush.* Notre Dame: Ave Maria Press, 1989.

_____. "Welcoming Marginal Catholics: Pastoral Challenges of Baptism and Matrimony." *Church* (Spring) 1989 3–8.

_____. "Why It's Not as Easy to Get Kids Baptized." *U.S. Catholic* (April 1982) 25–26.

Cole, Basil. "Is Limbo Still in Limbo?" *Homiletic and Pastoral Review* (March 1985) 56–64.

Connor, James L. "Original Sin: Contemporary Approaches." *Theological Studies* 29 (1968) 215–40.

Counce, Paul D. "The Deferral of Infant Baptism According to Canon 868 (1,2)." *Louvain Studies* 13 (1988) 322–40.

Covino, Paul. "The Postconciliar Infant Baptism Debate in the American Catholic Church." *Worship* 56 (1982) 240–60.

_____. "The Question of Infant Baptism in the American Catholic Church: 1965 to 1980." Master's thesis. Notre Dame, 1981.

Dallen, James. *Infant Baptism Today.* Glendale, Ariz.: Pastoral Arts Associates of North America, 1979.

Daly, Brendan. "Canonical Requirements of Parents in Cases of Infant Baptism According to the 1983 Code." *Studia Canonica* 20.2 (1986) 409–38.

Donlan, Paul A. "Second Thoughts on Delaying the Baptism of Infants." *Priest* (June 1977) 31–33+.

Dooley, Catherine. "Catechumenate for Children: Sharing the Gift of Faith." *Living Light* 24 (1988) 307–17.

Downey, Michael. *Clothed in Christ: The Sacraments and Christian Living.* New York: Crossroad, 1987.

Duffy, Stephen J. "Our Hearts of Darkness: Original Sin Revisited." *Theological Studies* 49 (1988) 597–622.

Duggan, Robert D. "The Age of Confirmation: A Flawed Proposal." *America* (June 5, 1993) 12–14.

_____. "The Great Confirmation Debate." *Church* (Summer 1991) 39–40.

_____. "Implementing the Rite of Christian Initiation of Adults: Pastoral-Theological Reflections." *Living Light* 17 (1980) 327–33.

Duggan, Robert D., and Maureen A. Kelly. *The Christian Initiation of Children: Hope for the Future.* New York: Paulist, 1991.

Dunning, James B. *New Wine; New Wineskins: Exploring the RCIA.* Chicago: Sadlier, 1981.

Ellsberg, Peggy. "'Let the Little Children . . .'" *America* (March 1993) 16.

Engel, William. "Pastoring Marginal Catholics: Another Look at Infant Baptism." *Church* (Summer 1990) 18–22.

Fourez, Gérard. "Celebrating the Spirit with Adolescents: More on Confirmation." *Living Light* 23 (1987) 199–206.

_____. "Toward a Pastoral Theology of Confirmation." In *Confirming the Faith of Adolescents: An Alternative Future for Confirmation,* ed. Arthur J. Kubick, 46–61. New York: Paulist, 1991.

Friedman, Gregory. "To Baptize or Not." *St. Anthony Messenger* (December 1980) 12–15.

Gallen, John. "American Liturgy: A Theological Locus." *Theological Studies* 35 (1974) 302–11.

_____. "The Pastoral Celebration of Initiation." *New Catholic World* 222 (1979) 148–52.

Garvey, John. "Turning People Away: More Fastidious Than Jesus?" *Commonweal* (December 4, 1981) 679–80.

Grippo, Dan. "Confirmation: No One Under 18 Need Apply." *U.S. Catholic* (August 1982) 31–32.

Guerrette, Richard H. "Ecclesiology and Infant Baptism." *Worship* 44 (1970) 433–37.

_____. "The New Rite of Infant Baptism." *Worship* 43 (1969) 224–30.

Gusmer, Charles W. "The Revised Adult Initiation and Its Challenge to Religious Education." *Living Light* 13 (1976) 92–98.

Guzie, Tad. *The Book of Sacramental Basics.* New York: Paulist, 1981.

_____. "Should We Cancel Confirmation? *U.S. Catholic* (July 1979) 17–23.

Haggerty, Brian A. "Adult Initiation and Infant Baptism." *New Catholic World* 222 (1979) 157–60.

Hamilton, William. "New Thinking on Original Sin." *Herder Correspondence* 4 (1967) 135–41.

Hellwig, Monika. *The Meaning of the Sacraments.* Dayton, Ohio: Pflaum, 1972.

Hovda, Robert. "Hope for the Future: A Summary." In *Made, Not Born: New Perspectives on Christian Initiation and the Catechumenate,* ed. Murphy Center for Liturgical Research, 152–67. Notre Dame: Univ. of Notre Dame Press, 1976.

Humbert, Greg J. "Welcoming Unmarried Parents: Mysterious Grace of Baptism." *Church* (Fall 1991) 15–17.

Irwin, Kevin. "Christian Initiation: Some Important Questions." *Chicago Catechumenate* (March 1981) 4–24.

_____. "Ecclesiology of Christian Initiation." *New Catholic World* 222 (1979) 176–79.

Ivory, Thomas P. "The Adult Catechumenate: Pastoral Application of Vatican II Theology." *Louvain Studies* 9 (1982) 211–20.

_____. "The Restoration of the Catechumenate as a Norm for Catechesis." *Living Light* 13 (1976) 225–35.

Kavanagh, Aidan. "Adult Initiation: Process and Ritual." *Liturgy* 22 (January 1977) 5–10.

_____. "Christian Initiation for Those Baptized as Infants." *Living Light* 13 (1976) 387–98.

_____. "Christian Initiation in Post-Conciliar Roman Catholicism: A Brief Report." *Studia Liturgica* 12 (1977) 107–15.

_____. "Christian Initiation of Adults: The Rites." *Worship* 48 (1974) 318–35.

_____. "Christian Initiation: Tactics and Strategy. In *Made, Not Born: New Perspectives on Christian Initiation and the Catechumenate,* ed. Murphy Center for Liturgical Research, 1-6. Notre Dame: Univ. of Notre Dame Press, 1976.

_____. *Confirmation: Origins and Reform.* New York: Pueblo, 1988.

_____. "Initiation: Baptism and Confirmation." *Worship* 46 (1972) 262–76.

_____. "The New Roman Rites of Adult Initiation." *Studia Liturgica* 10 (1974) 35-47.

_____. "The Norm of Baptism: The New Rite of Christian Initiation of Adults." *Worship* 48 (1974) 143–52.

_____. *The Shape of Baptism: The Rite of Christian Initiation.* New York: Pueblo, 1978.

_____. "Theological Principles for Sacramental Catechesis." *Living Light* 23 (1987) 316–24.

_____. "Unfinished and Unbegun Revisited: The Rite of Christian Initiation of Adults." *Worship* 53 (1979) 327–40.

Keating, Charles J. "Baptism Sets Our Boundaries." *New Catholic World* 217 (1974) 100–104.

Keifer, Ralph A. "Christian Initiation: The State of the Question." *Worship* 48 (1974) 392–404.

_____. "Faith Community Necessary for Adult Initiation." *New Catholic World* 222 (1979) 161–63.

Kemp, Raymond. "The Rite of Christian Initiation of Adults at Ten Years." *Worship* 56 (1982) 309–26.

Kiesling, Christopher. "Confirmation: The Rite Not the Age." *Church* (Summer 1987) 25–28.

_____. "Infant Baptism." *Worship* 42 (1968) 617–26.

_____. "The New Rite of Baptism for Children." *Cross and Crown* 24 (1972) 262–79.

Kinast, Robert. *Sacramental Pastoral Care: Integrating Resources for Ministry.* New York: Pueblo, 1988.

Krause, Fred. "Infant Baptism and the Domestic Church." *Priest* (June 1977) 25–28+.

Kubick, Arthur J., ed. *Confirming the Faith of Adolescents: An Alternative Future for Confirmation.* New York: Paulist, 1991.

Leystan, A. "New Rite of Infant Baptism." *Priest* (July–August 1970) 52–57.

Ling, Richard. "A Catechist's Vote for Infant Confirmation." *Living Light* 7 (1970) 42–56.

Lowery, Daniel L. "Should Every Baby Be Baptized?" *Liguorian* (July 1982) 14–19.

McDermot, Brian O. "The Theology of Original Sin: Recent Developments." *Theological Studies* 38 (1977) 478–512.

McManus, Frederick R. "Ritual of Infant Baptism." *American Ecclesiastical Review* 160 (1969) 190–99.

Maly, Eugene. "Why Baptize Babies?" *St. Anthony Messenger* (September 1978) 34–38. Reprinted as "Still a Case for Infant Baptism?" In *The Sacraments: Readings in Contemporary Sacramental Theology,* ed. Michael J. Taylor, 95–103. New York: Alba, 1981.

Mannion, M. Francis. "Penance and Reconciliation: A Systematic Analysis." *Worship* 60 (1986) 104–16.

Marsh, Thomas. "Christian Initiation: Practice and Theology." In *Confirming the Faith of Adolescents: An Alternative Future for Confirmation,* ed. Kubick, 13–24. New York: Paulist, 1991.

_____. *Gift of Community: Baptism and Confirmation.* Wilmington: Glazier, 1984.

Martos, Joseph J. "Let's Deny Baptism to Babies of Fallen-Aways." *U.S. Catholic* (February 1984) 13–15.

_____. "A Modest Proposal: Put Some Spirit Back into Confirmation." *U.S. Catholic* (October 1990) 30–31.

Mick, Lawrence. "Christian Initiation: Separate-But-Equal Doesn't Work." *Chicago Catechumenate* (July 1982) 14–18.

_____. *Understanding the Sacraments Today.* Collegeville: The Liturgical Press, 1987.

Miller, Edward Jeremy. "Confirmation as Ecclesial Commissioning." *Louvain Studies* 10 (1984) 106–21.

Mitchell, Nathan. "Christian Initiation: Decline and Dismemberment." *Worship* 48 (1974) 458–79.

_____. "The Once and Future Child: Towards a Theology of Childhood." *Living Light* 12 (1975) 422–36.

Murphy Center for Liturgical Research, ed. *Made, Not Born: New Perspectives on Christian Initiation and the Catechumenate.* Notre Dame: Univ. of Notre Dame Press, 1976.

O'Malley, William J. "Confirmed and Confirming." *America* 17 (June 1995) 16– 19.

Osborne, Kenan B. *The Christian Sacraments of Initiation: Baptism, Confirmation, Eucharist.* New York: Paulist, 1987.

Perrey, David Greye [pseud.]. *Baptism at 21.* New York: Vantage, 1973.

_____. "Let's Stop Baptizing Babies." *U.S. Catholic* (February 1972) 14– 15.

Peterson, Rockford. "Let's Baptize Babies of Nonpracticing Catholics." *U.S. Catholic* (September 1977) 14–15.

Quinn, Frank C. "Confirmation Reconsidered: Rite and Meaning." *Worship* 59 (1985) 354–70.

_____. "The Sacraments of Initiation and Christian Life." *Spirituality Today* (March 1982) 27–38.

Ramshaw-Schmidt, Gail. "Celebrating Baptism in Stages: A Proposal." In *Alternative Futures for Worship.* Vol. 2: *Baptism and Confirmation,* ed. Mark Searle, 137–55. Collegeville: The Liturgical Press, 1987.

Redmond, Richard X. "Infant Baptism: History and Pastoral Problems." *Theological Studies* 30 (1969) 79–89.

Reichert, Richard. "Adolescent Confirmation and the Paschal Mystery." In *Confirming the Faith of Adolescents: An Alternative Future for Confirmation,* ed. Kubick, 62–69. New York: Paulist, 1991.

_____. "A Catechist's Response to the Rite of Christian Initiation for Adults." *Living Light* 14 (1977) 138–46.

Resonance 6. "Baptism: Aspects of the Present Situation." St. Meinrad, Ind.: Abbey Press, 1968.

Rigali, Norbert. "New Theology and Infant Baptism." *Priest* (February 1974) 13–17.

Roberto, John. "Confirmation in the American Catholic Church." *Living Light* 15 (1978) 262–79.

Robertson, John W. "Canons 867 and 868 and Baptizing Infants Against the Will of Parents." *Jurist* 45 (1985) 631–38.

Sawyer, Kieran. "A Case for Adolescent Confirmation." In *Confirming the Faith of Adolescents: An Alternative Future for Confirmation,* ed. Kubick, 25–45. New York: Paulist, 1991.

_____. "The Confirmation Dialogue Continues." *Living Light* 22 (1986) 215–21.

_____. "Readiness for Confirmation." *Living Light* 24 (1988) 331–39.

_____. "Toward an Integrated Theology of Confirmation: Basic Principles." *Living Light* 19 (1982) 336–43.

Searle, Mark. *Christening: The Making of Christians.* Collegeville: The Liturgical Press, 1980.

_____. "Confirmation: The State of the Question." *Church* (Winter 1985) 15–22.

_____. "Infant Baptism Reconsidered." In *Alternative Futures for Worship.* Vol 2: *Baptism and Confirmation,* ed. Mark Searle, 15–54. Collegeville: The Liturgical Press, 1987.

_____. "Response: The RCIA and Infant Baptism." *Worship* 56 (1982) 327–32.

Searle, Mark, ed. *Alternative Futures for Worship.* Vol 2: *Baptism and Confirmation.* Collegeville: The Liturgical Press, 1987.

Sherman, Anthony F. "Baptism Preparation: Where Parents Are At." *Priest* (September 1980) 8–9.

Stasiak, Kurt. "Infant Baptism Reclaimed: Forgotten Truths About Infant Baptism." *Living Light* (Spring 1995) 36–46.

Torres, Joan. "Uncommitted Catholic Parents and Children's Baptism." *Church* (Winter 1989) 49–50.

Turner, Paul. "Baptism and Original Sin." In *New Dictionary of Sacramental Worship*, ed. Peter E. Fink, 81–83. Collegeville: The Liturgical Press, 1990.

_____. *Confirmation: The Baby in Solomon's Court.* New York: Paulist, 1993.

Upton, Julia Ann. *A Church for the Next Generation: Sacraments in Transition.* Collegeville: The Liturgical Press, 1990.

_____. "A Solution to the Infant Baptism Problem." *Living Light* 16 (1979) 484–96.

Vanbergen, Paul. "Baptism of the Infants of *non satis credentes* Parents." *Studia Liturgica* 12 (1977) 195–200.

Walsh, David. "Rite of Welcoming a Christian Child." *Modern Liturgy* (June–July 1980) 8+.

Wilde, James A., ed. *Confirmed as Children, Affirmed as Teens.* Chicago: Liturgy Training, 1990.

_____, ed. *When Should We Confirm?* Chicago: Liturgy Training, 1989.

II. THEOLOGY OF CHILDHOOD

Bédouelle, Guy. "Reflection on the Place of the Child in the Church: 'Suffer the Little Children to Come unto Me.'" Trans. E. Tillman. *Communio* 12 (1985) 349–67.

Frederick, J. B. M. "The Initiation Crisis in the Church of England." *Studia Liturgica* 9 (1973) 137–57.

Karay, Diane. "Let the Children Lead the Way: A Case for Baptizing Children." *Worship* 61 (1987) 336–49.

Rahner, Karl. *Holy Baptism.* Trans. Dorothy White. Denville, N.J.: Dimension, 1970.

_____. "Ideas for a Theology of Childhood." In *Theological Investigations 8: Further Theology of the Spiritual Life 2.* Trans. David Bourke, 33–50. New York: Herder, 1971.

Stevick, Daniel. "Christian Initiation: Post-Reformation to the Present Era." In *Made, Not Born: New Perspectives on Christian Initiation and the Catechumenate*, ed. Murphy Center for Liturgical Research, 99–117. Notre Dame: Univ. of Notre Dame Press, 1976.

_____. "Types of Baptismal Spirituality." *Worship* 47 (1973) 11–26.

Underhill, Evelyn. *The Fruits of the Spirit.* 2nd. ed. London: Longmans Green, 1942.

von Balthasar, Hans Urs. *Unless You Become Like This Child.* Trans. Erasmo Leiva-Merikakis. San Francisco: Ignatius, 1991.

III. THE PAULINE TEACHING ON ADOPTION

Dictionaries and Encyclopedias

Achtemeier, Paul J., gen. ed. *Harper's Bible Dictionary.* San Francisco: Harper, 1985.

Bromiley, G. W., ed. *The International Standard Bible Encyclopedia*. 4 vols. Grand Rapids: Eerdman's, 1979.

_____. *Theological Dictionary of the New Testament*. 9 vols. Trans. G. W. Bromiley. Grand Rapids: Eerdmans, 1964–. English trans. of *Theologisches Wörterbuch zum Neuen Testament*, ed. Gerhard Kittel and others. Stuttgart: Kohlhammer, 1933–.

Buttrick, G. A., ed. *The Interpreter's Dictionary of the Bible*. 4 vols. Nashville: Abingdon, 1962.

Brown, Colin, ed. *The New International Dictionary of New Testament Theology*. 3 vols. English trans. of *Theologisches Begriffslexikon zum Neuen Testament*, ed. Lothar Coenen, Erich Beyreuther, and Hans Bientenhard. Exeter & Devon, Great Britain: Paternoster, 1975.

Hastings, James, ed. *Dictionary of the Bible*. 5 vols. Rev. ed., Frederick C. Grant and H. H. Rowley, eds. New York: Scribner's, 1963.

Leon-Dufour, Xavier, ed. *Dictionary of Biblical Theology*. Trans. P. Joseph Cahill. New York: Seabury, 1962.

McKenzie, John L. *Dictionary of the Bible*. Milwaukee: Bruce, 1965.

Mills, Watson E., gen ed. *Mercer Dictionary of the Bible*. Macon, Ga.: Mercer Univ. Press, 1990.

Myers, Allen C. *The Eerdman's Bible Dictionary*. Rev. ed. Grand Rapids: Eerdman's, 1987.

Richardson, Alan, ed. *A Theological Word Book of the Bible*. 1950. London: SCM Press, 1957.

van den Born, A., ed. *Encyclopedic Dictionary of the Bible*. 2nd ed. Trans. and adapt. Louis F. Hartman. New York: McGraw, 1963.

von Allmen, J.-J., ed. *Vocabulary of the Bible*. Trans. ed. Hilda M. Wilson. London: Lutterworth, 1958.

Critical studies and Miscellaneous Works

* Byrne, Brendan. *'Sons of God' - 'Seed of Abraham': A Study of the Idea of the Sonship of God of All Christians in Paul Against the Jewish Background*. Analecta Biblica 83. Rome: Biblical Institute Press, 1979.

Cook, James I. "The Concept of Adoption in the Theology of Paul." In *Saved By Hope* (Essays in Honor of Richard C. Oudersluys), ed. James I. Cook, 133–44. Grand Rapids: Eerdmans, 1978.

* Hester, James D. *Paul's Concept of Inheritance: A Contribution to the Understanding of Heilsgeschichte*. Scottish Journal of Theology Occasional Papers 14, gen. ed. T. F. Torrance and J. K. S. Reid. London: Oliver & Boyd, 1968.

Lyall, Francis. *Slaves, Citizens, Sons: Legal Metaphors in the Epistles*. Grand Rapids: Zondervan, 1984.

Rossell, William H. "New Testament Adoption—Graeco-Roman or Semitic?" *Journal of Biblical Literature* 71 (1952) 233–34.

Schoenberg, Martin W. "St. Paul's Notion on the Adoptive Sonship of Christians." *Thomist* 28 (1964) 51–75.

_____. "Huiothesia: The Adoptive Sonship of the Israelites." *American Ecclesiastical Review* 143 (1960) 261–73.

_____. "Huiothesia: The Word and the Institution." *Scripture* 15 (1963) 115–23.

* Scott, James, M. *Adoption as Sons of God: An Exegetical Investigation into the Background of Huiothesia in the Pauline Corpus*. Wissenschaftliche Untersuchungen zum Neuen Testament 2/48. Tübingen: J. C. B. Mohr, 1992.

Theron, Daniel J. "'Adoption' in the Pauline Corpus." *Evangelical Quarterly* 28 (1956) 6–14.

Index of Authors:
The Discussion of Infant Baptism

This index includes the American authors cited or referred to throughout our work, as well as several other English-writing contributors to the postconciliar discussion.